RESTORING BROKEN VESSELS

Confronting the Attack on Female Sexuality

Victoria L. Saunders Johnson

Dabar Publishing Company

P.O. Box 35377   Detroit, MI 48235

Unless otherwise noted, scripture quotations are from the New American Standard Version. copyright © 1960, 1962, 1963, 1968, 1971, 1972, 1973, 1975, 1977, by The Lockman Foundation. Used by permission.

All definitions are from *Webster's New 20th Century Dictionary*, 1988, Jean L. McKechnie (ed.) New York: Simon and Schuster.

Lyrics from the song, *"I Can Begin Again"* Copyright © 1989 John T. Benson Pub. Co./ASCAP, LifeSong Music Press/BMI, First Row Music/BMI.

All Rights Reserved. Used by permission of Benson Music,Group, Inc.

Cover and Illustrations by Lynette Gibson
Typesetting and Interior design by William T. Florence

Library of Congress Cataloging-in Publication Data

Johnson, Victoria L.
    Restoring broken vessels: Confronting the attack on female sexuality/ by Victoria L. Johnson
        p.   cm.
    ISBN 1-880560-65-8
    1. Suffering-Religious aspects-Christianity. 2. Women-Religious life. 3. Consolation. 4. spiritutal life-Christianity. 5. Sexuality-Religious aspects I. Title

BV 4909.F57   1995   CIP 95-72232
248.8'43-dc20

Printed in the United States of America

Dedication To My Best Friends

To the **Lord Jesus Christ**, to whom I owe everything. You are the One who knew me when I was in my mother's womb, saw all my days, yet loved me then and still loves me now. You truly are my very best friend.

And to **Debralee Townsend** and **Jamie Saunders**, my two sisters, and closest women friends. You have sometimes laughed at my crazy ideas and tangled-up thoughts, yet you still listened and always ecncouraged me to do what I believed God was telling me to do. I am grateful to both of you.

ACKNOWLEDGMENTS

This book is not the product of a solo effort. It was indeed a team effort for which I am exceedingly grateful to my husband Curtis for his consistent encouragement. I also want to express appreciation to Lydia, my oldest daughter for her typing; Candacee, my youngest daughter and Andre my only son, for their energizing hugs and kisses. I also acknowledge the attributes modeled to me by my parents, James R. and Mattie Saunders. The early examples of my father's dreaming the impossible and my mother's hard work and commitment are, I believe, what propelled me through the road blocks to the completion of this project..

My words of appreciation also go to the many friends, and relatives who prayed for the success of this project. A special thanks to the various sources for permission to share their stories* in this book.

I am also indebted to David and Sharon Brickner, Helen Harris, Sandra McPherson, Lisa Sinclair, Andrell Sturdivant, Brenda Watkins, and numerous others who have contributed in one way or the other to the creation of this book.

Particular mention must be made of Clarinda Gipson for her priceless editorial work and input. Literally, Clarinda took this manuscript, a diamond in the raw and polished it through long hours of editing.

I also place on record my deep appreciation to Rebecca and Uwaifo Osaigbovo, publishers and godly friends for trusting the Lord with me and this book. Some of the wise insights inside these pages, especially those articulated in chapter 1, are the results of our conversations. I am thankful to them for sometimes going beyond the call of duty to make it possible for me to complete this project.

*The stories are true to life. The names are fictional. Some stories are composites of more than one person. Any resemblance to persons living or dead is coincidental.

FOREWORD

Resonating with insights from the Bible, *RESTORING BROKEN VESSELS: CONFRONTING THE ATTACK ON FEMALE SEXUALITY* is an excellent contribution to works addressing female sexuality. It not only enables the reader to understand the many complexities of female sexuality, it also gives a perceptive analysis on how to experience hope and healing through practical application of biblical teachings.

Victoria Johnson affirms how the Bible candidly deals with sex, more so than many modern sex manuals. She is forthright in establishing the biblical view that sex is a gift from God. Mrs. Johnson has brillantly blended episodes from her personal life with the voices of other women to tell the world a compelling story of human breakage and its intergenerational consequences on females. Readers will discover that her straight talk about sex is liberating and a long overdue resource for females of all ages, especially those who are held hostage by their sexual past and present.

Throughout the book, Mrs. Johnson reminds us of the reality of spiritual warfare and Satan's evil schemes designed for human destruction and ruin. Consequently, *Restoring Broken Vessels* can be likened to a personal survival kit for Believers to use to train themselves to spot and avoid deception. Satan's sexual attack on females is part of his equal opportunity plan. One could say that *Restoring Broken Vessels* is an Overcomer's guide to spiritual warfare.

When women reflect on their lives to evaluate their successes and failures, commonly expressed sentiments are, "If only I had . . . ." or "If I could live my life again I would. . . ." In retrospect, we spend much time seeking to identify specific points in our life journey where we could have avoided major problems if only we had made a better decision at that point. *Restoring Broken Vessels* presents for future generations a way to avoid these regrets.

Woven throughout each chapter Victoria has laid the groundwork for making clear-headed choices that will apply to any dilemma girls and women are facing regarding sexual matters and sexuality. She encourages you, instructs you, enlightens you and equips you to deal head-on with these intimate choices that all females must make at some juncture in life.

Restoring Broken Vessels is a remarkable book. It has the capacity to lead readers to an oasis within themselves from a variety of perspectives. For parents, Sunday school teachers and educators, it is a valuable resource for teaching children and youth how to live balanced and healthy lives, that also are pleasing to God. For women who are living in the prime season of adulthood, for those in the mid-life years and fear growing older, and for the elderly who still have contributions to make, *Restoring Broken Vessels* is a timely book which reaffirms their dignity and changes the perception of their value.

In specific areas of pedagogy, *Restoring Broken Vessels* has a special place. Victoria Johnson's message is relevant and timely for programs targeting women's studies, ethnic studies, parenting/childrearing, and related social science topics.

*Restoring Broken Vessel*s goes far beyond being just a book by and about the African American woman, it is a book about the daily struggles of females of all ages, classes, racial and religious groups. Every counseling center, seminary, church library, and minister of the Gospel should own this valuable document.

Victoria has made an exceptional contribution to the growing pool of theological views on women.

Anna Lou Blevins, Ph.D.
Professor of Education, Buhl Scholar
University of Pittsburgh

and

Associate Pastor
Lincoln Avenue Church of God
Pittsburgh, Pennslyvania

PREFACE

If you saw my oldest daughter, Lydia, the first thing you would probably say is, "She looks just like her mother."Not only does she look like me but she has similar interests and personality traits, and even some of her attitudes are identical to mine. As she approached her teen years, this began to scare me. I didn't mind observing the positive things she picked up from me. But when I noticed in her traces of the negative aspects of my personality,I began to pray fervently, "Lord what can I do to help her not repeat some of my past mistakes?

God clearly revealed to me some root causes of my ungodly behaviors in my past and present. I began to understand that at each stage of my sexual development, there was a demonic, strategic plan to destroy me. I found this very insightful, and it freed me from years of self-inflicted guilt and blaming my parents for things that went wrong. I started to realize what I needed to do in order to help steer Lydia in a different direction.

God, however, did not stop there.He made it very plain to me that Lydia and I were not the only ones to take advantage of this wise counsel. I was to write down what He had revealed to me for the benefit of other women. Reluctantly, I agreed. Little did I know that this writing project would take me almost two years to complete and would demand so much of my time and energy. Yet, it has been one of the most enriching spiritual experiences of my life.

Several times I sat at my computer and prayed, "Lord, I have no idea what you want me to say."But little by little God has provided the Scriptures, people, books, and all kinds of useful resources to help me accomplish His assignment. He prompted me to recall incidents from my life and to adapt stories from the lives of many others, to bring about a better understanding of what I perceive as a very difficult subject.

This book is exemplary of God's pattern in my life. Once He asks me to do something, He is faithful to pull it together and bring it all to pass. All praise and glory to my Heavenly Father. My prayer is that each everyone who reads this book will hear God speaking to him or her in a special way.

"The Son of God appeared for this purpose, that He might destroy the works of the devil" (1 John 3:8).

CONTENTS

Dedication
Acknowledgements
Foreword
Preface
About the Author

Section One: Satan's Attack on Little Girls
Chapter 1: Where It All Began   11
Chapter 2: Shame Originated In The Garden   23
Chapter 3: Normal Genital Exploration and Shame   37
Chapter 4: Satan's Fiery Dart Called Sex Abuse   49
Chapter 5: Families And Unidentified Victims   57
Chapter 6: The Effects Of Sexual Abuse   73
Chapter 7: From Victim To Victor   83
Chapter 8: The Church And Sexual Abuse   95

Section Two: Satan's Attack on Teenage Girls
Chapter 9: Sex Education God's Way   109
Chapter 10: Talking To Our Girls About Sex   121
Chapter 11: Ungodly Sex Education In Public Schools   135
Chapter 12: Teen Girls Are Hungry For Love   145
Chapter 13: Clearing Up The Love/lust Confusion   155
Chapter 14: Stopping Generational Curses   163
Chapter 15: Practical Help For Teenage Girls   171
Chapter 16: Broken Teens And Other Dilemma s   181

Section Three: Satan's Attack on the single woman
Chapter 17: The Enemy's Plan For The Single Woman   191
Chapter 18: Without A Mate But Not Alone   199
Chapter 19: The Single Woman With A Tainted Past   209
Chapter 20: Countering Satan's Attack On Singles   217

Section Four: Satan's Attack on Married and Older Women
Chapter 21: Intimacy In Marriage   235
Chapter 22: Lies Satan Tells To The Married Woman   245
Chapter 23: Battling Satan During Mid-life   259
Chapter 24: Sexually Alive And Over 75   269
Chapter 25: Conclusion   279
Appendix: Resources   284

ABOUT THE AUTHOR

The author, Victoria L. Saunders Johnson, was born in Joliet Illinois to James and Mattie Saunders. She is married to Curtis Johnson of Detroit, Michigan and they now reside in Milwaukee, Wisconsin.

Victoria is the mother of three children–Lydia , born in 1980, Candacee, born in 1984, and Andre, born in 1989.

Mrs. Johnson is a freelance writer and editor; and teaches for Moody Bible Institute Extension in Milwaukee.

Victoria asked Christ into her life as a teenager. She graduated from Ottawa University, in Ottawa, Kansas, with a Bachelors degree in counseling psychology, then accepted God's call to a full-time Christian vocation in 1977. She began her service to the Lord as a staff member of Campus Crusade for Christ and also worked at the Detroit's Afro-American Mission. She has counseled and discipled many women along with coordinating various women's ministry activities. She believes that God has given her the gifts and abilities to help women come to know Christ in an intimate way through His Word.

If this book has been a help or an encouragement to you, please write and let her know:

Victoria L. Johnson
P. O. Box 10105
Milwaukee, Wisconsin 53210

Section One

Satan's Sexual Attack
on Little Girls

SATAN'S PLAN IS TO DESTROY WOMEN

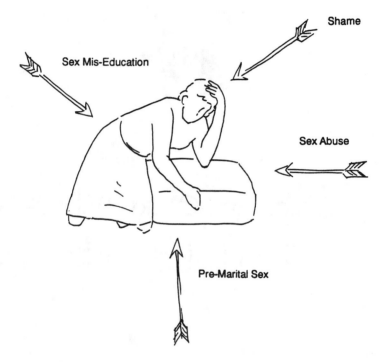

Chapter 1

Where it All Began

I'm single. I have been in and out of several relationships. A couple of times I even reached the point of engagement. But each time I found a reason to break it off. I go through a cycle after each relationship. I say to myself, "I'm just going to stay single. It will just be the Lord and me." That might last for a few months and then I meet someone. I date him for a while and if I like him, I start to press him for a commitment. If he does decide to make a commitment to me and he starts to get serious, I'll find a way to begin to sabotage the relationship until the friendship or engagement is broken. Afterward I am discouraged and depressed for months. I'm angry with myself and angry with the guy for not hanging in there with me, even though I destroyed the relationship–and I'm angry with God because this part of my life is such a mess. Then the cycle starts all over again with me telling myself, "I'll never get involved again." –Mary

I divorced several years ago and I still blame myself for the marriage not working out. I loved my husband. In fact, I try to love everybody. But every time I turn around I'm getting my feelings hurt, especially by the people I love the most. I often question myself about whether I have any right to have feelings about things, especially hurtful things. Instead of confronting people I usually stuff the pain down on the inside. I often use food to make myself feel better. I either overeat or eat the wrong things, and sometimes it's difficult to stop. As you can imagine, I have a weight problem which takes a toll on me physically and emotionally. It's hard to admit these things to myself. I realize now that the eating and the way I feel are connected, but I'm not really sure that I understand how or why. –Eileen

I started stealing at twelve. I aborted my son at thirteen. I started using drugs at fourteen. I married at nineteen. I was an adulteress right away. I even lived with another man for a time while married. I left my husband when I was twenty-six. I have experimented with group sex involving both men and women. I have had, at times, more than one man a night. I have had sex in public. I have slept with over sixty men in this lifetime. I have gone to every kind of club, juke joint, and disco in the country. I have lied, deceived and hurt people. I have used people, partied myself into a near coma, and tried to fool God. I have tried to hide from God and blamed everyone, including God, for my problems. –Tammy

On the surface it appears that these woman are dealing with entirely different issues. However, behind each of these dilemmas there is one common problem, one that not even they are aware of or understand. Though these stories show few similarities, the root of the problem for each of these women is the same. Let me take you back to how it all began.

***

"I now call the convention of Hell In Action to order," Lucifer angrily banged his gavel on the long oblong table. The noisy demons jumped, then sat attentively. "We've got a big problem. And I mean a really BIG problem." Lucifer twisted his face and his eyes darted back and forth.

Lucifer repeated, "I said we have a BIG problem." He shouted and banged the gavel on the table again. No one dared to make another comment. They had never seen Lucifer so upset. Usually he was cocky and overly self-confident. But today was different.

"Did you hear what happened today?" All the demons shook their heads, for they were still afraid to speak. "You bunch of good-for-nothing imps. Do I have to keep watch over everything around here? Where were you idiots when God was talking to Adam and Eve after the fall?"

"God has put the woman on us!", he shouted.

One demon with a chuckle in his voice asked this question, "Are we to fear...the woman?"

Lucifer pushed his chair over, and proceeded to kick him unmercifully, shouting, "Yes, the woman! Yes, we are going to have to deal with the woman!" Lucifer said this with great vehemence and rage. Each time he said the word "woman," he kicked harder and the demon screeched at his feet. "God has made her and us arch-enemies. She will hate us. She'll do whatever she can to destroy us. The woman is our number one problem!" Finally Lucifer retreated to his seat at the head of the table. He was hot and sweaty from his great outburst of anger.

"God said that he would put *enmity* between us and the woman. Of course you stupid idiots have no idea what enmity means, so let me break it down so your pea brains can grasp it. Enmity means deep seated hatred, hostility, and violence.... It means war-r-r-r!" Lucifer spit out the word and let his head roll back.

Another demon on the far right side of the table felt that he was far enough away from Lucifer–if he said the wrong thing he would not be hit–and so he timidly spoke up. "Please pardon me, sir, if I am still ignorant in this, but doesn't that mean we get to attack her?"

"Yes, yes. I'm not worried about that part," Satan said quickly. "But she gets to declare war on US! That would not be a big problem either, except God will be on her side. Somehow we've got to orchestrate a plan to keep her away from God."

"Didn't you see the woman in the garden?" Lucifer closed his eyes as if he were replaying the scene in his mind. "Did you see her influence and power over the man? She simply held the fruit out in front of Adam and he just took it and ate it. She has power, the power of influence. If she teams up with God, she can influence the man in all kinds of ways. I tell you, God has some special plans for the woman. Why else would He make her our enemy? I bet He is going to talk to her and have her doing all kinds of little special favors for Him. If she's in love with God, she'll do anything for Him. O-O-O-!" Lucifer growled. "She must not be allowed to be in close communication with Him! She has got to be stopped!"

Lucifer sat back in his chair. "I was able to get to Eve by just talking to her in the garden about the fruit. Did you notice that? Words must be very important to her, and I can talk to her often. But the problem is that God will also talk to her. And once she hears God, she will do what He wants," Lucifer scoffed. "And did you see the way Adam looked at Eve once God's glory departed from her?" Lucifer continued. "When Adam saw the fruit and saw the change in Eve, he was affected by it, too. We were able to use Eve to separate them both from God. I just have the feeling that God is going to try to use her to get Adam reconnected. If she learns how to live by God's power, the man will see it and want it. This is a very dirty trick."

"What if both the man and the woman," one of the brave demons spoke up, "begin to live their lives with God's power?"

"Shut up!" Lucifer said sharply, "We can't think of such things. You know what that means for us! They will be an unstoppable team for God." Lucifer talked faster and his anger intensified. "We can't have it! A spirit-filled man and a spirit-filled woman!"

Lucifer lay out on the table, whining like a wounded animal. "We cannot allow it."

Once Lucifer composed himself again, the brave little imp who always had a question spoke again, "Sir, I do beg your pardon. I don't mean to be ignorant, but I just don't see what all the fuss is about. There are just two of them. Look at all of us. Certainly we can handle two little humans. Remember, they are separated from God. Wasn't that the purpose of getting Eve to disobey God? Or did I miss something?"

"There will be more than two!" Lucifer said, thrusting two long fingers in the little imp's face. "God told them to multiply," Lucifer said in a frustrated whisper. "God told them to cleave and come together. He said her seed will bruise my head" Lucifer tucked in his chin and frowned. "We've got to destroy her seed. That's all there is to it."

"How many of them will there be?" the little imp inquired again.

"I don't know." Lucifer was growing impatient and starting to stomp around the table. "But God told them to fill up the whole earth. The whole earth! That's a lot of humans."

"Well, we won the first round," a demon named Power Thirst piped up. "But don't think God will let it stay this way. He has plans to get humans back with Him. It involves this woman and her seed. It won't take many humans on God's side to be a big problem!"

With a semi-approving look in Power Thirst's direction, Lucifer said, "Well, I'm glad somebody is finally getting my point and realizing we have a very serious situation on our hands. We have got to come up with a plan that will create division between men and women. It has to keep women from being too close to God. It has to prevent women from being the visible examples of godliness. It has to obstruct women from understanding the power they hold. It has got to be a long reaching-plan. We've got to plan things that will go from generation to generation. Think, you bunch of bumbling idiots. Think!... The woman is the one responsible for the seed that will come. She could really shape every human that comes into this earth. And she has already blown it with God, so she will want to be in his good graces. We have got to destroy her influence and affect all her seed," Lucifer mused.

"We've got to think of a way to make her a tool in our hands, fulfilling our purposes. If we don't get her into our camp we will have to at least neutralize her, make her ineffective for God."

"Meet me back here tomorrow," Lucifer was already heading toward the door. "And each one of you had better have an idea of how we can either neutralize or use her. Now out of my sight."

The next day many ideas were brought forth. Each idea was good, but none quite the solution to their problem.

After hours of shouting, arguing and fighting to get their ideas approved, Power Thrist had finally suggested they would so influence humans to be like demons that God would destroy them.

"Stop!" Lucifer stood up and shouted. He had had enough. "Is this the best you can do? Remember that this woman is teaming up with God to destroy our kingdom. It's got to be an airtight plan."

Lucifer was quiet for a moment then reluctantly said, "Ok, Ok, Power Thirst, since we have no better plan, I'll put you in charge of destroying all humans. But if this does not work, you can forget about being my right hand demon."

Several hundred years passed. Power Thirst's idea had almost worked.God had destroyed most humans. However, Noah and his family had survived the flood. Another emergency meeting was scheduled. After enduring hours of Lucifer's ranting and raving about the failed plan, a demon called Jealous spoke up slowly and carefully. "We've succeeded in separating the woman and man from God. Now all we have to do is separate the man and woman from each other. She'll have no place to turn. The way to do that is to break her up inside. She'll be separated from HERSELF and we can accomplish what we want."

"How do you expect to accomplish that?" sneered Power Thirst.

"I have spent these years observing women. I have felt that there must be a vulnerable part in them—a place on the inside where, if we can get to it early enough, we are guaranteed that they will forever focus on it and not God. I have looked for something that will cause women to doubt and not trust God. I wanted to make sure they would not have the energy to even look in God's direction, let alone listen and do what He says. On the outside the woman will look good, but inside she will be one big pile of broken pieces."

"Well, did you find it? What is that place inside of her?" Lucifer inquired. "You could get promoted with this one if your plan is any good!"

"Her S-E-X-U-A-L-I-T-Y is the key." Jealous began to smile. "Hit her at the core of her being, and it ties in to everything God wants to use her to do. It will break her heart into tiny pieces. It will emotionally cripple her for the rest of her life. She will never recover."

"You had better have very good reason why you think sexuality is the key." Lucifer scowled.

"Well, her sexuality is intertwined with her spirituality," the confident Jealous continued. "Sexuality encompasses all of her soul, her thoughts, desires, and her emotions. With her sexuality intact, she has some semblance of wholeness. But if we attack her sexuality, she'll be broken in pieces and won't even know it."

Impatiently Lucifer almost shouted, "I'm listening. Go on."

"By attacking her sexuality, we will definitely affect her ability to trust God and man," Jealous explained, feeling more and more confident. "This alone will accomplish most of what we want. Without trust in God, she will not be close to God. She will not be able to hear Him warn her of our plans. She will not bring Him into her affairs. She'll just try to handle things on her own. Plus, we can make sure she passes this distrust along to her seed so that they won't hear God, either.

"We'll use our bitterness, unforgiveness, and hate troops. I believe we can actually have a vicious cycle of hate going—women hating men and men hating women. We'll use men in our plan. Since men like power, we'll trick them into using it to oppress and damage women." Jealous paused again to let his words sink in. Then he added, "Don't worry. The men will help us."

Lucifer began to get excited." Yeah! We can assign demons whose only job is to work in this arena. We can lead humans into all kinds of acts of perversion, lewdness, and abuse! Much of these things will be humanly intolerable. We will work constantly to make this happen! I can see a day we can even have fathers sexually abusing their children! It may take some time, but I believe we can do it."

"Yes," Jealous continued. "A lot will depend on how much humans call upon God's help and seek to follow His regulations. We'll use guilt and lies to keep women away from God. We can eventually set an atmosphere in which our ways are the norm. Then they will totally ignore God's way's. They won't even know the difference. God wants to keep this sex stuff within the confines of marriage, but that will be the biggest joke around— once we have our way."

"It's great! That's it!" Lucifer could no longer contain himself. "I see it! I love it! When they do it our way, we'll be in control. They'll be under our clutches. Why didn't I think of this? We'll just keep inserting more pain. They will be so frustrated, they won't have time to serve God."

"Certainly," replied Jealous, now with his chest stuck out. "The more they walk away from God's way, the more inroads for us to do what we want with them."

"This is just excellent! But we've got to do it in such a way that they'll never know we're behind it all," said Lucifer.

Jealous continued, "I see a day when these humans will no longer be spiritually sensitive. We can talk them out of believing in our existence. Even those who believe we exist will no longer think about us and what we are capable of doing. This whole plan will need a sub-plan, someone to take on indoctrination with our philosophies. We need a special group who will be responsible to put out our propaganda. They will be responsible for getting out lies, vicious lies, the more lies the better, until we cover all of humanity. Ha! Ha! Ha! Lies about women, lies about sex, lies about God's love. But humans will accept them. Believe me. If we work hard they'll be doing what we want them to do."

"Yes! Yes! This is it!" Lucifer started to laugh uncontrollably.

"But we won't stop at this," Jealous beamed. "We'll cause so much confusion. Instead of families that God planned, we'll destroy the family unit. We'll make sex recreation. We'll take away the sacredness of it. We'll remove all God intended. We'll use the pleasure aspect. We'll kill the pleasure of sex if necessary. We'll do whatever we can to make sure women are broken. We'll make having seed such an inconvenience they'll begin to destroy it."

When he was finished, everyone gave Jealous a standing ovation. Not appreciating the attention given to Jealous, Lucifer quickly took over. "Listen up, everyone. We have much planning to do. We have to break into plenary sessions! Let's discuss our strategies. Group one, plan your attack on infants and little girls. Your task is to see to it that eventually they are sexually shamed, fondled, molested—even raped, if possible. Remember, you have to work closely with the philosophy and indoctrination demons to get acceptance of the lies that will make your job easier.

"Group two, figure out how you can miseducate girls at a young age to help us influence their minds and cause damage later on in life.

"Group three, go after the pre-teen, teenagers, and single young adult females. Entice them any way you can to have all kinds of sexual experiences with several different partners before they get married. That will surely confuse them.

"And Group four, you work undercover. Plant seeds of destruction in areas they will never suspect—like shame about normal childhood experiences, distorted ideas pertaining to sex in marriage—and try your best to destroy them in their mid-life years. Oh yes, this is a wonderful strategy. I see thousands of bitter, angry women messed up for life because of our destructive operation. Nothing will be able to remove the shame or wash away their evil behavior. Oh, they'll be just like us. Isn't this great? Are there any questions?"

"How many women do we attack?" one demon who sat next to Lucifer asked.

"EVERY SINGLE ONE OF THEM. We'll make a plan to attack every single woman on the face of the earth and in some way attempt to destroy her sexually." Lucifer was wringing his hands with joy. "Any more questions?"

"What about God? Won't He confront our attack on female sexuality?" asked Power Thirst, hoping to get a chance at saving face. "I don't care about God. I don't care about the Seed. We're going to do this! Forget God. Our plans will work. Humans still have free will." Lucifer was now very cocky, arrogant, and confident. "Power Thirst, you're demoted; take charge over the group assigned to lust and perversion. Jealous, you're now my right hand principality. I put you in charge of 'Operation: Attack Female Sexuality.' You are all dismissed until tomorrow."

The little ignorant imp piped up, "One more question, Boss. How long does our sexual attack on women continue?"

"Until the very end of time."Lucifer began to laugh."Until the end of time!"

***

This Satanic convention was imaginary and speculative, but the Satanic attack is not. Since the beginning of time, women have been reeling from Satan's vicious assaults in the sexual area of their lives. (This is not to say Satan does not attack males as well, but our concentration is primarily on women.) Is there hope? Can we overcome such savage assaults? Can women who have been sexually violated as children ever be whole again, or are they irreparably scarred for life? Is there a way to protect our daughters from premarital sexual experiences, or do we resolve to stock up on condoms and hope for the best? Can there be sexual fulfillment in marriage and the senior years of a woman's life?

Talk shows, book authors, music, and movie media–everyone seems to have plenty to say about sexual abuse, sex education and miseducation, sexual behaviors, problems, and perversions. Isn't it time we listen to what God has to say? After all, He is the creator of our sex organs and He had the original plan on how they are to be used. This book is His opportunity to speak. I have found that the Word of God has a wealth of information, encouragement, and healing for women in the sexual area.

In this book, I attempt to expose you to Satanic attacks upon women. It is my firm belief that once Satan's work is explained and understood from God's perspective, you will walk away armed with knowledge for the future benefit of you and your family. You will have the assurance that regardless of your past experiences, sexual pain, and brokenness, God can make you whole.

ADDITIONAL INFORMATION

Several places in the book will suggest counseling. I realize when the word "counseling" is used, different images come to mind; from a woman stretched out on a psychiatrist's couch, telling her whole life story, to a woman sitting in a room alone praying, claiming God as the only counselor she will ever consult. To follow our method throughout this book, let's look at what the Word of God has to say on the matter.

The word. Counsel (*Ya'ats* and *'etsah* in Hebrew and *boule* and *sumbolion* in the Greek) basically means to advise, admonish, direct, resolve, plan, or to consult with one another, counsel together, or to be advised.

Another Hebrew word (*tachbuwiah*) that means counsel is used very specifically to mean good or wise counsel. "Where there is no guidance [counsel] the people fall, but in abundance of counselors there is victory" (Proverbs 11:14).

From these definitions, various events in the Bible, and principles in God's Word, we can establish what God thinks and wants us to do about counseling.

God wants Himself, Jesus, and the Holy Spirit to be our primary counselors. Whenever God's counsel was received and followed, God's people were successful, problems were solved, and everything eventually worked out all right.(Joshua 1:8; Psalm 16:7; 33:11; 73:24; Jeremiah 23:18)

Jesus is called our Wonderful Counselor (Isaiah 9:6). One of the Holy Spirit's responsibilities is to lead and guide believers into all truth (John 16:13). We are to look to these two sources to escort us through the perils of this life. The Persons we consult first–the leaders of our counseling team, and the final authority in any course of action in our lives–should always be the Godhead.

God wants us to use the Bible as our main counseling manual. There are a lot of books on the market designed to give us step by step instructions about what to do concerning problems in our lives. But once again, just like the Godhead, the Bible should be our place to go for guidance, information, and the final authority over any other words on a printed page. I have yet to find a problem that does not have specific information or a guiding principle to apply to it. *"Thy testimonies also are my delight; they are my counselors"* (Psalm 119:24).

Every child of God should be regularly reading, studying, and learning God's word, individually and with other believers. So when a problem arises you will not have to scramble to find the passages that are applicable to your problem; they will come to mind from your past study. If you are a new Christian or not familiar with God's word, consult one who is more knowledgeable and have them find the passages for you.

A woman whose husband recently died asked me to give her all the scriptures in the Bible on widowhood. She said that they comforted her, assured her of God's presence, and gave her specific guidance in certain areas of her life. *"Thy word is a lamp to my feet, and a light to my path"* (Psalm 119:105). There are times when we will not need to go any further than the Bible for what we need.

There are a variety of counselors. We have already looked at the Godhead and the Word of God as counselors. But the Bible also indicates that counseling can come from other sources (Proverbs 11:14; 15:22; 24:6). For example, older women are to be encouragers and teach the younger women how to love their husbands and their children (Titus 2:3-4).

At times the Lord will lead us to others who can help with a particular problem. We should see the body of Christ as a rich source. In fact one of the gifts God gives to His people is the gift of exhortation. (*Parakiesis in Greek means to call to one's side or to aid another person for the purpose of strengthening, encouraging, and establishing them in the ways of God.*)

A believer in the church can have knowledge and expertise in a certain area that will help us come up with a godly solution for a problem. I really enjoyed hearing a Christian doctor talk about women's health issues at a women's seminar. She was knowledgeable in her field but also brought in the biblical aspects of health. You may not know all the different Christian professionals in your church or community, but your pastor may be able to direct you to someone that can give you information and help with your particular problem.

A mature Christian may be able to have a Bible study with you on a particular subject and be committed to support you until the problem is resolved. For some problems, a prayer partner who is committed to praying for and with you will work. You may need one or all of the above sources mentioned to find a solution for your particular problem. The key is to be led of the Lord as to where to go and who to talk to about your situation.

We should see those in authority over us as sources of God's counsel. A wife should consult her husband. Even if he is not a Christian, God may be able to use him to speak to her about a particular matter. "The king's heart is like channels of water in the hand of the Lord; He turns it wherever He wishes" (Proverbs 21:1). (Of course, one has to be wise and prayerful if the problem involves the husband. For example, if you suspect your husband of sexually molesting your children, you need to talk with some other people and know what you are dealing with before you confront your husband.)

The church to which you have committed yourself should have a godly shepherd whom you respect as a man of God and who is able to give you biblical advice. Our pastors are put over us to help guide our lives. *"Obey your leaders, and submit to them; for they keep watch over your souls. Let them do this with joy and not with grief, for this would be unprofitable for you"* (Hebrews 13:17).

Whether you choose your husband, pastor, or someone else be prayerful before you go to them. Ask God to guide what they say to you and help you to be discerning if they are suggesting something that God would not have you do.

We are not to follow counsel that is ungodly. *"How blessed is the man who does not walk in the counsel of the wicked, nor stand in the way of sinners, nor sit in the seat of scoffers"* (Psalm 1:1). I do not believe this passage is saying that we should never go to a secular counselor or any non-Christian resources for help. But I believe it is saying that we are not to follow advice of which our divine counseling team does not approve.

There was a case of a Christian woman who had an abortion and needed support to get over it. There was a support group that met to help women with this kind of problem. The group was not Christian but the woman learned a lot about what happens after a woman has an abortion and how to get over the mistake. But when a group member discussed yoga and other forms of ungodly meditation as a solution to negative thoughts, the woman knew that this advice was not biblical and she did not follow it. She proceeded to follow the Bible's instructions about ridding her mind of negative thoughts. She also knew she would not stay in this group for long. She would get the information she needed and then join a women's Bible study to get the encouragement and support she needed from other godly Christian women.

Chapter 2

Shame Originated in the Garden

THE EARLY IMPRESSIONS

I will never forget the day I was talking with my neighbor in the kitchen and my oldest daughter came bursting into the room. "Mama," she said excitedly, "Bobby is teaching Candacee how to change a diaper." Bobby was my next door neighbor's three year-old little boy. My youngest daughter, Candacee, was about two at the time. While we were talking, the two children had been playing in the bedroom. Bobby decided to invent a new game called "change the diaper," making himself the baby. At some point, most parents have had to deal with this kind of situation. It is a normal part of a child's growing up years.

There is, however, an enemy lurking in the background watching these innocent beginnings in childhood. Satan's job description is to take these natural activities and sow negative seeds in the early developmental stages. These seeds of destruction may never bloom until an individual has reached adulthood. The enemy is Satan, and some of the negative seeds he plants in those early developmental years are false guilt and shame.

SATAN'S SEEDS OF SHAME

In this chapter and the next we will discuss where shame originated, how it affects little girls in childhood and possibly later on in adulthood, and practical ways parents and other adults can keep Satan from damaging our little girls with shame in their early innocent stages of life.

A world without shame. In the second chapter of Genesis, the word "ashamed" is mentioned for the first time in the Bible.

"For this cause a man shall leave his father and his mother, and shall cleave to his wife, and they shall become one flesh. Both were naked and not ashamed" (Genesis 2:24–25).

God created Adam and Eve in the garden of Eden. Then He performed the first wedding ceremony. The couple became one flesh by coming together physically, with the goal of harmonizing intellectually, spiritually, and emotionally. God made this additional comment after creating man and woman: *"And the man and his wife were both naked and were not ashamed"* (Genesis 2:25).

In that short phrase, God communicated two important facts about what He desired before sin entered the world. First of all, Adam and Eve were not encumbered by clothing. They were able to experience and feel the beauty of God's creation with their whole bodies. I can imagine this first couple enjoying their honeymoon by rolling down hills of fragrant flowers and soft grass.

Secondly, they were not ashamed of their bodies. The root of the word "shame" (*buwsh* in Hebrew) means to "become pale or blush." When we feel the blood rushing to the face, on the inside we are saying, "You just caused me to be self-conscious, embarrassed, or confused." When Adam and Eve looked at each other's nude body, they could do so without blushing. Also, in God's presence, they did not drop their heads in shame or have an urge to run and hide because of their unclothed state. It was not until after the fall when sin entered the world that man began to experience negative feelings about being naked.

When the woman saw that the tree was good for food, and that it was a delight to the eyes, and that the tree was desirable to make one wise, she took from its fruit and ate; and she gave also to her husband with her and he ate. Then the eyes of both of them were opened, and they knew that they were naked; and they sewed fig leaves together and made themselves loin coverings. And they heard the sound of the Lord God walking in the garden in the cool of the day and the man and his wife hid themselves from the presence of the Lord God among the trees of the garden. The Lord God called to the man and said to him, "Where are you?" And he said "I heard the sound of thee in the garden, and I was afraid because I was naked; so I hid myself" (Genesis 3:7–10).

Shame's entrance into the world. When Adam and Eve disobeyed God, they became aware of their bare bodies. Shame made its entrance into the world. It is an emotion or feeling that says, "I have done something I know I was not supposed to do and I feel bad about it." God had given

Adam instructions. Every tree in the garden was available to the first couple except one. They ate from the tree that God forbade them to eat. God's standard was disregarded. Now Adam and Eve feared God's response.

Before Adam and Eve sinned, they were in perfect harmony with God. Now, feelings of being disconnected and distant entered their minds. What was God going to do now that they had displeased him? Would they ever be able to face Him again? They had knowingly displeased God. Hiding behind the fig leaves was an attempt to cover up not only their naked bodies but their bad inner feelings as well.

The shame I just described is the result of an individual deviating from a known standard. In this case, God established the guideline. Adam and Eve crossed over the line. Shame resulted. But there is another kind of shame referred to in the Bible. This second kind of shame (*Kalam* in the Hebrew) is inflicted upon a person from an outside source. It results when an innocent person, who has not done anything wrong, is insulted, taunted, or wounded. People would not experience this shame if it were not for something or someone else causing them to experience it.

When King David took the throne of Israel, for example, he desired to show kindness to Hanun, the king of Ammon (2 Samuel 10:2). David sent servants to this new king to console him because his father had just died. But instead of the young king appreciating and receiving David's kindness, he listened to bad advice from his subjects, who told him, *"Have not his servants come to you to search and to overthrow and to spy out the land?"* (1 Chronicles 19:3). Hanun then took David's servants, shaved off half of their beards, and cut off their clothes in the middle as far as their hips. This was considered a great humiliation for an Israelite. When these events were reported to David, he told them to stay outside the city until their beards grew back.

David's servants had no personal reason to be ashamed. They were following David's orders and not breaking any known laws. Because of the insecurity of this new king and his administration, shame was inflicted on these innocent men. They were insulted because of another person's insecurity.

THE RESULTS OF SHAME

Disconnectedness. Whether the person is shame-filled because of disobedience or because he or she is violated, it results in a feeling of disconnection from God and/or from other people. This is one of Satan's main goals for women; to isolate them from God and to ensure they never fulfill God's purpose and plan for their lives.

Adam and Eve were no longer harmoniously connected to God or one another. Before the fall, they had a close relationship with God. They welcomed His presence, communication, and association. Now there was a backing away from God. Sin had come into the intimate relationship.

The Bible says in the book of Romans, *"The wages of sin is death...."* which means a spiritual separation from God because of disobedience (Romans 6:23). This separation can be experienced after we die, meaning we will not live with God in heaven but in hell, eternally out of touch with God. This verse also means spiritual separation from God in our lives presently. Although God's presence is always surrounding Christians and non–Christians alike, if we disobey God's instructions we will ignore His presence; and like Adam and Eve, we will want to run and hide.

Adam and Eve also had been close to each other. After the entrance of shame, we see the man despising the woman, blaming her for eating from the forbidden tree, and making her his scapegoat before God. Sin had severed their close relationship as well.

David's servants suffered humiliation about their beards and clothes being cut off. Because of it, they temporarily disassociated with the rest of the people in Israel. They stayed away until their beards grew back and they felt presentable among the public again.

Confusion. Both Adam and Eve, as well as David's servants, also experienced confusion, another result of shame. Confusion occurs when something is unsettled or not in place. The Bible informs us that *"...God is not a God of confusion"* (1 Corinthians 14:33). God created the world and set everything in its proper place (Genesis 1-2). Satan works hard at upsetting God's intentions. God wants a woman to be used as a vessel, displayed to bring honor and praise to Him. Satan's job is to shatter God's woman into a thousand pieces and convince her that she will never be whole again. He does this by using people to cause situations which make a woman think that God is unconcerned and distant, that God must think she's an awful mess. His job is to disrupt things and knock them off kilter. *"The thief [Satan] comes only to steal, and kill, and destroy..."* (John 10:10). But you will see as you continue reading this book that God is able to heal and restore shattered vessels.

Guilt. Guilt is another result of shame. Often the words "guilt" and "shame" are used interchangeably, but if you look up both words in the original language in the Bible, they have different meanings. Guilt (*rasha* in Hebrew) is a legal term. It is the predicament or state of one who has broken the law. When individuals stand before a court of law, they are either declared guilty or not guilty. There is a violation that can be pointed to that has been disregarded.

Shame (*buwsh* in Hebrew) means to "become pale or blush" as was mentioned earlier. These are internal messages and emotions that cause us to be self-conscious, embarrassed, or confused. Adam and Eve experienced shame emotionally after they disobeyed God. They also were, however, in a state of guilt. They broke God's law. God distinctly told Adam, "Do not eat of this tree." Adam consciously disobeyed. Guilty! No court of law, no judge or jury was needed in the garden to declare it. Adam and Eve knew what they had done. Shame entered their emotions and guilt was their condition.

In contrast, David's servants did not break any laws when they went to the King of Ammon. Emotionally they experienced shame as a result of what happened to them. They were not guilty, however.

ADULT PROBLEMS AS A RESULT OF SHAME

Unhealthy relationships. As discussed earlier, shame causes feelings of disconectedness. This state can be very lonely. Women sometimes suffer with this kind of negative emotion. I've often heard people in church comment, "I can't understand it; this nice young single woman was growing in the Lord and doing so nicely in the church. Then along comes a man and bam! It seems as if she loses touch with reality. She latches on to him and no one is able to get through or reason with her about the damaging relationship or the destructive person who has come into her life."

In an attempt to get back in connection with someone or something, women will often latch on to the wrong things. Satan is an expert at telling single women, "You need a man," or at whispering to married women, "You need a different kind of man, one who is more sensitive, loving, and who understands you." If the woman does not take the time to pray and ask God about these seemingly true messages, she may begin to embrace the wrong enticements that bring false security and no lasting satisfaction.

Feelings of disconnectedness might be avoided if issues and situations related to sex were properly handled during a child's development. A young woman might be saved from many years of life on the wrong path. A person also often is spared from improperly imposed shame and guilt, which could lead to problems later in the marriage bed.

> I could never enjoy sex with my husband. I always felt guilt every time he touched my private parts. Something in my head kept saying, "This is wrong, nasty, dirty." As far as I know I had never been sexually abused as a child. I was a virgin when I married, and I never allowed a man to

take advantage of me as a teenager or young adult. But I did play with myself and play doctor with other children a lot when I was growing up. This is the only place I can imagine I picked up these negative feelings. I can't believe they followed me all the way into adulthood and into my marriage. I never imagined having to have counseling for something like this. –Lois

Poor self-concept. In the early stages of development, children are not able to discern. A little girl may not know, for instance, if her parents disapprove of her as an individual or if they disapprove of her behavior. The child may wonder, "Am I a bad person? Is there something wrong with me?" If the message that the child is "bad" continues to play inside her, the child will think less of herself. Adults who have poor self concepts may have picked up this tendency in childhood, and perhaps with improper parental responses to normal body explorations as a contributing factor.

If parents react negatively or punish this activity, it can cause adverse effects which may surface immediately or later on in life. Instead, a parent needs to help the child understand and appreciate her body as a good part of God's creation.

When I was about five years old, my cousin, who was about the same age, hid me under a coat and started to play inside my panties. He was looking inside my pants and checking things out, so I started to play around in his. We wanted to see how everything worked. My mother saw us and she spanked me unmercifully. I remember a very angry look on her face. She never did explain to me what was so wrong about what we did. I just knew it had to be awfully bad. From that day on, I felt that I could never do anything to please my parents, not even my dad, because I was sure my mother told him about what happened. I remember feeling that it was something that I would never live down, and just when I would think that I had gotten over it, something would happen to make me have those bad feelings all over again.

I spent the rest of my time in my parent's home trying to be the perfect child. I tried to eat the food no one else would eat, I did my homework and my chores, I tried not to bring any negative attention to myself. My discipline paid off in the form of excellent grades in school, but the whole experience made me very serious and sensitive. Anytime I was criticized for anything, it took on monumental proportions.

To this day, my mother does not know how much that spanking affected me. I have since, though, taken the whole experience to God. I have

forgiven my mother, because the more I learn about her, the more I realize that she probably had some similar negative experience of her own. She did what she knew to do. And I have asked God to help me accept that I am not a bad person and to not carry any baggage related to this experience. As I go through the days, giving my feelings to Him, I must say that He has been most loving and patient in making me feel whole again.
–Abbie

Hiding. When Adam and Eve reached for a way to cover up their sins, they reached for fig leaves to cover their bodies. People today already are wearing clothes, but they reach for other things to cover up their embarrassment for breaking God's law or for being ashamed. Defense mechanisms such as blaming others, withdrawal, and anger are a few of their symbolic coverings. Alcohol, drugs, food, and sex are other forms. What people think they are reaching for is simply something to make them feel good. Unfortunately, they are often seeking to hide from bad feelings of shame.

HOW TO OVERCOME SHAME

As we observe how God dealt with Adam and Eve and their shame and guilt, it will help us know what to do in similar circumstances.

Confess. When God came upon Adam and Eve hiding He asked them, "Where are you?" And later He asked, "Who told you that you were naked?" Keep in mind, God is sovereign and omniscient. Surely, God knew the whereabouts of Adam and Eve. He even understood exactly why it seemed necessary for them to hide. God heard every word of the conversation between this first couple and the serpent. Then, why did He ask the questions? God wanted to prompt a confession from their lips. This is the first step in dealing with shame and guilt as a result of a known offense. Confession means to agree with God concerning a matter. Confession is encouraged: *"If we confess our sins, He is faithful and righteous to forgive us our sins and to cleanse us from all unrighteousness"* (1 John 1:9).

Most of the time, we think of confession as telling God about what we have done wrong. However, confession is also agreeing with God about what is true concerning ourselves and others. When we confess about our own genital exploration as children and our feelings about it, or when we confess our own reactions as parents to our children, we may need to say something like this: "Lord, I as a parent have acted out of ignorance" or "My parents did not handle genital exploration correctly. Therefore, I'm not handling my children and their sexual exploring correctly," or "Lord, I feel really uncomfortable when I see my children touching the sexual parts of their bodies."

These kinds of feelings may be difficult for some to admit. When a child suffers from imposed shame from a parent, ironically, the child's response is often to protect and defend their parents. It is hard for adults to admit shortcomings on the part of a parent. We are taught as Christians to honor and respect them. Therefore, to say that our parents were wrong or acted unwisely toward us at any point in our child-rearing years would appear to be disrespectful or even a sin. This kind of thinking can cause us to harbor unhealthy emotional feelings and continue negative behaviors toward our own children.

If our parents shamed us, said nothing about normal genital exploration, or never gave proper sex education at home, THEY WERE WRONG. They may have acted or failed to act out of ignorance. Nonetheless, they had a responsibility and let us down at this point. Parents are not perfect. All parents have made their share of mistakes with their children. It is not only appropriate but healthy when we can acknowledge that fact, forgive them, and move on.

Accept forgiveness. God gave Adam and Eve a clean slate. He allowed them to start afresh and anew. They did suffer the consequences of their sin, but God didn't kick them out of the garden and make them fend for themselves. He sat down at His sewing machine and made the first fur coat for them to clothe themselves. He taught them how to use the plants and animals around them to survive. We, too, can always begin again in God.

I remember specifically praying about my sexual relationship with my husband before I got married. I realized the garbage of my childhood experiences–feeling shame about genital explorations, heavy petting during dating, and premarital sex experiences. I was a sexual mess. But I asked God to wipe it all clean and allow me and my husband to experience our intimate life together as if none of it had happened. I believe God answered my prayers. –Julie

Get a fresh perspective. God took the sin of Adam and Eve and shaped it into a cross called Calvary. Since the beginning of time God has been reshaping negative experiences into positive experiences for His glory.

A neighbor boy went well beyond the normal point of genital play. I was uncomfortable with it, but I was twelve before I told my mother and it was stopped. I felt trapped. As a result of that experience, I made a vow that no one except my husband would ever touch me sexually or even kiss me. That vow kept me a virgin until I got married. –May

May's negative childhood experience is living proof of the verse in Romans 8:28, *"And we know that God causes all things to work together for good to those who love God, to those who are called according to His purpose."* As we bring shabby pieces of our childhood to the Lord, He is able to make something clean and new from them. We do not need to continue to berate ourselves. Once we confess to God, we need to forgive ourselves and our parents, and continue to progress with our lives.

Examine your feelings. Parents who feel uncomfortable discussing with their children such topics as exploring the body, including the sex organs, may need to free themselves from their own negative thoughts on the subject stemming from the past. Scripture says, "And you shall know the truth and the truth shall make you free" (John 8:32). Some adults may need to hear it said, "When you touched your sex organs, you were not wrong. If an adult punished you or made you feel ashamed for this, they were wrong!" The book, *How and When to Tell Your Kids About Sex* by Stanton and Brenna Jones, has an excellent chapter called "Taking Stock: Knowing Your Strengths and Weaknesses as a Parent."[1] It has a number of questions parents should ask themselves honestly before the Lord in order to give their children a healthy perspective in this area. For example:

- What were your parents' attitudes toward sexuality and nudity? Were they comfortable talking about sex?
- Were you taught about sex as a child? What did you learn? How was it conveyed?
- Did any crucial experiences shape your feelings about sex in childhood (for example, engaging in sex play with another child and being caught or punished by parents)?

This kind of personal examination is good. It is unhealthy for a person to walk around feeling uncomfortable about a child's developmental stage which includes body curiosity and not become aware of the source of these awkward feelings or past wounds. Admitting your personal inner conflicts can "be enough to improve your functioning as a parent, and it can put you on the road to healing as you lift your weaknesses up to God."[2]

Praise and thank God for your sex organs. God did not create ninety-five percent of our body parts, then sit back and allow Satan to design and make our sex organs. When He fashioned man and woman, He was pleased with the complete final product (Genesis 1:31).

Nevertheless, some girls are told never to touch their genitals directly, only with a tissue or towel. They are taught or pick up the implication that their vaginal area is dirty or nasty. Once a young girl starts her menstrual cycle, she may again harbor the impression that because blood comes from the vaginal area it is unclean. These women tend to grow up and experience problems with sexual intimacy in marriage. Little boys, on the other hand, handle their penis regularly when they urinate, and are probably more comfortable and feel more positive about their body parts.[3]

Wrong ideas are also communicated to a child when sexual parts are called various names. We may say to a child, "This is your nose, these are your fingers, and these are your toes." Then we refer to the private parts by non-anatomical and even misleading names: "This is your 'peter,' 'ding dong,' or 'pussy cat.'" The child begins to think differently or negatively about these areas of the body.

For the sake of yourself and your children, destroy all the old recordings in your mind which play back harmful messages that the private parts of the body are dirty or nasty. Maybe your parents did not communicate unhealthy sexual connotations to you but you picked up these associations from other adults, television, peers, or even from a bathroom wall. Dismiss them now. It is time to have a praise and thanksgiving session over your sex organs and the sexual parts of your spouse and your children. These are all good things God has given us. *"I will give thanks to Thee, for I am fearfully and wonderfully made; wonderful are Thy works, and my soul knows it very well"* (Psalm 139:14).

NOTES

1. Stanton and Brenna Jones, *How And When To Tell Your Kids About* Sex, (Colorado Springs: NavPress, 1993), 35.
2. Ibid., 38.
3. Ibid., 82.

WHAT'S NORMAL?

Chapter 3

Normal Genital Exploration and Shame

S atan knows the potential damage that can be done when an adult inflicts a little girl with shame and guilt for normal genital exploration. This is one of Satan's devious sneak attacks. The negative side of shame and guilt can fragment and cause damage in a woman's relationship with God. That is the deceiver's whole purpose. Satan, therefore, introduces these concepts early in the child's life. He methodically chips away at these little baby vessels, bit by bit. He has plenty of time because he knows by the time a girl has developed into womanhood, practically every room in her emotional house will probably eventually give way. As an adult, there may be need for extensive reconstruction.

WHAT IS NORMAL?

In infancy. When a child is born, she is just like Adam and Eve in their pre-sin days. She has no negative thoughts or feelings about the body at all. It is not until a parent slaps or pulls the hands away from the sex organs that the child begins to experience *inflicted* shame.

Surprisingly, recent ultrasound studies suggest male children may experience an erection of the penis inside the womb–before birth! Also, one might notice an erection shortly after birth, when an infant has a full bladder, or while the baby is breast feeding. Female babies are also physiologically capable of responding in what may appear to be sexual ways by firming the clitoris and producing vaginal lubrication. This probably happens because infants experience pleasure with their whole bodies.[1] Although this seems unusual, it is normal.

It is fascinating to watch newborns discover their world. Once infants determine the mouth gives pleasurable sensations, in go the fist, toes, or anything else within their grasp. Babies attach themselves to soft, warm, security blankets or a favorite cuddly toy. These developmental activities are perfectly normal.

An infant learns to hold on to things at about five months old. It is not uncommon for a little boy that age to discover and touch his penis. He plays with it just like he does his big toe.This is an ordinary part of baby's examining his body.

By the end of the youngster's first year, some form of random genital play will be observed in both males and females. Children may not always use their hands for this type of stimulation. Another means of gratification involves rubbing their thighs together. Girls in particular are inclined to stimulate themselves by rhythmic movements of the buttocks while lying down.

This behavior is typical for a small child. Even though the child may seem to thoroughly enjoy this experience, there are no erotic or sexual connotations to the act. This will not cause the child to be overly sexually stimulated or desire genital play more than a child who does not engage in this kind of activity. This is all very normal.[2]

Babies usually consistently wear a diaper. It is only while bathing or changing the child's diaper that genital exploration occurs. At this age, such play should be ignored and regarded as typical infant behavior.

> My son seemed overly stimulated when he was a baby. I would just touch
> him lightly in that area and he would have an erection. I thought, "This
> can't be good, what do I do?"–Marie

Some parents are uncomfortable even with a baby touching his or her genitals. They may respond by trying to distract the infant or by constantly moving the hands. Even at this early stage of development, parents can transmit negative feelings to the child and the infant can sense a parent's discomfort. If this kind of response is consistently displayed, it won't take long for the child to comprehend that there is something wrong with this part of his or her body.

The parent's disapproving actions establish a standard: "Children are not to play with their sex organs. If they do, it results in objection by the parent." Now, if she does it again–which, in all likelihood, she will–the child is "guilty" because the parent has stated the rule either verbally or by action. The child understands that she is not to do it, but continues to fondle her private parts anyway. As the infant moves into toddlerhood and continues this genital play, it is now accompanied with a great deal of guilt.

Earlier in the century, parents were told erroneous facts about children touching their bodies and were warned not to allow their children to touch the genital area. Myths even prevailed that childhood masturbation could cause mental retardation, physical deformity, blindness, poor physical and mental health, facial pimples, hair on the palms of the hand, homosexuality, and sexual perversions.[3]

A description of masturbation quoted from 1890 says, "Children who masturbate become visibly emaciated and anemic, remained backward in their bodily and mental development; they develop an apathetic expression and placid muscles. The become indifferent to the amusements which they once enjoyed and withdraw from all society, preferring to be alone, in order to indulge their passion. Their gait becomes unsteady and cumbersome and the knees fall inward. The penis increases disproportionately in length and thickness. Paralysis of the lower extremities is occasionally an effect of this practice."Treatment methods advocated fifty years ago included cauterization or burning of the clitoris, blistering of the vulva, and sending the child away from home.[4]

Thankfully, these myths are no longer believed. However, parents are usually still uncomfortable with a child exploring the genitals or demonstrating sensual behavior.

Toddler Activity. Around the second birthday, a child begins to derive a great deal of pleasure from the senses. The feel of messy, gooey things fascinates children. This is why making oatmeal or mashed potatoes into a shampoo and then massaging it into the hair is more pleasurable to a toddler than eating it. Children this age reach out to feel soft fabrics, instantly turn away from bright lights, and spit out food not pleasurable to taste.[5]

Toddlers constantly want entertainment-type experiences repeated. It is impossible to swing a two-year-old up in the air just one time. The bundle of joy will scream and cry each time you stop and demand that you continue swinging until your arms are sore. In the same way, once the toddler realizes the genital area feels good, fondling the penis or rubbing the clitoris–he or she might repeat this stimulating behavior.

By the toddler stage, the child is capable of understanding simple limitations and can be easily distracted. By setting simple guidelines and keeping the child occupied, the parent can handle a potentially embarrassing genital-play situation.

Close supervision is essential when small children are playing together. Provide them with exciting games and toys. Toddlers quickly get bored with television. They will independently find something more interesting to do if a parent is not present to make a suggestion, especially if the child is hyperactive.

When unsupervised, for example, children often will engage in sex play with each other. The incident I mentioned earlier involving my daughter and my neighbor's son was never tried again. The neighbor and I decided that whenever we talked, the children would be in the same room with us, or we would check on them often if they played in another room.

Parents also need to be on the alert for other significant adults or siblings in the child's life who may be inflicting unnecessary shame and guilt when they observe normal genital play. Unfortunately, not all relatives and friends will respect a parent's decision about genital exploration. If other adults or older children are babysitting your child or live in your household, be firm with them about the way you have decided to handle your child's behavior in this area. Make sure you are consistent regardless of the circumstances or who is present, and give the child plenty of positive affirmation.

If you do find your child involved in sexual play or genital exploration, for the sake of your child, it is better to stay as calm as possible. Do not make a big scene. Tell the child, "I realize this may be a fun game, but you are to keep your clothes on. A person's private parts are to stay covered. I prefer that you play something else." Then make a few suggestions and see to it that they are carried out.

John Nieder in his book, *What You Need To Tell Your Child About Sex*, advises parents about genital play: "Don't ignore it and don't condemn it. Take the opportunity to communicate your love, acceptance and understanding...of the human body as God created it." Nieder spells out a way to talk to your child:

> It feels good to touch your body's private parts, doesn't it? God made you that way. As you get older, you will understand why. Your body happens to be a magnificent machine that God designed for you to use in order to work for Him. Because our bodies are special to God, we should take care of them. [6]

Another example from *How and When to Tell Your Kids About Sex* is to say something like this:

> I understand exactly why you are interested in other people's bodies and they in yours. We all know inside that those parts are special, and we want to know about special things. It's like wanting to unwrap a Christmas present before Christmas! It's just natural to feel that way. And it's also natural to want to know more about private things; it makes us feel grown up to know about private things. But even though it is a fine thing

to be curious, I don't want you to show your penis (vagina, privates) to other kids. And I don't want you to ask to see theirs. If you keep those parts of you private and special, it will help you to always feel that God made you in an especially wonderful way. [7]

Parents should understand a child at this age is simply curious and attempting to learn. She is mystified about the private areas of the body; her own, her peers, and adults. When you find your child exploring her body or that of another child, this may be a good time to say, "You seem to be interested in the private areas of your body. Let's find a book that will help you learn about them, rather than playing this way."[8] Many good books and booklets are on the market to help you explain the sexual areas to your child. (See the resource list at the end of this book.)

At this point, the child may begin to ask sex-related questions. Parents should be prepared to give the child simple, brief answers. A child is less likely to excessively engage in sexual play if she is appropriately educated for her age on sexual matters, understands the parts of her body (perhaps by observing elementary biological pictures of the reproductive organs), and is given explanations by a loving, caring adult. She may not need sexual play because her curiosity needs have been answered.

This is also a time when children are learning Bible stories. As simply as you can, explain God's approval of sex in marriage. For example, in the creation story, point out that Adam and Eve were naked and this was all right with God because they were married. God approved of all that He had made, including our sexual parts. There is nothing bad about God's creation. Many children pick up negative messages about sex and sexuality. This way, they are hearing from you and the Bible that our sexual parts and their appropriate functions are good in the sight of you and God. If the child has been given negative messages in this area, then they can be countered with truth.

As we are teaching privacy of sexual parts to our toddlers, we also need to model this before them as parents. We should also be keeping our private areas covered. The child will get mixed messages if we make a habit of walking around the house in skimpy underwear or revealing night clothes. This may cause the child to be sexually aroused and unable to understand her feelings at a young age. Arousal may also occur when parents have sexual intercourse in the same bed or in the same room where a child is supposedly sleeping. Some women report feelings of shame, negative thoughts about sex, or early erotic feelings because of sounds, vibrations, or observations of the sex act. Parents should not assume a child is sleeping or unaware of their activities and should only have sex in private.

Parents should also be careful not to embarrass children in ways that relate to their bodies or sexuality. Some fathers may spank their daughters and make them pull their panties down as part of the spanking. Mothers with little boys may also do the same thing. Or they threaten to pull a little girl's panties down or spank her in the tub with no clothes on. Although these practices may sound harmless, they may cause negative thinking about the body and sex later on. A spank on the bottom through a pair of underwear can be just as effective as hitting a naked bottom.

In keeping with the above suggestions, give your child her privacy as quickly as possible. Once she is at the age where she can function in the bathroom, let her go alone. Teach her to knock before she enters a closed door. You, in turn, give her the same respect.

Preschoolers and sexual curiosity. Genital exploration in preschool years is probably the most intense. One mother shared a comment from her three-year-old daughter. "I tried several times to get my daughter to keep her hands out of her panties," she said. "But she would argue with me, 'This feels good, Mama. It's my favorite thing to do.'"

During the preschool stage, the child's tight-fitting diaper is replaced with training pants. This type of underwear is easy to reach into or take down. When a preschool child is potty training, there is more access to the genital organs. The child's fascination increases even more in the sexual area when the child learns about urination and defecation. By the time a child is in regular school, this type of activity may still be occurring, but should be diminishing. The children find other means of satisfaction outside their own bodies. [9]

WARNINGS SIGNS

Although genital exploration in the early stages of childhood development **is** normal, excessive activity in this area is not. Dr. Grace Kettermen, author of *How to Teach Your Child About Sex,* gives these warnings:

> Due to excessive curiosity from either too much, too little, or the wrong sort of sex education, many children will explore each other's bodies while at play. Some of this exploration is natural, but it can be both frightening and guilt producing to a child. Few parents are prepared to handle such a situation well.... Children can become sexually excited, and to become involved in experiences that create such intense feelings so prematurely may cut short the carefree simple joys they deserve. [9]

Even though it is normal for young children to explore in "body curiosity" type of behavior privately or with other children, parents should also be on the alert for certain situations.

Children acting out adult sexual behavior.   Children today are exposed more to sexually explicit materials and could be engaging in activities that are not "child's play," but reenactments of adult sexual behavior.

> The seven-year-old from the new family had enticed the younger kids to act out the movie he saw. He had wheedled, bullied and induced the younger kids to do what he directed them to.... Becky, the three-year-old from across the street, had acted out intercourse with the new five-year-old...though she had kept her panties on. [11]

This type of behavior is becoming more common among children. Exposure to explicit sex scenes on television, videos and movies, access to a parent's pornographic materials, exposure to seductive lyrics in songs, or even watching parents, older siblings, a babysitter, or others involved in sexual activities, can give a child the instructions as to how to carry out certain adult sexual behavior. With this in mind, it is important that we understand when ordinary childhood developmental experimentation crosses the line into inappropriate behavior or even sexual abuse.

An older child with a younger child. The older child might be taking advantage of a younger child and forcing the small child to engage in sexual play with which the younger one is not comfortable. Adolescent sexual abuse is on the rise. A parent should be very leery about allowing an older male child to be with a younger girl alone.

Aggressive children. If another child is insistent on sex games or engaging in adult sexual activities with your child–TALK WITH THE PARENTS. You may be instrumental in helping the child get help with a serious problem before he is accused and arrested for sexual abuse. It also may be necessary to keep your child away from certain children for a time, (and perhaps even explain why). Most children do stop such behavior after a while. But do not allow your child to be a victim while waiting on behavioral changes.

POSSIBLE REASONS FOR EXCESSIVE TOUCHING
Physical Problems. If a child continues to excessively touch his or her private areas in public, physical reasons should be explored first. Does the child have an infection or rash? This can easily be treated or ruled out by a pediatrician. Is the child's skin sensitive? A special soap or medication may

be required. At bath time or during toilet wiping the area may be rubbed too harshly. There could be some kind of physical cause, like itching. When frequent public genital play continues and physical problems have been ruled out or solved, then begin to examine other possibilities.

Attention. Most parents do not ignore this kind of activity. Thus, if little Suzy discovers that she will always get attention from an adult if she starts to fondle her genitals, she may engage in it more frequently to be noticed by an otherwise occupied parent.

Is a new brother or sister taking more of the parent's attention away from the child? Is someone ill in the family and requiring extra care from the parent? Rarely do children understand these kinds of changes. They still want their needs met and will find ways to accomplish this goal. If some of these events have occurred, include her as much as possible in the baby's or sick person's care. This might reinforce her importance and provide the necessary attention she may be craving.

Frequent genital stimulation lessens significantly when parents increase physical contact with the child. Hugging, holding, wrestling, and other games which involve a great deal of body contact can be helpful for the child.[12] The purchase of a dog for the child to aggressively play with may also help.

Allow me to add this side note. Some parents shy away from this kind of physical parenting activity because they have experienced sexual arousal when in physical contact with the child. Commonly, mothers may have experienced this while breast feeding her infant. A father may have an erection when a child is playing horsey on his lap. This validates the fact that we are sexual, not sinful, beings. When sexual parts are touch or rubbed, sometimes a certain sexual response happens, whether we want it or not. Such a response does not mean you are destined to be a child molester or that you have perverted sexual drives. However, parents need to be honest with themselves, have an understanding about what may be causing the feelings, and focus the meeting of their sexual needs in the marriage relationship, not with the child.[13]

If you find that you are encouraging physical activity with your child solely to get a sexual arousal, if you begin to feel overwhelming sexual desires or thoughts toward the child, or if you have been sexually abused yourself, it may be a good idea for you to confess this feeling to your spouse, a trusted friend,or someone who is knowledgeable in the parenting field. Do not leave your child starving for physical affection because of your insecurities or the fleshy thoughts Satan may be trying to force into your head. Physical touch is necessary for your child's emotional well being.

Pray that you can find the help that you need so you can give your child healthy, parental affection that most children seem to crave.

Trauma. A parent should observe if the child seems happy in her surroundings or relationships. Has the child been frightened by something? Has there been a separation or a divorce? Has she just started day care? Did the mother begin to work outside the home? These are just some of the things that can cause a child to use genital stimulation for comfort.

Other Issues. When children excessively stimulate their genitals, investigate to determine if there is a relative, friend, or schoolmate engaging in this type of behavior and being observed by the child. Is there exposure to sexually explicit materials? Is the child simply imitating a bad habit she picked up from someone else? Is the child hyperactive and using genital stimulation for tension release?

While these concerns are being investigated, the child needs to feel understood. Without inflicting guilt and shame, she needs to be reassured. Begin by saying, for example, "Touching yourself is not necessarily bad. But when you do this in public this way, it makes people uncomfortable." This kind of support from parents may result in eliminating or reducing the activity immediately. If the excessive genital stimulation continues, you may want to talk with someone who is knowledgeable about children's developmental stages and familiar with this kind of behavior. Some choices are a school counselor, a teacher, a counselor who deals with children or even a parent who is older or more experienced with children. Any or all of these sources may be able to give you insight.

Parental Considerations. Some children may seem to have a genital play problem when, in fact, it is the parents' excessive preoccupation with their child's genital play that creates the problem. In those cases, the parents need help with their problem first. Review the suggestions in Chapter 1 and the exercises at the end of this chapter to become better prepared to help your child.

When I was growing up, my sister and I often played a little game called "girlfriend and boyfriend." The game always included fondling each other's genitals. It seemed we had a lot of time to ourselves. Our mother seemed to be busy at the other end of the house. When other children came over we often included them in our game. I still can remember the look of satisfaction on this little boy's face as my sister and I caressed his penis.

I never remember my mother catching us or talking to us about this kind of activity. Now that I have children, when I see them engaging in this

kind of play, I'm very uncomfortable with it. I usually don't handle it well.
–Lynn

Parents need to come to grips with their attitudes about genital exploration–and the earlier in the child's development the better–especially if
they are responding to this childhood activity with extreme embarrassment
or anger. If you are unable to talk to your child about these activities in a
calm unemotional way, this could be an indication that you may have a
problem related to these same issues. You may still be suffering from the
insensitive or harsh manner a parent dealt with you when you engaged in
normal genital exploration. Anxiety in this area could also stem from your
own experiences as a victim of sexual abuse.

Whatever the root of your discomfort, get to the bottom of it in order
to better deal with your child. Before you do anything pertaining to what
you perceive as a problem with your child or yourself...PRAY! Seek God's
direction. He knows you and your child inside out. God will directly give
you the help you need or direct you to someone who can.

NOTES
1. Stanton and Brenna Jones, *How And When to Tell Your Kids About Sex,* (Colorado Springs: NavPress, 1993), 78-79.
2. R. Johnson, *Masturbation In Children,* (Focus On The Family, 1993) (Fact sheet), 1.
3. Ibid., 2.
4. Ibid., 2.
5. Grace Craig, *Human Development*, (Englewood Cliffs N.J.: Prentice Hall, 1976), 1993.
6. John Nieder, *What You Need to Tell Your Child About Sex*, (Nashville: Thomas Nelson, 1988), 165-166.
7. Jones, *How and When to Tell Your Kids*, 92-93.
8. Nieder, *What you Need to Tell Your Child*, 165-166.
9. R. Johnson, 2.
10. Grace Ketterman, *How to Teach Your Child About Sex,* (Old Tappan, N.J.: Fleming H. Revell, 1981), 95.
11. Jones, *How And When to Tell Your Kids,* 98.
12. Ibid., 23.
13. Jones, *How and When to Tell*, 80.

EXERCISES

1.Take time to read and think about these verses in scripture and what God thinks about our bodies. Genesis 1:27; 2:7; 21-22; 1 Corinthians 12:12-25 (especially verse 18); Psalm 139:14.

2.Write down all the things that you have experienced which caused you to feel shame or guilt when you were a child in the area of sexual exploration. Then ask God to show you the truth about each one. The next step is to forgive all persons involved as related to these matters. Pray for a new beginning.

3.Write down all the mistakes you may have made with your child in this area of sexual exploration. Pray and ask God if you specifically need to ask your child's forgiveness about anything. If so, do it!

4.What do you plan to do differently?

Chapter 4

Satan's Fiery Dart Called Sex Abuse

GOD'S ORIGINAL PLANS FOR SEX

Before we look at the mishandling of God's precious gift called sex and how Satan has distorted it through sexual abuse, let's examine what God initially had in mind when He created it.

Sex is to help eliminate isolation and loneliness. Before God created the first woman He declared, *"It is not good for man to be alone; I will make a helper suitable for him"* (Genesis 2:18). One purpose this "suitable helper" was to fulfill was to be sexually compatible with the man. Sex in marriage was to enhance and help deepen the couple's relationship.

Sex is for procreation. In Genesis, God told the first couple to be fruitful and multiply (Genesis 1:28). The method Adam and Eve and the rest of mankind was to employ in bringing more human beings into the world was sexual intercourse.

Sex is for pleasure. After God performed the first wedding ceremony, Adam and Eve became "one flesh." This meant to come together physically, and eventually blend together spiritually and emotionally as well. The next line in the verse reads, *"And the man and his wife were both naked and were not ashamed."* This verse confirms that God fully approved their physical union. His marriage bed is undefiled.

In other places in Scripture, it is emphasized that this physical union is to bring pleasure and satisfaction to the married couple. In Proverbs, Solomon says, *"As a loving hind and a graceful doe, let her breast satisfy you [the husband] at all times..."* (Proverbs 5:19). Most of the Song of Solomon emphasizes the pleasure of the intimate physical relationship between husband and wife.

I'd always heard, "Sex is for the man; women just have to endure it." I was a virgin when I married and from the first night my husband and I were together on our honeymoon, I was pleasantly surprised. We really seemed to connect sexually and I have always gotten a lot of pleasure in it. At first I thought something must be wrong with me. Then I studied Song of Solomon in a couples class. I found Solomon's wife seemed to have the same feelings about sex as I did. So now instead of thinking something is wrong with me, I think something is wrong with other women who talk negatively about sex in their marriages. –Marge

Marge is not only right from a biblical perspective but also the physical. If you look at the human body, you will see that God designed certain parts of the body for sexual pleasure. For example, at no other place on our bodies (except the mouth) do we have as many nerve endings that cause intense delight. The woman's clitoris has no additional function other than to give her satisfaction in sex. Men don't even have such a unique area. God's design is for us to intensely enjoy the sexual experience. Ladies, God wants us to have sexual pleasure. Thank God that we are fearfully and wonderfully made!

Our sexual organs are to bring glory to God. The Bible calls our bodies "vessels." God wants to set apart and use our vessels (or bodies) for His honor (2 Timothy 2:21). Paul reminds the Corinthians, while warning them against sexual sin, that their bodies are members of Christ and that believers house the Holy Spirit. The body is to glorify or bring praise to God, not shame. This encompasses every part of our body–including the sex organs. The Bible strongly speaks against sexual misconduct. In one passage, Paul reminds the Corinthians that the body was not made for sexual sin. We must run from it, because no other sin affects the body like this one (1 Corinthians 6:13, 18).

Women's bodies are special–they are used by God as a conduit to bring forth life itself. Men don't have this unique purpose. When a female's body is placed on Satan's altar and misused (instead of in God's place of sacrifice, see Romans 12:1-2), God is grieved and the woman is violated.

Sexual misconduct weakens the woman's vessel, like a crack in a wall. Before you know it, this one crack causes a hole, and eventually the whole building falls apart. Sexual sins effect the entire body and life of the woman. The body of Christ also feels the rippling effect of sexual offenses. The body (the woman's and God's people) can no longer be all that God intended it to be. Satan is delighted when God's purposes and plans are hindered. Yet Jesus came on the scene to counter the plans and destroy them. *"...For the* _devil has sinned from the beginning. The Son of God appeared for this purpose, that He might destroy the works of the devil_" (1 John 3:8).

SATAN'S INTENTION TO CREATE SEX ABUSE

Pastor Myles Munroe wrote a book and has a tape series outlining seven principles for purposeful living. In principle number four he says, "Wherever purpose is not known, abuse is inevitable."[1] In other words, if one does not know how something is to function, it might be used incorrectly. When people do not know God's intentions and designs for sex, the result is usually abnormal activity (out of the context in which it was created) or sexual abuse. Satan's job is to see to it that sex is taken outside of God's instructions and is put into operation to hurt and destroy people's lives, not enhance a loving relationship in marriage. If it is true that sex plays a vital role in God's plan and purposes—and it is—then it makes sense that women would especially be attacked in this area. Why? Because God has given women some very special and unique roles in his work based on our physical and emotional make-up.

I hate to commend Satan, but he has done his job well during the last thirty years in America. He has made sure that his perspectives are widespread and that ungodly sexual activity flourishes. Satan has influenced people to believe several of his lies, and this has led to widespread sexual abuse.

Sexual abuse occurs when sex is seen as recreation. The sexual revolution in the sixties moved behavior intended for the privacy of a married couple's bedroom into the realm of "sex any time, any place, and with anybody, for any reason." The attitude became, for many, that if you are thirsty and need a glass of water, get one and drink it. If you want to satisfy your sexual urges, grab anything, a plastic dummy, your neighbor's wife, a vibrator—or even an innocent little girl.

Sexual abuse occurs when women are seen as sex objects for man's sexual pleasure. In spite of all the women's rights activities in recent years, women are still seen as sex objects. Women are still sexually exploited, especially in the media, but also in what should be loving relationships.

Shortly after we were married, I discovered my husband regularly read pornographic magazines and occasionally watched "X" rated movies. I admit, at first, I watched them with him. He would immediately want to try whatever we had just seen on the screen. Somehow this made me feel less than human. –Shelly

After I pick her up in my car, use up my gas, then I spend my money on a nice dinner and maybe I spend some more money if we go out to a club..., she had better give up something before I take her home.–Ace

Sex abuse occurs when people think sexual desires cannot be controlled. If you don't have sex, you will break out in hives or a bad case of acne; you will be stressed out and uptight all the time; you will lose the desire and the ability, and the list goes on. Satan is out to convince people, especially men, that they cannot keep their sexual desires under control. This gives them a license to live promiscuous lifestyles, sometimes at an early age. A junior high school student, however, who has the charm to talk his girlfriend into experimenting with sex in the back seat of a car, may end up becoming a high school "date raper" who feels he has the right to have sex with every girl he takes out.

I'm going to give it to you straight. I've just got to have it [sex]!–Ace

I've been "getting" it on with the women ever since sixth grade. I can't give it up now–Joe

A man has certain needs that need to be taken care of...understand?–Ed

THE SEXUAL ABUSE ISSUE
What God has to say. God has never been silent on the subject of sexual abuse. Yet, He is not considered by most people as a leading expert to turn to in sexual matters, abuse or otherwise. Nor has the Bible been regarded as the manual to consult to avoid sexual abuse or to know how to handle the situation when it does occur. Because God's counsel has been disregarded, sex abuse problems and all other kinds of relational and family malfunctions continue to exist and even increase.

Whenever sexual activity transpires outside of the heterosexual marriage union, it reeks with God's displeasure. For example, the Old Testament laws prohibit sex with (or even looking upon the nakedness of) family members (Leviticus 18:6-17). In the New Testament, Paul strongly chastises the church at Corinth for ignoring an incestuous practice (1 Corinthians 5:1-5). God's children were continually told that their sexual behavior was to be pure, holy, and undefiled–unlike those in the rest of the world. Unfortunately, these standards were sometimes ignored in biblical times, and they are very definitely being ignored today. (Many other Scriptures in the Bible express God's displeasure with other non-incestuous sexual relationships outside of marriage. More on this later.)

What is sexual abuse?

I grew up in the south. Our house did not have hot and cold running water. On Saturday we took turns taking a bath in the kitchen. When I was about nine or ten my mother started putting a curtain over the kitchen door and telling my brothers (I had seven brothers and I was the only girl) to let me have my privacy. Well, the Saturday night game for my brothers became who could pull the curtain down when Mamma wasn't looking. My brothers never bothered me sexually in any other way. But this little game made me feel very ashamed. –Esther

There was one uncle in my family who hugged and kissed me while he rubbed and patted my behind. When my breasts developed, he began to fondle them as he kissed me on the cheek. He always made sure no one was around when he gave these seemingly added touches of affection. The older I became, the more uncomfortable I felt with his behavior. But I never said anything to him or anyone else about it. –Ann

Growing up, my mother had men coming in and out of our house all of the time. Sometimes my mother would leave me at the house alone with them, or fall asleep while they were there. When she did that I sometimes became the object of their sexual pleasures. –Della

Each of these acts would be considered childhood sexual abuse. The National Center on Child Abuse and Neglect (NCCAN) generally defines child sexual abuse as "contacts or interactions between a child and an adult when the child is being used for the sexual stimulation of that adult or another person."[2] This interaction or contact can also take place by an adolescent who is five years older than the child, or by an abuser who is one of the child's own peers. From the child's point of view, this person has power or control over her.

Of all the subjects in the book, CHILDHOOD SEXUAL ABUSE will be covered more extensively because it IS ONE OF SATAN'S MOST VICIOUS ATTACKS ON WOMEN. It is estimated that one out of three girls (in comparison to one out of five boys) will experience some form of sexual abuse by age eighteen.[3] Considerable evidence exists to show that at least 20 percent (with significant increases each year) of American women experience some form of sexual abuse as children.

Sexual abuse can be broken down into two basic categories: touching and non-touching. Touching is used to arouse sexual desire in the victim or the offender. This can be intercourse, oral, or anal sex. (About 25 percent of victims suffer this kind of violation.) Another type of sexual abuse occurs when the person is fully or partially clothed and is stimulated vaginally, the breasts are fondled, or any form of imitation intercourse occurs. (About 40 percent of sexually abused victims suffer this kind of abuse.) It is also considered sexual abuse when the victim is forced into sexual kissing or touching clothed breasts, buttocks, thighs, or genitals. (36 percent of sexual abuse victims have been subjected to this kind of abuse.) Of this last category, 74 percent of the victims report severe damage later on in life.[4]

Non-touching sexual abuse is visual or verbal abuse. This could entail such situations as a child being forced to watch an adult undress, or being told intricate details of a dirty joke intentionally by her grandfather, or being watched by a peeping tom.

It is a myth that mere fondling or non-touching sex abuse are less traumatic than actual intercourse or oral sex. As we will see in the next chapter when the victim is specifically discussed, a single incident of sexual abuse can have lasting damaging effects on a little girl.

When the female victim is older at the time the abuse starts, she may build up more defense mechanisms to emotionally handle the abuse. At an older age, the victim is more conscious of what is right and wrong. When a child endures sexual abuse for a long period of time and/or when the abuse is someone the child is close to and trusts, more defense mechanisms will probably surface. One victim, now an adult stated, "When somebody sexually abuses you, they don't just invade your body; they invade your soul."[5]

Satan is delighted when a little girl's vessel is damaged in the sexual area because he knows this kind of break heals very slowly, if ever. He also will use her wounds like a hand puppet, influencing her to do things throughout her life that are detrimental to herself and displeasing to the Lord. Therefore, it is necessary to understand sexual abuse, how it affects girls and their families, and what we can do to prevent it. The following chapters will help us do just that.

> I was about twelve when my father forced me to have sex with him. Thirty-eight years have passed, but the pain and confusion are as fresh as if it were yesterday. –Eliase

NOTES

1. Myles Munroe, *In Pursuit of Purpose,* (Shippensburg, P.A.: Destiny Image, 1992), 31-32.
2. Bill Anderson, *When Child Abuse Comes to Church*, (Minneapolis: Bethany House, 1992), 31.
3. Ibid., 9.
4. Ibid., 31.
5. Lynn Heitritier and Jeanette Vought, *Helping Victims of Sexual Abuse*, (Minneapolis: Bethany House, 1989), 22.

THE SHAME OF SEXUAL ABUSE

Chapter 5

Families and Unidentified Victims

I had two boys and a girl already, all within six years, so babies were nothing new to me. But when the nurse placed my second daughter, Marie, in my arms for the first time, I felt like there was something special about this child. As she grew and developed, the Lord confirmed it in my spirit. We said grace before every meal and I read Bible stories and had prayers with the children before they went to bed at night. Usually the older children took the lead; the younger ones just did as they were told.

But little Marie was not just following. Even as a toddler, when we said grace, she kept her head down longer, as if she and God were having a private conversation. At night when each child prayed, I could tell they were just mimicking prayers that they had heard from me or their father. But Marie prayed from her heart, like she really knew God already and she always had a lot more to say than all the rest.

When Marie was around two years old, we moved. An older couple at the church seemed to identify with my plight of four children all under six and another one on the way. They began taking the children for us on several occasions so I could get a break or my husband and I could go away together. That year Marie began to change.

At first I thought it was the "terrible two" stage setting in, the adjustments of a move to a new home, or the fact that I was pushing her to grow up because another child was on the way. I tried to shrug it off. But something kept saying to me, "Something is wrong with my Marie," so I started to pray.

The Lord laid it on my heart that Marie was being abused. This scared me. She was not in a day care center. I was with the children most of the time. We only went to church and church functions. Where? How? Who? I had no idea what to do with this thought. I called two women from my church and asked them to be in prayer with me about a special family concern. One said out of the blue, "The Lord's been laying it on my heart to pray for families whose children have been sexually abused." Then I knew the Lord was trying to get my attention.

I just happened to know someone who worked in children's social services, so I casually asked her what parents should do if they thought their child had been abused. She gave me some specific questions to ask. One day at bath time I asked Marie as I bathed her, "Has anyone ever touched your here?" I couldn't believe it when she nodded her pretty little head yes, as if she had been waiting patiently for someone to ask, for someone to rescue her. I questioned her further about who it was and where, but a two-year-old mumbles so much, and by this time she was crying. But I knew my child had been harmed in this way.

After a long ordeal we found out that my daughter had been molested, not once, but several times, not by one person but possibly by three or four. We found out that the man of the couple who had been so nice to us when we first came to the church had a problem in this area and had molested Marie–sometimes right there in the church, in our presence, while he held her a certain way on his hip. And she was sexually misused again by a woman, also from the church, who came by to help me with the children and to clean from time to time. Sometimes she brought her teenage children and possibly they too molested Marie. I was devastated.

I've cried many nights and days over this. It has upset everything in our household. I've felt guilty. Could I have prayed more? Shouldn't I have known? How could such a thing happen to a Christian family, with supposedly Christian people in the church? But throughout all the turmoil (and as the turmoil continues) God has given me a peace and somewhat answered the many questions on my heart. I saw something special in my child on the day of her birth. Obviously, Satan saw it too, and he went to work to set this child up and put her in the path of those who would attempt to do her severe harm. He wanted to stop whatever work God had planned for her to do. This may sound crazy, but that is exactly what I believe. Thank God that He, not Satan, is controlling the destiny of this child's life. –Dee Dee

As we saw in the last chapter, Satan especially targets his sexual abuse darts at little girls. God, however, does not leave us defenseless and scrambling in the dark for protection. Once again, God's Word is there to give us insight, solutions, and forewarnings.

A biblical example. God allows us to take a peek in the window of an Old Testament family to examine their history and the events that led up to a sexually abusive situation. Usually, sexual abuse does not just happen. Hopefully, as we observe Lot's family, we will see potential danger signs and will be on the alert for Satan's attack.

In this first biblical example of sexual abuse, incest (sex among family members) occurred and women were the predators. Note that sexual abuse is a broad term that includes incest along with abuse by non family members. There is rising evidence of women abusing boys. Unfortunately, some men who are abusers were abused themselves as boys by women. Since, our focus is how Satan harms females, our examples will deal with females as victims. This is still by far the most prevalent problem.

Tragedy in the family's past. "Terah had three sons, Abram, Nahor, and Haran. Haran had a son named Lot. But Haran died young..." (Genesis 11:28). Lot's life started out with calamity. His father died at a young age. Lot traveled with his uncle Abraham (Abram) and grandfather Terah from Ur, their hometown, to Haram. He piggy-backed on the promise God gave to Abraham: "I will lead you [Abraham] to a country [Canaan] and make you and your descendants a great nation" (Genesis 12:1-3). But before they reached Canaan, Terah, Lot's grandfather, died.

A family that ignores God. The scriptures do not tell us how old Lot was at the time of his father's and grandfather's deaths, but usually death affects human behavior and thinking. Many individuals respond in one of three ways: (1) they draw closer to God; (2) they blame God and aggressively turn away from Him; or (3) they passively ignore God and attempt to go on with their lives.

Lot's record indicates that he probably chose number three. Not one place in Scripture do we find Lot thanking God for His blessings, seeking God's guidance, or uttering any kind of prayer, negative or positive, to God. These childhood losses may have caused Lot to make some ungodly choices. This tending to make bad choices seems to have followed Lot once he got married, and it was imitated by his wife and daughters. In fact, as the historical account about this family progresses, the behavior of the wife and daughters seems to validate that the entire family lacked an intimate connection or understanding of God. In the book of 2 Peter, Lot is called "righteous." Thank God He looks beyond our faults.

Bad choices. Even though Lot lost his father and grandfather, he was not totally abandoned. Abraham took him in. Scripture confirms the fact that when God deals with one member of the family, He does not just want the allegiance of that one individual; He wants the entire household to become believers. I think God wanted Abraham's nephew, Lot, to follow Him in the same way Abraham did.

God blessed Lot materially, as he did Abraham. But when it was time for Lot and Abraham to separate (because their livestock were too abundant to continue sharing the same land), there is no evidence that Lot prayed or asked for God's divine wisdom. Nor did Lot ask his godly Uncle Abraham for advice. I am sure Abraham and God would have been more than happy to help Lot decide where to settle his family.

Lot's silence toward God did not discourage God from speaking to Lot. Two divine beings (angels) stayed in Lot's home overnight.

They saved him from a dangerous incident with the men in the city and performed miracles right on his front porch. They warned him about the impending destruction of Sodom and personally saw to it that his family was removed before the annihilation of the city.

Lot's family was told to leave Sodom, and not look back. Lot's wife disobeyed and when she did turn around, she became a pillar of salt. Death and tragedy entered Lot's life again. Lot, however, did not turn to Abraham. Instead, after his devastating loss, he wandered around in "no man's land." Here is where the tragic incestuous incident took place.

> One day the older girl said to her sister, "There isn't a man anywhere in this entire area that our father would let us marry. And our father will soon be too old for having children. Come, let's fill him with wine and then we will sleep with him so that our clan will not come to an end." So they got him drunk that night, and the older girl went in and had sexual intercourse with her father; but he was unaware of her lying down or getting up again.... The next morning she said to her younger sister, "I slept with my father last night. Let's fill him with wine again tonight, and you go in and lie with him, so that our family line will continue." So they got him drunk again that night, and the younger girl went in and lay with him, and as before, he didn't know that anyone was there. And so it was that both girls became pregnant from their father (Genesis 19:31-38).

Hopelessness. Lot's two daughters felt hopeless and fearful about their future. Therefore, they carried out a devious, heathenish plan. They both had sons. The older called her son Moab and he was the father of the Moabite nation. The younger called her son Benammi and he was the father of the Ammon nation. Both of them were ungodly people and continually caused the nation of Israel grief.

The two girls, like so many other sex offenders, thought pessimistically about their state of affairs and were inwardly frustrated. This type of thought process can drive the person to destructive behaviors. Satan gladly presents a variety pack of deviant behaviors to people who are helpless.

Certain families (or family members) are fertile breeding ground for major problems including possible sexual abuse. They have certain characteristics or behaviors in common: one or more tragic past incidents, unbelieving homes, choices made contrary to the will of God, and a sense of helplessness about the future.

Keep in mind, however, these signs mentioned may be kept well under cover within the family. Some wives may not be aware of their husband's past family secrets and dysfunctions. Even church congregations have been shocked to find that upstanding, committed families have been involved in sexual abuse for years. It is necessary to take a closer look at one's family members.

The Victims People Usually Do Not View as Victims
When my daughter told me that her father had been sexually molesting her for two years, nothing in our family was ever the same. It was as if someone turned my whole household upside down. My husband went to prison, which made me a single parent. I had to now carry the financial load. My sons blamed my daughter for their father being taken from them. They thought she should not have told and they fought constantly. I went to my church for help but they had never had a situation like this and gave me unwise advice and very little support. I eventually had to find another church. I had so many mixed emotions it was hard for me to cope day after day. Other than God's daily grace, I don't know how I did it. –Sylvia

In sexual abuse situations, we usually just think of the victim and the offender. Yet, when Satan strikes in this particular area, his goal is not only to victimize a child but to damage the lives of as many persons as he can. Like Sylvia, whole families are affected–even entire churches and communities can feel the negative ramifications of sexual abuse.

The offender. We would like to think we could recognize a child abuser if we saw one. But the truth of the matter is that they come in all shapes, colors, and sizes. They cut across all socioeconomic and cultural lines. Some of us picture sex offenders as "dirty old men" who live on the wrong side of town, appear out of nowhere, wearing an oversized filthy raincoat, glasses, and walking bent over. This is far from the truth. Unfortunately, about 95 percent of sex offenders are family members or some person the victim knows and trusts. Also, one study showed that half of all abusers were under age thirty-one; only 10 percent were over age fifty.[1]

Most sex offenders have pleasant personalities and publicly give the appearance of nice teenagers, good fathers and husbands. They are usually hard-working, law-abiding, church-attending individuals. These persons, however, may have grown up in homes where there was no positive male role model, substance abuse was prevalent, or where they were themselves physically or sexually abused.

Pedophiles are adults who prefer to have sex with children. There are two kinds of pedophile: (1) fixated offenders who relate only to children, and (2) regressed pedophiles who have experienced normal sexual relationships with adults but, usually due to some overwhelming stress in their lives, regress to desiring sex with children. Most likely, the situation is that a man takes advantage of a little girl.

It is important to note that the regressed pedophile could be having regular, satisfying sexual relationships with his wife and is still sexually abusing a child. A wife should not feel that if she had been more submissive or better in the bedroom this would not have happened. A person who sexually abuses children is emotionally sick and no matter what a wife might have done in the couple's relationship, the abuser still would have acted out this kind of dysfunctional behavior.

There is another increasing group of sex offenders–those under the age of eighteen. The adolescent sex offender is usually the nice, quiet person who keeps to himself. For various reasons he may be isolated from his peers, have a low self-esteem, and a history of sexual abuse. Interestingly, he is often asked to babysit or work with children because of his kind, gentle personality. His victims often are very fond of him and may cooperate with the sexual activities for a long time before the secret is told.

Since the offender's mind is often twisted or confused, he may be unable to distinguish between love and sex, regardless of his age. To him, sexual activity could be justified as emotional support. He may even convince himself that his daughter's or a little girl's invitation for ordinary parental or adult affection is a sexual come-on. Girls are usually in love with their daddies. They may hug and kiss them in a sensual way. They are NOT, however, asking for an adult sexual relationship. An emotionally stable and mature man will not take advantage of this innocent affection. But one who has emotional difficulties will often become a repeat sex abuse offender.

Sometimes sex offenders are blind to their own inner pain. It is too uncomfortable to face their problems, not perceiving that they have a problem.They may be too insecure to seek the emotional support and help they need outside the home. Many times the wife may know something is wrong but has no idea what it is or how to help her husband. Therefore, an innocent child becomes the prey. One offender describes his struggles from the past.

I was repeatedly sexually molested by an older woman. She threatened me and so I never told anyone. Somehow my mother eventually found out. My mother threatened to kill the woman. Shortly after that, the woman died. In my mind, I killed her. I felt somehow responsible, even though she died from a natural illness. My father died a year before this all happened. Then about five years later my mother died.

All of these deaths occurred before I finished high school. I got married right after high school. I thought everything was going to be okay. But then I went to Vietnam. It was traumatic. I was just a country boy. I could never get used to the idea of killing people or people dying all around me.

After I got back from Vietnam, I blamed God for all of these deaths—my parents, the woman who molested me, and the people in Vietnam. I was filled with anger, but at the time I didn't know what it was, how to talk about it, or what to do.

One of my ways of coping with all of this rage inside me was committing adultery on my wife and eventually sexually abusing my daughter and my stepdaughter.

I believe being sexually molested when I was twelve started things rolling. I'm fifty now and I'm just now beginning to understand what was going on inside of me. I've finally stopped blaming everybody and everything else for my anger. I'm attempting to put the puzzle pieces of my life together and desiring to understand the rage I've held inside all these years. I've had to admit I've hurt innocent people who should not have suffered from my problems. This is a lot of hard truth to swallow. –J.

The offender's offense.   Many times sex offenders will do what is called "courting" a child. They will take time to develop a relationship with the child and build their confidence in them before they ever sexually abuse the child. This way, it is harder for the child to tell on such a special friend or relative. Also, they often deceive those who are around the child into thinking, "Oh, isn't it wonderful that Mr. Jones is taking so much time with little Sarah." Very few people will suspect someone of sexual abuse who has been so nice to the children and willing to spend time with them.

My husband "courted" his stepdaughter for several years before he began molesting her. She adored him. He showered her with gifts and attention. I was sick to learn that he did all of this just to eventually molest her. –Sylvia

David Finkelhor, a researcher in the field of child sexual abuse, gives four preconditions that must be met before an adult will sexually abuse a child[2]. First, the offenders must have sexual feelings about children. This can develop from pornography and advertisments which sexualize children. Secondly, the offender must ignore any internal inhibitors, such as conscience. Alcohol or drugs are effective means of overcoming internal inhibitors. Thirdly, the abuser's external inhibitors, such as the presence of other adults, must be overcome. This provides the opportunity for the abuse and prevents interference with it. Finally, the resistance of the child must be broken down.

After the first sexual abuse act, the offender most likely will feel guilty and may vow within himself never to allow it to happen again. Unfortunately, the sensation of pleasure is sometimes stronger than the guilt. The offender finds himself repeating the sexual abuse every time the opportunity presents itself. At this point the abuser finds it difficult to stop. In fact, the urge seems irresistible. He continues to feel empty, hopeless, and trapped. The more the outside pressures which initially led to the sexual abuse fail to improve, the more he will abuse.

Offenders may be insensitive and unaware of the needs of others. This insensitivity is often reflected in their inability to perceive the harm and pain they cause their victims. Their rigid defense system of denial and rationalization can dull their consciousness to the point that they do not perceive that what they are doing is wrong (and as stated earlier, some offenders know it is wrong and constantly say that it will never happen again). One of the main purposes of this book is to alert people about the devastating effects of sexual abuse and the severe damage that can be done by seemingly insignificant sexual acts.

> When I asked my grandfather why he molested me as a child he said, "If I'd known how it was going to affect you, I never would have done it."
> –CJ

One would think that sexual abuse occurs predominantly in non-Christian homes; however, Christians are influenced by the world. Unfortunately, some believers embrace sensual entertainment, pornography, ungodly educational systems, anti-Christian worldly philosophies, and overindulge in alcohol and drugs. These are the factors that may contribute to dulling sexual inhibitions. (*Penthouse* magazine claims 35 percent of its readers are born-again Christians. That is 2.67 million Christians!)[3]

The offender's needs. The offender is often looking for unconditional love and acceptance. He wants someone to help him through the struggles of this life. These needs are only met with a personal growing relationship with Jesus Christ. When people do not establish this relationship they begin to look elsewhere–the wrong places–to satisfy their desires for love that only Christ can give. Satan is right there to convince them, nonetheless, that fondling an innocent child is a non-threatening way to get those needs met.

THE NON-OFFENDING CARETAKER

> My grandfather molested me when I was a toddler. When I asked my grandmother, "Did you know about this?" she sadly replied, "Women in our day often knew about things, but we didn't always know what to do"–Jan

Who is she? The non-offending caretaker could be the mother, grand-mother, aunt, or someone close to the victim. She is either completely oblivious to the sexual abuse or fully aware of what is taking place. Sometimes the non-offending caretaker is absent or incapable of functioning in the home due to a substance abuse problem, divorce, illness, death, or a job.

> I was a victim of child abuse. I married a man who physically abused me. I tried desperately to drink away my problems. While I was hopping from bar to bar, my husband would be home molesting my children. I was so busy trying to deal with my pain, I could not see the pain of my children. –Ruby

Many of the mothers of abuse victims have been abused themselves. Also, victims tend to marry immature, domineering, controlling husbands. When a victim then has a daughter of her own, self perception may be extremely distorted. She may be so laden with emotional problems and sexual dysfunctions that she cannot rationally view the world around her. Such a mother's low opinion of herself may cause her to not only miss clues of sexual abuse by her husband, but also to believe that she cannot live without her husband despite his dominance and other shortcomings. A woman with such a background may, in fact, suspect incest between her daughter and husband but may choose to ignore it. She has too much to lose. The daughter may understand her mother's plight, even better in some respects than the mother, and may be willing to suffer to keep from hurting her mother and upsetting the home.

Remember Lot's family as they fled Sodom and Gomorrah? This was a very hard situation indeed. Lot's wife died because she refused to obey the angel's direct command not to look back. She did not believe the divine message and could not let go of the past. She wanted things to stay the way they were, even though God was very displeased. At the least she longed for the comfort of the known, compared to the uncertainty of her future. She died trying to hold on to what God chose to destroy.

There are many women today like Lot's wife. They would rather hold on to something familiar, even when it's unhealthy, than to face a new world. Some homes are so dysfunctional that women, especially Christian women, are misguided about what should happen there. Chrisitian women often are taught to submit totally to the husband's every command. For them, divorce or leaving their spouse is out of the question, regardless of the situation, and a dominating husband is merely asserting his God-given right and authority. Sometimes in these kinds of homes, the wife is being physically abused and disrespected as a woman. The daughter may also be a victim of physical or sexual abuse.

Another sad state of affairs occurs when a wife stands up to an angry, abusive husband in an attempt to set limits to lessen or stop abuse directed toward her. She finds out that her husband then begins to take out his frustration through physical or sexual abuse on the children.

> I was beaten and emotionally abused by my ex-husband. I left for six months, but when he saw a counselor and promised reform, I returned. I was not beaten after the return, but I found that my four-year-old daughter was—and sexually abused by him as well. The pastor I spoke to, the counselor I saw..., all Christians, preferred to believe I was lying, or at least to blame for the trouble.[4]

In a situation like this, it is not wise to attempt to protect your husband, the family name, your church, or to keep the family intact. Your child is defenseless and needs you to come to her aid. I would recommend that you get help for your child and yourself. An offender may promise it will never happen again, but it usually does. The offender rarely goes for help unless he has been turned in to the authorities and the court requires it. Turning in an offender may be the best thing you can do to help the person.

While you are in the process of working through what to do about the sexual abuse or suspected abuse, make sure your daughter or girl in your care or household is protected from any other potential danger or harm. Maybe at an earlier time there were very few places to turn with this problem. But today, crisis lines, hotlines, counseling centers, and a general awareness of the sexual abuse problems are common. No onlookers—

whether teacher, parent, neighbor or friends has an excuse for not seeking help for young victims.

Many Christian women stay in abusive situations or continue to allow their children to be abused, believing that they are doing the right thing. They think that if they endure, eventually their husbands will come to Christ; and if they are already Christians, they want to stay while believing that the husband's behavior will change. This sounds very spiritual but is not faith; it is denial and/or co-dependency.

> Turning my husband in for molesting my daughter was one of the hardest things I've ever done in my life. It has taken years for our family to recover from the repercussions. It has been extremely hard for me and my children. But it is also one of the BEST decisions I ever made. It had to be done. I had to think about my child. God has seen us over this difficult time. We are all still healing but I know it would have been worse if I didn't do anything and allowed it to continue. –Sylvia

The caretaker who does not act on her suspicions about child sexual abuse is being tormented by Satan, like the victim. Satan sees to it that she suffers in fear, regret and constant anxiety. He knows that abuse, unchecked, will ruin the life of the victim, and strikes hard also to destroy the lives of those around her.

There are, of course, some non-offending caretakers who are completely oblivious to the sexual abuse.

> I was shocked when my teenage daughter told me my husband (her father) had been sexually abusing her for several years. She said he would wait until I was asleep, out running errands, or gone to church, then he would molest her. She was angry at me because she thought I should have known what was going on, but I had no idea. My husband and I had our difficulties in marriage but during the time he was molesting my daughter everything seemed to be at a good point. I would have praised him for being an excellent husband and father. –Ruby

Caretakers who were not aware of the abuse in their families may suffer with guilt, feeling as if they should have known. These individuals should keep in mind that sex offenders can be very manipulative and secretive about their activities. Not every unsuspecting parent has looked away from telltale signs. Sexual abuse is not a commonly discussed subject and not all parents are aware of the signs. (The signs of sexual abuse and information about the victims and how to help them are discussed in Chapter 7).

ADDITIONAL INFORMATION

Interview with an offender. When a sexual abuse victim is attempting to sort out what has happened to her and why, she will usually ask two main questions about the offender: (1) Why would someone sexually take advantage of a helpless child–especially if that little girl is their daughter? (2) What goes on in the mind of a sex offender? The following interview might provide some insight.

What happened?

When my stepdaughter was seven, I masturbated while looking at her private areas. I thought she was asleep but later I found out she was not. She was very aware of what I was doing. After it happened I felt guilty. I said to myself, "Al, you've crossed the line." But there was no undoing what I had done.

Next day, my stepdaughter asked me, "What are we going to do about last night?" Initially I denied it. Then I eventually said, "It will never happen again." My wife had taught my daughter if anything like this ever happened to her she was not to keep it a secret and she didn't. Right after she talked to me, she went straight to her mother and told her all about it. I feel like my daughter was the most courageous of all of us.

When my wife confronted me I swore up and down that it didn't happen. My wife did not believe me and she reported the incident to the authorities.

My stepdaughter was examined and there were no physical signs of sexual abuse. But I was still made to leave the house. Two or three days later, I did admit the whole thing to my wife. At that time I didn't realize I was facing twenty years in jail.

Do you think the authorities should have been brought in?

I'm glad my wife called the authorities; they should have been brought in. Men who have this problem don't necessarily need jail but they do need counseling. My wife did not press charges. I had a deferred prosecution, which meant if in two years I had not had anything else happen, no sexual crimes, got into counseling, and stayed in a sex anonymous group, nothing would appear on my record. The penalties for this type of crime are getting stiffer, though, because it is happening more often–or people are reporting it more.

What happened to your family after this incident?

My wife and I split up. There were other problems in the marriage. As far as I know, my stepdaughter went to counseling and is recovering well.

Why did you do it?

This is still a mystery to me. Maybe it was a new sex territory to explore. Another step on the ladder. I had never done anything like this. I was into pornography pictures and videos. I even watched porno movies with my wife. Maybe it happened because of the crowd I hung out in. I used marijuana and drank but I was not drunk or high the night I abused my stepdaughter. Maybe it was because of my lack of concern for anyone but myself. At that time I had drifted away from God.

Before the incident happened I did talk to a friend about what I was planning to do. He said it was normal; my daughter was a very pretty little girl. I wasn't obsessed with the thought beforehand, but I did plan it. I waited for her to go to sleep. Most sexual activities are planned. You have to look for porno or a prostitute. A person usually starts thinking about their sexual need, then how they are going to satisfy it. When a person is angry, lonely, or tired, these kinds of things can begin to trigger lustful desires.

What has happened to you as a result of this incident?

This incident happened about three years ago. Right now, I pray for my stepdaughter's recovery. I am out of her and my wife's life. If any good came out of what happened, I am closer to the Lord. I realize I do have a problem. I committed an offense against a little girl. Several things have helped me overcome my problem. I did admit what I did to my family and friends. They are supportive and stand behind me. When I say I don't want to do drugs, participate in pornography, or any other kinds of things, they respect me for that.

I also got into a Christian men's support group which emphasizes these kinds of problems. That really helped a lot. I realized I wasn't the only one struggling with these kinds of things. Through the group I realized that other guys out there thought porno and masturbation were okay, but all have problems because of them.

Christian counseling really helped, I'm still getting counseling. I found out about several issues that I needed to work through. I found out that anger is related to sexual problems. It is good to express anger, but the question is how do we express it. I needed to learn to control my anger, and also work out and understand some of my anger issues. Anger can trigger sexual desires. Also, I found several scriptures where God speaks about sex, recovery, and love. Sex should only be done in marriage. It's a sin otherwise.

Do you still struggle in this area?

Even though I have gotten all this help, I still have a daily struggle with sexual temptations. Some days are easier than others. Besides working everyday, I intentionally keep myself very busy. By the time I get home I'm exhausted. I very rarely watch television. The shows and commercials are too sexually explicit. I stay away from women who wear seductive perfume. I don't allow myself to sexually fantasize. I don't gawk at improperly clothed women. These are things I have realized cause me problems and I start thinking about them later on. I have to stay close with God and stay busy.

What would you suggest to men like yourself and others who do not want to repeat your mistake?

What would help men like me is for porno to be completely eliminated. There is no good reason for it. The magazines, videos, nude dancing, and the places that have these things should be shut down. People are fighting for free rights and freedom to choose, but if you are not following God, you have no rights. Most of the sexually explicit materials are seen by men. This hurts the women in their lives. It is extremely demoralizing to women. It does not help the relationship between men and women.

Women need to be educated about how men operate, their chemical testosterone levels. And men need to learn about them too, and how to control themselves. Men need to understand that alcohol and drugs make them more loose with their morals. Women need to realize certain ways they dress cause men to be tempted and to lust. Summertime is very difficult for me. Both sexes need to be more careful in their thinking and watching. More and more women are in beer and car commercials. It's a fact that beautiful women sell products. The advertisers know this and they use them.

And I don't think fathers should bath their little girls or let girls sleep with them. Parents need to help their children become independent early and learn how to do certain functions like dress themselves, use the bathroom, and take their own baths.

Men must learn to be honest with their wives and themselves. A husband should be able to admit to his wife, "I'm horny today, I don't think I should dress our little girl." Good communication is needed between the husband and wife and the parent and child.

The child needs to be educated. My stepdaughter was told, "If someone ever does something you are uncomfortable with, no matter what, you come and tell someone." You should tell the child over and over again. Good communication between the parent and child makes it easier for them to talk to a parent. My daughter came to me and then she went straight to her mother. She knew how to handle it, and it kept her from probably more harm.

I've learned not to live life in the past. I had a good Christian upbringing; that has helped. Sexual problems do not have to be overwhelming. I'm learning everything is in the Bible. All the answers I need are there. I'm continuing in therapy. It's an ongoing battle, but there is victory in Christ! –Al

NOTES

1. Bill Anderson, *When Child Abuse Comes to Church,* (Minneapolis: Bethany House Publishers, 1992), 47.
2. David Peters, *A Betrayal of Innocence*, (Waco, Texas: Word Books, 1986), n.p.
3. Nieder, *What You Need to Tell Your Child About Sex,* 89.
4. James and Phyliss Alsdurf, *Battered Into Submission*, (Wheaton, Ill.: InterVarsity Press, 1989), 65.

Chapter 6

The Effects of Sexual Abuse

There were two small bedrooms in the house. We called one the front room and the other the back room.... My sister, then fifteen, was moved to the front room to sleep with our mother. I was to sleep in the back room with my father.

Anyone can imagine what might result from such circumstances: a man whose sexual needs had not been met for years, sleeping with a little girl, not his own, while trying to cope with long days of hard work and an alcoholic wife.

In that little room my innocence was mutilated over and over again. The physical pain, the fear and the shame were unspeakable. The knowledge that there was nowhere to go, no one to tell, horrified me. I wanted to run, but he held me down; I wanted to scream, but he told me I must be quiet. So over the years, in that desolate bed, I learned to cry out to God. With tears running back into my ears and my father asleep at my side, I stared at the ceiling and prayed.[1] –Glenda

THE VICTIM

Glenda's experience is not unusual. One-fifth of all American families are involved in some form of child abuse.[2] In the United States, the average age for sexual abuse is around eleven years old, although some victims are infants or in their late teens. Little girls are usually sexually abused early in childhood, between the ages of five to eight years old. The abuse commonly goes on for three to five years.

I have met very few women who have not experienced some form of sexual abuse. As stated in chapter 1, I believe Satan sets out to see to it that every woman experiences sexual abuse at some point in her life. Because women are God's vessels of compassion and restoration, Satan works especially hard at seeing to it that they get thrown off course in the early years by causing such atrocities as sexual abuse. Through the perpetrator, he elicits physiological responses in a little girl's body which should only by awakened on her wedding night, thereby causing her much confusion and shame. Sexual abuse forces cracks into her fragile spiritual being. These breaks open and usher in negative feelings, and allow the spiritual oil of a young girl's inner being to spill away. This leads the way for open emotional wounds to erupt and fester within other areas of her life. In this chapter, we will discuss some of the emotional struggles of the sexually abused victim and prayerfully give her hope that she can operate as a wonderful vessel of God, completely whole again.

Just one incident of childhood sexual abuse can have immediate devastating effects upon a little girl. After or even during the first experience, instantly several emotions come to the surface. David Peters in , *A Betrayal of Innocence,* sights six of these emotions: fear, confusion, betrayal, shame, anger, and false guilt. [3]

Fear. Fear is usually the initial and prevailing emotion that surfaces when a child is molested or sexually abused in any way. Childhood should be a carefree experience. The moment a child is sexually abused, she is immediately loaded with burdens a child should never have to carry. The offender has to make sure the victim never exposes his activities. Therefore, he might make such threatening statements as, "If you tell your mother, it will make her very unhappy;" or "If someone finds out what I've done, I might have to go to jail;" or "You might have to go and live somewhere else." The child and not the adult offender, is now concerned about the well-being of her mother and the rest of her family. Parents are a child's God-given protectors. They are responsible to see to it that no harm comes to the child. Sexual abuse turns the tables. The child now attempts to protect herself from an abusive parent, as well as hold the family together.

> I wanted desperately to tell my mother that my stepfather was abusing me, but he told me if I ever told he would kill my mother. I also feared that my mother might kill him if she found out. I thought, either way my brothers and sisters and I would have no one. I didn't want our family to fall apart, so for years I keep it a secret. I thought it was better for me to suffer than my whole family. I did tell my mother when I got older. By that time my stepfather had died. We cried and hugged. That seemed to release something inside of me.–Jan

Confusion. A warm parental embrace perhaps results in inappropriate touching. The child is frightened and uncomfortable. The offender may show signs of excitement or obsession. The child does not know how to mentally assess what is happening to her. "What is going on?" "Should I tell?" "Is this right or wrong?" "Why is he doing this to me?"

> My father got sick and died when I was around five years old. A friend of our family who lived down the street seemed to feel sorry for me and started paying me a lot of attention. It really filled the gap my father's death had left. For almost a year he would come by my house at least once a week. He'd bring me gifts, take me to the movies, or just sit and listen to me chatter away. Then one day he took me by his apartment. He said instead of going to the movies we would just stay there and watch television. At first he just held me on his lap like he had done on several occasions, but then he began to fondle me. I didn't know what to do or think. I adored this man. I felt uncomfortable with what he was doing but I didn't want to tell on him and lose him as a friend. But he continued to abuse me, and my mother noticed a change in the way I behaved around him. She never asked me anything, but she made him stop coming around me. –Liz

Feelings of betrayal. As was mentioned in the previous chapter, the sexual abuser will often first "court" his victim. He may give the child special attention, favors, or gifts. A little girl's heart is usually tender toward a man or older boy who pays her a lot of attention. It does not take long to win her affection. When the tragic event occurs, often the child is simply cuddling on a parent's lap, snuggling up to a parent in bed, or going to a special place with that special friend. After such an experience, a girl will find it hard to build a trusting relationship with men.

> My father molested me as a child. He and my mother later separated. My father's friend started to come around. I began to build a relationship with him, only to be molested by this friend. Then, my father died. I turned to my pastor for counseling and comfort only to be molested again. I don't think I can ever trust another man again. –Diane

Shame and false guilt. Even at an early age, a child senses that this sexual activity is wrong. The offender may try and reassure the victim, "This is okay for a daddy to do," or "I'm just teaching you about sex, where babies come from." Yet something within the child says, "This is not okay; this is bad." The incest victim is overwhelmed with feelings of humiliation and disgrace. She wishes it had never happened.

> Before my uncle molested me, I loved to play outdoors with the other children. After that incident, I didn't want to go outside. It felt like everyone was looking at me and knew what happened. My parents kept

asking me what was wrong, but my uncle told me not to tell. If I did, he would deny it and no one would believe me. For years I held my head down, trying to hide from the world. –Lilly

A little girl full of shame says, "I wish this had never happened to me." A child who feels false guilt takes that thought one step further and says, "I must have done something to have caused this." Guilt seems to be a universal feeling among sexual abuse victims. They wonder if they could have stopped or avoided the abuse somehow. They may have experienced some pleasurable feelings during the abuse and feel guilty about it. Or they may somehow feel that *they* are bad because the abuse happened to them. Some victims even feel guilty because they have both love and hate toward the offender or because they disrupted the family if the father was removed from the home.

When I was about eight years old my mother started working nights. I had a bad dream and I went into my father's room because I was scared. He allowed me to climb in bed with him and he began to fondle me. Each time my mother went to work at night after that, he would come to my room and molest me. I always thought it was my fault. I started it. I should never have gone into his room that first night. –Deanna

Up to this point, we have been examining some of the immediate effects of a single sexual occurrence. Unfortunately, it is extremely rare for an offender to stop after only one incident. The sexual abuse may go on for years. Also, some victims tell stories about being abused in different situations by several different men, as if someone had given them a name tag that said, "I'm available for sexual abuse."

My mother moved us around a lot to different apartments. Each time we moved, some man in the building would sexually molest me. It was as if someone called ahead each time and told them I was coming and described what I looked like. Finally, when I was older I ran away from home. But out on the streets on my own the same thing happened. Different men raped me over and over again. –Pat

LONG-RANGE EFFECTS OF SEXUAL ABUSE

Interpersonal relationships. The abuser may isolate the child from her peers. He fears that she may tell their secret. If the offender is the father, when the daughter becomes a teenager and takes an interest in boys, he becomes jealous and keeps her from dating and other social functions. In some cases the girl may never learn how to socially relate to those her own age.

A sexual abuse victim often grows up too fast. Her behavior may become manipulative or seductive with her peers or other people, because this is the way she has learned to deal with her offender. (In fact, seductive, sensual behavior, too mature for a young girl's age, can be a signal of sexual abuse.)

In some incest situations the girl may take on the mother's responsibilities.For some reason, the mother is absent or unable to function as the wife and mother.The daughter takes her place.These bossy mannerisms may carry over into the child's relationships with her peers, and are usually not well received. The victim is further isolated.

Once the victim becomes an adult, she commonly takes on one of three unhealthy characteristics which cause further broken relationships: (1) This woman condemns herself even when she is not responsible. She says to herself, "Everything is my fault." (2) She believes she has no power to accomplish anything and constantly calls on people to meet her needs. She tells others, "I'm helpless. Please help me." (3) The victim has had so many things go wrong in her past that she does not tolerate any mistakes in herself or other people. "I have to be perfect and do everything perfect and so does everyone else around me," she might insist.

When women exhibit these kinds of mannerisms, people tend to shy away and leave them without any friends at all. The stories in Chapter 1 are a perfect example of women who have these characteristics which are indicative of sexual abuse in one's past.

Some victims, because of their past, are more at ease with causal sexual encounters. This could result in promiscuity or prostitution. Three-fourths of adolescent prostitutes are victims of incest. This may happen because some victims of abuse may find intimate, lasting relationships frightening.

A distrust of men is also a natural response from most female sexual abuse victims. In some cases, it is possible that these same women might not have received nurture and care from their mothers when they were little girls. The combination of these two factors has also caused some women to turn to lesbianism. In so doing, they are rejecting men and securing the care they missed from their mothers.

> A neighbor boy molested me when I was about four or five. That started a long line of all kinds of relationships with other young boys, men, and women. I just wanted someone to love me. –Susan

Family relationships. Not only is Satan out to attack women because of their special role as nurturers, encouragers and conduits for bringing life, he wants to destroy the entire family, the very social structure which God ordained and put in place. Sexual abuse acts like a termite. It slowly eats away at the family structure. By the time the sexual abuse is reported and help is available, the damage seems almost beyond repair.

In abuse situations, the mother-daughter relationship may be tense. The mother may be jealous of the father's attention toward the daughter. The daughter may hold resentment toward her mother because she is absent when the abuse happens. She is angry that her mother does not come to her rescue.

> My daughter was extremely angry at me because I did not detect that she was being sexually abused by my husband. I had no idea until she told me about it. I just thought she was going through some typical teenage attitudes toward her father. It has taken her years to forgive me.
> –Ruby

The father-daughter relationship could turn into a pseudo husband-wife relationship. The husband may become physically or emotionally attached to the daughter instead of his wife. Often the daughter hates her father for violating her in this way, even after the father is no longer abusing her, or the girl is no longer in the home or the place of abuse. Even after the father has died, the daughter still may hate him.

Siblings can also be affected by sexual abuse. The other brothers and sisters may be jealous of the victim, who could be receiving special treatment from the offender. They also may resent her because she takes on the role of the mother, especially if she and becomes bossy or unfair. If the sexual abuse is reported and the father is removed from the family, often the victim is ridiculed because she disrupted the family or brought hardship or shame upon them.

The victim's future marriage relationship also may be affected. Even potentially strong marriages have survival difficulties when incest has been involved in the past. An innocent husband may cause an extreme negative reaction from the victim when he approaches her sexually. She may see sex as immoral or dirty. A victim may feel shameful about the sex act if she experienced any sexual pleasure during her abuse. One way the victim deals with the abuse is to habitually shut out those feelings even when they are desirable and legitimate. Now that she is married, she still may not enjoy the sexual sensations.

My first husband did not understand. I'm not sure if I understood it all at first myself. When we first got married, I kept telling him not to touch me in certain places. We always argued about sex. Neither one of us enjoyed it. There was always tension. That's one of the reasons we split up. I don't think I'll ever find anyone who understands what happened to me and how I feel. –Lilly

On the other hand, some women who fell prey to sexual abuse may want to have sex all the time.This type of response may be an attempt to overcompensate for the offender, who kept her away from other men. She may also be trying to receive the parental affection she did not receive as a child.

When I was about seven or eight, my mother died. When my father worked, he left me with a family in the neighborhood. Another girl from the same neighborhood came over often to play with me and we were left alone quite a bit. She was older than me and she forced me to do lesbian sexual activities with her. She showed me pictures in pornographic magazines and forced me to imitate what I saw. One day the older sister of the family who baby-sat me walked in on us and witnessed our sexual interaction. She made the other girl go home. Then she started to yell all kinds of things at me, "Do you want to be like that? Do you want to have sex with women?" She never asked me my side of the story. I was never given the opportunity to say that I was forced into it. I never forgot her words. So as soon as I was out on my own, I set out to prove to myself that I was not a lesbian. I had sex with every man I possibly could. –Maggie

Generational factors. One statistical fact is that women who have been abused usually marry abusive men who take advantage of them and their children.[4] This phenomenon is a mystery.There is no explanation given for it. Yet it happens repeatedly.

Sometimes, when a daughter reaches the age at which the victim was molested, a mother may become jealous of any attention the husband gives to the child. She may become paranoid and suspicious of her husband. This is especially problematic when there is no real reason to be suspicious.

I was sexually molested as a child. My husband has given no indication of doing anything like that to any of our children. But I never have left any of our daughters alone with him. This lack of trust in our marriage has caused all kinds of problems. But the pain was so great for me as a child, I just don't want any of our children to suffer in the same way. – Carol

Finally, a mother who has unresolved conflicts about her childhood abuse could end up abusing her children physically and sexually herself. *The iniquities of those who came before us do continue down through the generations* (Exodus 34:7). Unfortunately, childhood has a way of locking certain behaviors, both good and bad, into the subconscious. Even with the best of intentions, if a parent has unresolved issues and given enough stress, she may find herself abusing her child, the very thing she may have vowed never to do.

SPIRITUAL DAMAGE

Children cannot fully comprehend the idea of God. So when they attempt to picture what God is like, they look to their parents. To a child, parents represent God's love, affection, limits, and discipline. Can you imagine the misrepresentation in the mind of a child when a parent sexually abuses her? Her spiritual vision of God can become grossly distorted.

Some children are abused in God's name. They are told, "This is God's will," or "This is the way God wants you to learn about sex," or "God will get you if you tell." Some feel God is punishing them with the abuse. They constantly ask, "What did I do so wrong that God would punish me this way?"

> My father was a preacher. He would sexually abuse me on Saturday, then preach in the pulpit on Sunday. I hated him and God. I could never understand why God would allow him to do it. –Amy

Like Amy, some children blame God and turn away from Him because they do not understand His inactivity in their dark, helpless hour. The sexual abuse victim is usually spiritually damaged.Even a dedicated Christian woman who has been abused as a child can have (and usually does have) a distorted image of how she sees God and how God sees her. She is unable to feel personally intimate with Him or unconditionally accepted by Him. This could be a woman who seriously prays and studies the Bible, is active in the church, and seen by everyone else as a wonderful Christian. Still, she is not experiencing a real sense of intimacy with God.Though she looks very "religious" on the outside, she doesn't have the peace of God inside. In fact, much of her religious activity may be an attempt to cover up for how dirty she feels inside. Her constant striving to work her way into God's favor borders on perfectionism.

Satan is pleased with all the damage he does to the victim in her relationships, but damaging her relationship with God is his ultimate goal. If he is able to keep a woman doubting God's love and care for her, her spiritual foundation is left shaky, a vessel of God, but full of holes. But there is hope and help, and you will be able to turn your pain into a tool to be used by God.

Glenda, for example, at the beginning of this chapter, developed a deep and abiding relationship with God as a result of her experience and eventually wrote about it. The back cover of *Glenda's Story* proclaims:

> "Ultimately, Glenda's afflictions became the cord with which God drew her to Himself. Receiving His salvation, she understood that God had saved her from her own sinfulness as much as He had saved her from her horrid conditions. This story of hope is an amazing account of our merciful Savior, who brings light out of darkness, joy out of sorrow and peace of pain." [5]

God, who is not a respecter of persons, offers the same peace to you.

NOTES

1. Glenda Revell, *Glenda's Story,* (Lincoln: Gateway to Joy, 1994), 30.
2. David Peter's, *Betrayal of Innocence*, (Waco, Tx: Word Books, 1986), 48-66.
3. Lynn Heitritter and Jeanette Vought, *Helping Victims of Sexual Abuse,* (Minnesota: Bethany House, 1989), 15.
4. David Peters, *A Betrayal of Innocence,* (Waco, Tx: Word Books, 1986), 59-60.
5. Revell, Glenda's Story, back cover of the book.

FROM VICTIM TO VICTOR

Chapter 7

From Victim to Victor

Whose hand is this that fondles the bare, flat chest of a little girl? Whose fingers linger upon the flesh he helped to create? Why has the love that should be mama's come to snuggle under daughter? "Someone tell me how to rinse the feeling of fingers off my mind?"[1]

Sexual abuse is a difficult subject. As I was researching and writing this book, these four chapters on sexual abuse were the hardest for me to write. But I want desperately for women to know that although Satan has attempted to destroy them as vessels fitting into God's plan, God is more than willing, fully able, eager, and desiring to fix every single piece that is broken.

Facing the reality. The first step for a woman to be healed from the painful memories of childhood sexual abuse is to admit that she is a victim. Keep in mind that sexual abuse is not always as brutal as a little girl being forced to have intercourse with a man. The four components of childhood sexual abuse are: (1) the person is a child or a teenager. (2) Is <u>forced</u> by someone (an adult, older child or teenager, or even peers). (3) Into a sexual situation in which they are uncomfortable. (4) To satisfy another person's sexual curiosity, sexual desires, or sexual perversion. If you have been in a situation like this, you have been sexually abused and most likely have some wounds that need to be healed.

To admit that one has experienced sexual abuse opens a pandora's box of confusion, anger, and fear. Most of us want such boxes to stay closed. It is easier to deny or ignore painful incidents in the past.

Don't look for problems that don't exist. But if you know you have been in one of the situations just described (even if the specific details are now foggy in your memory and you have never dealt with the feelings of uneasiness or insecurity you sense are related to these incidents) take the courage in Christ and open the box. Let God also have the fragments you do know about, and He will begin to heal you.

Here are the sad words of a young woman who is facing memories of abuse perpetuated by her father, a respected pastor:

> "I'd rather be dead than face the truth of the memories. If I admit the memories are true, I'll be totally abandoned by my parents, family, and church. If I continue to live a lie, I'll slowly rot from the inside out, pretending all is well when I know I'm a zombie." [2]

Her choices were clear: lie and die slowly, or talk and be immediately cut off. This woman's vision had been distorted by Satan's worldly and unspiritual perspective. In reality, the truth is always liberating.

Deciding to deal with sexual abuse in the past is like a situation that happened with my sister last year when she broke her leg. It was a bad break, fractured in two places. She had a cast from her hip to her ankle and was on crutches for several months. For a mother of two young children and an active teenager who could not drive, this was very inconvenient. When the cast came off, the break still had not healed sufficiently. Her leg swells, her knee stiffens, and she experiences intense pain from time to time. The doctors advise that she allow them to break the leg again and reset it. They believe this is the only way it's going to get better. My sister says, "No way!" She will never allow her leg to be broken again. Instead she has learned how to live with the swelling, stiffening, and pain. To her, that is much easier to deal with than several more months in a cast.

This is the way most sexual abuse victims feel. They have learned to live with whatever the dysfunctions are in their personalities. For most, thinking back on negative sexual experiences, labeling those experiences sexual abuse, and admitting the sexual abuse victim's identity is too disturbing. I wish I could give reassuring words to encourage you, like "It won't hurt a bit," or "It will be over in no time," but that is not true. In the words of Dr. Dan B. Allender, author of *Wounded Heart:*

> "Marriages will need to be reshaped; sexual relations may be postponed.... The fabric of life will need to be unraveled piece by piece as the Master reweaves the cloth to His design. This process would be difficult even in an ideal world with supportive partners, friends, and churches....The external battle is dramatically difficult because others would prefer the nice woman remain sweet, the competent woman remain in control, and the happy-go-lucky woman remain the life of the party....Change is bumpy and messy...." [3]

So why even attempt to go down this road that promises such complications and heartache? Why bother to pick up the shattered pieces that seem impossible ever to put together again? Because God always requires that we love Him, serve Him, and worship Him with a whole heart. Sometimes it seems impossible to love God or anyone else, and childhood sexual abuse can be a major factor. It causes our hearts to be fragmented, wounded, and broken into several pieces.

Because of past experiences, many Christian women are not experiencing the satisfying, abundant life Jesus promised to give not just when we get to heaven, but right here and now. Too often women live in defeat, constantly battling frustration, depression, loneliness, bitterness, and anger. (See the list of resources at the end of the book for more information on these and other characteristics of a broken heart.)

Seek the one who can heal you. The Lord is our *Jehovah-Rapha*, the Lord who heals by taking the bitter waters of our lives and making them sweet. God's name, Jehovah-Rapha, is mentioned for the first time in the Bible in the book of Exodus (Exodus 15:22-26). *Rapha* means "to mend, to cure." It is translated "to repair, repair thoroughly, make whole." In Genesis, it is translated to mean *physicians* (Genesis 50:2).

Jehovah-Rapha is mentioned the first time in the Bible when the children of Israel had been in the wilderness three days without water. When the Israelites came to Marah, the water was bitter and they were unable to drink it. The congregation began to grumble but Moses cried out to the Lord. The Lord told Moses to put a branch in the water which made the water sweet and the peoples' needs were met. God called this a test. He was attempting to communicate this lesson in essence to His people: *"When you are given the bitter waters of life, call on Me; I am the fixer. I am the healer."*

God is our great physician. Many of us can testify about how God physically completely healed us or someone we know. But do we believe God can make us whole emotionally, even from the trauma of childhood sexual abuse? Is Jehovah-Rapha the One we are seeking for our healing?

When I speak of *healing*, I'm not implying that the individual will never experience pain again or that past memories will never surface. But when God heals us we can be *"more than conquerors."* We will have God's solution as to how to deal with our hurts. Satan can no longer manipulate us through our wounds. We will begin to see how this affliction is resulting in our good and for the good of others.

Believe that you can be made whole. I was talking to a woman who was molested by her stepfather as a child, practically everyday for years. She told me that her sexual abuse experience continues to haunt her daily and affects almost every area of her life. I assured her that it was possible for her to experience complete healing and be made whole. She stared at me in unbelief. "If I can just experience one day without feeling the pain of what happened to me before I die," she said, "I would be satisfied." Oh, my sisters, let me assure you; a lifetime of freedom is available to you, not just one day.

Telling women who have been sexually abused that they can never be whole again to think and function like other women is one of Satan's most damaging lies. Listen to a letter from a woman who had been the victim of incest since infancy:

> In a book I am reading, the author wrote of her personal experience with incest and how much her journey with God has helped her. The only thing I took discouragingly was her analogy of an amputee–saying that's how *a victim is,* missing something that can never be replaced. Several days ago I saw a Christian program on abused children and they expressed the same opinion. I must admit it hit hard at first. I felt my Light, Hope, and Faith pulling away from me for a moment, til I remembered what I read in God's Word about being born again, being a new creature, about all things being past and gone.

> What I got out of all this is that I'm slowly getting to be like Jesus. I have His mind. To me Jesus isn't a cripple, so I'm not. I am the only thing between God and being a whole person. I am the problem.

> You may correct me if I am wrong, but I'm holding out for all of God's promises. I will not settle to learn only how to adjust, cope, and function. I'm holding on to the promise of abundant life. I believe God can heal totally. I have the faith and hope that I will arrive at that point. That's my goal–to be all Jesus says I can be and wants me to be. Without that goal, if I believed what these two sources said, I'd stop growing. I'd settle, because there is no hope if I'll always be a cripple. I said you may correct me if I'm wrong, but you needn't do that in this case because I know I'm right.[4]

Talk it out. If you want to deal with your deep dark secrets of the past and to experience healing, you need to "have a little talk with Jesus." He knows all about them already. He is a Wonderful Counselor who will keep our information confidential, He understands your situation completely, He is always available, and He doesn't charge a cent.

Not only is Jesus willing to listen, but the Holy Spirit will help us talk it out. *"The Spirit helps our weakness; for we do not know how to pray as we should, but the Spirit Himself intercedes for us with groaning too deep for words"* (Romans 8:26). We may have a hard time articulating the words or allowing ourselves to speak about the violation but the Holy Spirit has promised to assist in explaining our anguish to God.

Once you have talked it over with Jesus, then find a person with whom you can share your secret. A good choice might be someone who has also experienced sexual abuse and won't find your story hard to believe or condemn you for the way you feel. For many women their inner healing begins after they are able to pour out their story to God and one other sympathetic person. For some, getting help from a professional or other person knowledgeable in the field of sexual abuse may be necessary.

Reprogram your thinking. When one is sexually abused in childhood, not only does the victim communicate negative perceptions about herself, but she also creates mistaken perceptions from others ("Everyone thinks I'm a terrible person;" "No one will ever love me because of this;"or "I deserve to be treated badly"). Her view of God is distorted ("If God loved and cared about me, He would have never let this happen;" or "God is distant and powerless;" or "I can't trust God"). All of these messages are lies. Satan loves to keep lies going, add on to them, and use them to keep people from moving closer to God and enjoying the life He desires for us.

The Word of God is the only effective cleanser and rearranger for the mind. *"All Scripture is inspired by God and profitable for teaching* (Lord what do I do now?), *for reproof* (establishing new convictions), *for correction* (knowing where you went wrong and how to change it), *for training in righteousness* (thinking and functioning the way God wants instead of the way you automatically think because of the abuse) (2 Timothy 3:16). In fact, God has sent His word for the purpose of healing and deliverance from our destruction (Psalm 107:20).

Decide to Forgive. Doris (Doris is her proper name: Dorie is her nick name) Van Stone in her books, *Dorie* and *No Place To Cry*, tells the tragic story of her past life of physical, emotional, and sexual abuse. For years she was brutally beaten and rejected by her mother. Then her mother abandoned her and she was placed in an orphanage. In the institution she was beaten regularly by the caretakers, mistreated by the other children, and forced to participate in perverted sexual activities with one of the female workers. Dorie was later placed in several foster homes and once again physically, emotionally, and sexually abused for several years. Later on in Dorie's life she was able to find her father. She had the opportunity to get to know him and even live with him for a short time. Initially, they had a great relationship, but when she decided to become a missionary he turned his back on her and disowned her as his daughter.

If anyone has the right to hold on to anger, bitterness, hatred, and anger, it is Doris. But this is not the case, however. One chapter in *No Place To Cry* deals exclusively with forgiveness.

Doris makes it very clear that each person must forgive at her own speed. Personalities and each individual situation will dictate whether the process will take months or even years. The thought of forgiving a grown man or any other person responsible for taking advantage of a young defenseless child seems impossible, but remember "nothing is impossible with God." Most victims would like to skip this step. But in order to experience emotional and spiritual healing, forgiveness must take place. Doris gives four principles that helped her forgive her many offenders: [5]

- See the offender as human. It is easy to think of those who sexually abuse children as dogs. But the offender probably has suffered abuse and never was able to work through his hurts. Therefore, he is incapable of coping with life and, in turn, abuses an innocent child. Truly he had a choice, but sometimes the offender cannot see his alternatives and feels trapped by his selfish desires, hostilities, and lust.

- The victim must realize that she can forgive without surrendering her desire for justice. *"Vengeance is mine says the Lord, I will repay"* (Romans 12:19). There will be a court date for all those who have abused children. God will be the judge and He will mete out the punishments according to the crimes. He has seen and recorded it all. God is a righteous judge, not like earthly judges who may be insensitive, lack all the details, or unable to render due punishment because of the limitations of the law. Therefore, the victim must leave the retaliation to God.

- Realize that forgiveness is not an emotion but an act of the will. Forgiveness is our choice. Whether we feel like it or not (and most likely we will not), we can say as Dorie did, "In the name of Christ I choose to forgive!" As Dorie asked one victim, "Why should your abuser continue to ruin your life? Hasn't he done enough damage to your soul?" Harboring anger and bitterness eats away at us on the inside. Forgiveness is something the victim does in order to become the victor.

- Forgiveness is not a one-time act but a process. Some victims of abuse are reminded of the violation when they see certain activities (like father hugging a daughter) or certain places or colors might that bring rake up bitterness from the past. It may take time for that bitterness to release its hold on you. But if you are determined to continue to forgive your offender(s) eventually when the hostility rises it will not be overbearing, nor harbor in your spirit for a long time as it once did.

Move from why to what. Glenda, who was molested repeatedly by her stepfather shares her personal healing process (also in chapter 6) in a book called *Glenda's Story:*

> I have heard people ask, "How can God be loving and kind when He allows such suffering in the lives of innocent children?" The answer lies in perspective. As any loving parent knows, he must sometimes withhold seeming good things for the ultimate good of His child.
>
> I know that God did not forsake me during my dark night of sorrow. All the time He was drawing me to Himself by peeling away, one by one, those objects of my longing, that, if given, would have kept me from longing for Him. God was on my side. His strong arm, which, in His great wisdom, sorely bruised me, would eventually, in merciful tenderness, gather me into His bosom.
>
> If the Lord had not been on our side when men attacked us, when their anger flared against us, they would have swallowed us alive; the flood would have engulfed us, the torrent would have swept over us, the raging waters would have swept us away. Praise be to the Lord, who has not let us be torn by their teeth. We have escaped like a bird out of the fowler's snare; the snare has been broken, and we have escaped. Our help is in the name of the Lord, The Maker of heaven and earth. (Psalms 124:2-8) NIV [6]

Those who sincerely turn to God for healing of their damaged past can overcome the scars of their past, but those who reject and repeatedly blame God for the abuse continue down a spiral of self-destruction. They turn instead to other behaviors–overeating, excessive spending, alcohol or drugs to name a few. Some have even taken their own lives because they saw no way to repair the emotional damage. Some spend time in and out of mental hospitals, unable to face reality.

There are some things God will not explain to us until we meet Him face to face. It is in our best interest not to continue to ask "Why, Lord?" but "What now, Lord?"

The first question "Why Lord?" keeps one agonizing. Satan wants to keep us in torment. He knows if he can keep the victim questioning, blaming, bitter, and wailing in self-pity, her life will be his. She will probably never be fruitful for God; she has no time to think of building His kingdom. All of her attention is on the rubble and rocks of her past. Satan will bring the memories back repeatedly. She sits with him reviewing the pictures and wishing the whole thing never happened. He has trapped her inside her own little prison. He empathizes with her and makes her feel as if he understands; but in private, Satan laughs.

The second question, "What now, Lord?" gives the victim a reason and the power to go on. God is full of help and hope for those who have been fragmented by the tragedy of sexual abuse. Satan will always attempt to upset God's plans for people to live productive, happy lives. But God will denounce whatever scheme Satan devises with Romans 8:28, *"All things work together for good to those who love God and are called according to His purposes."* If asked, God will faithfully guide the incest victim away from the horror of the past and use that experience to lift Him up and draw others to Him.

I want to conclude this chapter by briefly giving parents some things they can do to prevent their daughters from becoming victims of child abuse.

WHAT PARENTS CAN DO TO PREVENT SEXUAL ABUSE

Prayer. Childhood sexual abuse definitely needs to be fought politically and socially. Child protection agencies need to do more to fight on behalf of sexually abused children. Laws need to be changed and stiffer penalties for offenders need to be put in place. The root of the sexual abuse problem, however, is spiritual. Satan is the ultimate instigator of this crime against women because he sees it as a way to destroy us and our families.

The chief weapon against sexual abuse is prayer. We need to pray for our children's protection. We cannot follow them everywhere, but God can. If sexual abuse strikes our family or a family we know, prayer for wisdom is needed. God's direct assistance will be needed for decision-making, to give courage to face the challenges ahead, and provide healing for the victim and her family.

Prevention. Many sexual abuse situations can be avoided or cut short, if parents are alerted to signs. The following are some suggestions to keep this destructive trick of Satan out of your family. (Specific signs will be listed in the Additional Information section following this chapter.)

- Educate yourself. Sit down and read a good book on the subject. You are fooling yourself if you think this could not happen to your child or to someone you know. It is good to have the facts and to know how to handle a situation before it arises.

- Educate your child. There are various resources available in bookstores to help you tell your child about appropriate and inappropriate behavior from adults.

- Work at having a good open relationship with your child. Talk to her daily about her day and the events that happened. If someone is making inappropriate advances toward your child or if sexual abuse happens, she must feel comfortable telling you about it.

- Be careful of so many commitments which leave your child unattended or constantly in the care of others. If it is mandatory that you work, ask God to provide you with a job which allows you to be with your child as much as possible to give her the nurturing support she needs. Do not sacrifice your child on the altar of materialistic gain. If you have to leave your child with a caregiver, make sure the person is competent. Don't just leave your child with a family you hardly know. Teach your child not to go into anyone else's home. Have a reputation as a mother who is outside when her children are outside, or constantly checks on their whereabouts in the neighborhood, at school, day care center, or even in the church nursery.

- Engage your child in quiet activity at night. Do not allow her to watch or read scary stories at night. Be firm about her sleeping alone in her own bed. Additionally, to place an unclothed or partially clothed girl in close contact with an adult male is asking for trouble. This kind of sleeping arrangement, especially when mixed with alcohol, loneliness, stress or emotional immaturity could lead to a sexual abuse situation.

Protection. If a sexual abuse situation has occurred the main concern should be for the victim. If you suspect, or if your child reports a sexual encounter, allow the child to explain what happened. Keep yourself calm as possible. Do not ignore her confession; believe your child. Rarely do children make up sexual abuse stories. At this point the child needs to be protected from any further harm. Assure her that you will see to it that she is not abused again.

ADDITIONAL INFORMATION

The following list is compiled from *A Betrayal of Innocence* by David B. Peters and *When Child Abuse Comes to Church* by Bill Anderson.

HOW TO DETECT SEXUAL ABUSE IN YOUR DAUGHTER:

Behavioral Indicators of Sexual Abuse in Infants, Preschoolers and Older Children:

1. Uneasiness around previously trusted persons
2. Sexualized behavior (excessive masturbation, sexually inserting objects, explicit sex play with other children)
3. Fear of rest rooms, showers, or baths (common locations of abuse)
4. Fear of being alone with men or boys
5. Nightmares on a regular basis or about the same person
6. Abrupt personality changes
7. Uncharacteristic hyperactivity
8. Moodiness or excessive crying; constant unexplained anxiety, tension or fear
9. Aggressive or violent behavior toward other children or any other abrupt personality change; inability to relate to peers
10. Difficulty in sleeping or relaxing; nightmares on a regular basis or about the same person
11. Clinging behavior which may take the form of separation anxiety; unusual need for assurance of love
12. Passive or withdrawn behavior
13. Specific knowledge of sexual facts and terminology beyond developmental age
14. Wearing multiple layers of clothing, especially to bed; or wetting of bed after being "broken" of that problem
15. Parentified behavior (acting like a small parent)
16. Frequent tardiness or absence from school, especially if male caretaker writes excuses; or reluctance to go home after school
17. Attempts to make herself ugly or undesirable (such as poor personal hygiene)
18. Eating disorders (obesity, bulimia, anorexia)
19. Self-conscious behavior, especially regarding the body
20. Toys or money acquired with no explanation
21. Tendency to seek out or totally avoid adults
22. Running away, especially in a child, is normally not a behavioral problem. In addition to the above mentioned behavioral indicators, you may

be–but not always–able to detect physical indicators of child sexual abuse. Some of these physical symptoms include pain or itching in the vaginal area; vaginal discharge; difficulty in walking or sitting; bruises or bleeding of external vaginal or anal regions; venereal disease, especially in young children; swollen or red cervix, vulva or perineum; torn, stained or bloody underclothing; unusual or offensive odors; and pregnancy, when the child refuses to reveal information about the father or when the child is in complete denial about her pregnancy.

Additional Behavioral Indicators of Sexual Abuse in Adolescents:
1. Sexualized behavior (promiscuity, prostitution, sexual abuse of your children)
2. Drug and alcohol abuse
3. Suicidal gestures or attempts; self-mutilation
4. Extreme hostility toward a parent or caretaker; or defiance or compliance to an extreme
5. Self-conscious behavior, especially regarding the body
6. Delinquent behavior; school problems (academic or behavioral)
7. Friends tend to be older

Behavior Indicators of Sexual Abuse in Adults:
1. Sexual difficulties (usually regarding intimacy issues)
2. Distrust of the opposite sex
3. Inappropriate choice of partner (chooses a dependent partner she can mother or one who abuses her or her children physically or sexually)
4. Progressive breakdown of communication and eventual emotional detachment from children.
5. Multiple marriages
6. Extreme dependence upon or anger toward a parent
7. Sexual promiscuity (or alternating between periods of preoccupation with or revulsion by sexual activity)
8. Drug or alcohol abuse
9. Extremely low self-esteem
10. Nightmares or flashbacks
11. Continual victimization (seemingly unable to assert or protect herself)
12. May see self-worth only in sexuality
13. Eating disorders (usually obesity)
14. Self-punishing behaviors
15. Homosexual orientation
16. Body shame (extreme self-consciousness)

Family Indicators of Child Sexual Abuse
1. Role reversal between mother and daughter
2. Extreme overprotectiveness or jealousy toward a child by a parent (parent sharply restricts a child's contact with peers and adults outside the home)
3. Inappropriate sleeping arrangements (child sleeps with a parent on a regular basis or with both parents where she is exposed to sexual activity)
4. Prolonged absence of one parent from the home (through death, divorce, or illness, for example)
5. Mother who is often ill or is disabled, even if home
6. Extreme lack of communication between caretakers
7. Inordinate participation of father in family (father may interact very little with family members or may insist on being in charge of all family activities)
8. Extreme parental dominance of spouse (for instance, mother is not allowed to drive or talk to school personnel)
9. Work or activity schedules which result in a caretaker (especially male) spending large amounts of time alone with a child or children
10. Extreme favoritism shown to a child (father may spend a lot of time and attention on one daughter)
11. Severe overreaction by a parent to any sex education offered a child
12. Caretaker has been sexually abused as a child
13. Geographic isolation of family
14. Overcrowding in a home
15. Family has no social or personal support systems.
16. Alcohol or drug abuse within a family

NOTES
1. T.D. Jakes, *Woman Thou Art Loosed,* (Shippensberg Pa.: Treasure House, 1994), 22.
2. Dan Allender, *The Wounded Heart*, (Colorado Springs: Navpress, 1990), 26.
3. Ibid., 26-27.
4. Kay Arthur, *Lord Heal My Hurts*, (Portland: Multnomah Books), 1989, 43
5. Doris Van Stone and Erwin Lutzer. *No Place To Cry*, (Chicago: Moody Press, 1990), 77-81.
6. Glenda Revell, *Glenda's Story,* (Lincoln: Gateway to Joy, 1994), 61-63.

Chapter 8

The Church And Sexual Abuse

An abused woman was told by her pastor that she was to forget the past and stop pitying herself because many people have had a lot worse things happen to them than being abused by their father. This advice made any reflection on the effects of the abuse selfish and illegitimate. His comment felt as painful to her as the original abuse.[1]

A woman was told by her friends that she was tempting the judgment of God because she was taking her abuser to court. She was told that her desire to bring him to justice was unloving and vengeful. She wryly remarked that a friend had recently received a sizable out-of-court settlement for an accident, and no one batted an eye. It appeared to be acceptable to use the court system for a damaged car, but not for a damaged soul.[2]

A woman...was part of a charismatic church connected to a national healing and miracle ministry, which makes an assumption that sexually abused persons are demon-oppressed. The memories may be the concoction of the demons, thus discounting the validity of the past abuse; or the memories may be actual events that are kept in the mind by the evil host that inhabit the victim. In either case, the strategy is to cast the demons out through the ritual of exorcism....She eventually endured several exorcisms where she experienced her handlers as abusive and demeaning, though for a time she felt relief and rest. That period ended when she required constant assurance and drug-like jolts of emotional enthusiasm to keep her wavering and transient faith stable.[3]

The pastor, several of the church leaders, and various members in the church knew my sisters and I were being molested by my father. No one in the church said or did anything. I heard plenty of sermons and Bible lessons on why girls should not have sex before marriage. But I never heard anybody preach a sermon or give a warning to fathers about not having sex with their daughters. –Pam

"Brethren, this ought not to be!" (1 Corinthians 5:1-2) This was Paul's response when he found out about an incest situation that was known among the congregation and nothing was being done about it . Because of the church's silence on the subject of sexual abuse or mishandling of sexual abusive situations, many girls have been left wide open to Satan's vicious attack. The church can no longer pretend the problem does not exist. Failure to act on behalf of suffering young girls and these hurting families is to cooperate with Satan and his demonic plan to destroy women.

THE CONGREGATION'S RESPONSE TO SEXUAL ABUSE

The book of Judges includes a sexual abuse incident that demonstrates the way God's people should respond to this kind of offense. Judges was written in a time when *"In those days there was no king in Israel; everyone did what was right in his own eyes"* (Judges 21:25). Even the people of God were not governing themselves according to God's instructions. This is very similar to the world we live in today. This is fertile breeding ground for sexual abuse.

The historical event starts out with a priest who married a concubine from the tribe of Judah (Judges 19). As he traveled home with his concubine he had to stop for the night. He chose a place within Israel and an old man invited him to spend the night in his home. While there, several homosexuals surrounded the house and demanded that the man be brought out so that they could have sex with him. The old man refused to send the man out but he did give them the man's concubine to be raped instead. The men of the city abused the concubine all night. The next morning, the man found her at the door of the house–dead.

The man was outraged by what happened to his concubine and he took her body on to his home. There he cut her body up into twelve pieces and sent one piece to each of the twelve tribes of Israel. The congregation was also outraged and took extreme action against this tribe (Benjamin) in which the tragedy happened. They attempted to see to it that nothing like this ever happened again in Israel. At first the nation of Israel demanded that Benjamin send out the wicked men who did this awful act, but Benjamin refused. Therefore, they declared war on the tribe and almost wiped them out entirely (Judges 20-21). I believe there are several principles we can learn from the actions and reactions of Israel to this horrid act of sexual abuse and murder.

Congregations should hold leaders accountable.
Nowhere in Scripture does the law condone a priest having a concubine. This priest was not following God's instructions in the area of relationships with women (Leviticus 21:13-14; Ezekiel 44:22).

This is also true today with many pastors and church leaders. There are numerous sex scandals involving our church leaders. Often a congregation will joke about the pastor who has been with several women in the congregation, or laugh about the "dirty old man" on the deacon board. But these are no laughing matters, especially for a girl who might be the victim of these leaders' advances. When the leadership is ignoring God's instructions concerning sexual purity, it opens a gateway for all kinds of sexual sins to come into the congregation, one of which is surely to be childhood sexual abuse!

> When I was in seminary, there were about fifteen of us in one dorm and we were all pretty close friends. Only three or four of us were committed to celibacy. Those of us who thought this way were considered odd and endured our share of ridicule about our stance. The others had women in their rooms Saturday night, and would go for preaching engagements on Sunday morning. –Jason

> Our school sponsored a Christian student conference and one of the keynote speakers challenged those of us training for the ministry to stay sexually pure. This was the only time during my seminary years anyone ever addressed the issue and spoke plainly about what the Bible said. That helped take some of the pressure off of those of us who had already made that commitment; however, the women still spent the night on the weekends. –John

It is unfortunate, many men in the ministry have not learned how to live the victorious life as it relates to sexual matters. Perhaps it has to do with generational curses and certainly a lack of teaching and modeling of the spirit-filled life made available to us. In some cases, there is not even a desire to be obedient to the Word of God in the sexual areas.

Many of these men of God are struggling and do not find help because they are expected to be above these problems. They do not know where to go for help and few people pray for them. It is true that some are in the ministry without even knowing God. But there are those who know God and have genuinely experienced a definite call to serve Him. I realize God does not call men who are perfect into the ministry. In fact, He seems to mostly call those who are afflicted and God demonstrates His power through them. However, this particular weakness needs to be seriously addressed among our clergy and church leaders because it has such devastating effects on women who have been victimized.

> My daughter was a very strong Christian as a teenager. But now she despises the church. She does not follow the Lord. She has had a child out of wedlock. She was in counseling with our pastor as a teen and some inappropriate sexual things were said to her. She has not gotten over it to this day. I think what hurt her the most was when she started to take the right steps to confront the matter, the pastor seemed to be the one who was protected instead of her. –Shane

> A deacon at my church told me he could satisfy my sexual needs if I had any as a single parent. I was so disgusted with this comment. When I confronted him about it, he told me he was just teasing. But I think he would have taken me up on it if I had responded favorably. It has been a struggle to keep myself sexually pure after becoming a Christian as a widow. It almost makes you want to give up the struggle of a high standard when you have to deal with these things. But I've decided I need to do what God wants me to do no matter if all of the deacons and pastors in the world don't want to go God's way. –April

Men of God are in positions to influence many people. When they fall sexually, many people stop following God. The enemy will seek to set them up for a fall more often than the average Christian. There are tremendous sexual pressures on ministers. This need to be understood by all Christians– especially ministers' wives.

Women who are married to pastors often have to contend with other women who flaunt themselves before their husbands. Some women are specifically sent into churches by the enemy to set up a snare. The counseling chamber for example, is a very effective trap. Many pastors testify to affairs starting in this environment. Michelle Obelton has an excellent chapter specifically addressing this issue in a book called *Woman to Woman.*

> The pastor's wife is extremely important to her husband's ministry.... Pastors' wives need to understand that they are in spiritual warfare everyday. If Satan could creep into the garden way back in Genesis chapter three and single out Eve to frustrate God's plan for mankind, he can still creep into churches and single out the pastor's wife to frustrate God's plan for the church....

> A pastor's wife may have a keen radar to detect the needy people that come to the church, especially needy women who have great admiration for the pastor. While admiration for a member of the opposite sex can be healthy, there is a point where it leads to danger. The pastor is often viewed by many as a strong

spiritual giant, who is able to solve all their problems. Women who admire strong male leadership are attracted to the pastor. A pastor's wife is often aware of these attractions, and also knows that in the sexualized society we live in today infidelity has become commonplace. She realizes that a needy woman, better known as "the other woman," can pose a serious threat to her family as well as the church. Satan can use this kind of woman to destroy a man of God.[4]

Mrs. Obleton then goes on to offers biblical and practical help to deal with this problem, such as keeping yourself spiritually in tune with God through personal Bible study and prayer, working at keeping your marriage healthy, and being willing to confront the pastor if she has concerns.

As wives, mothers, daughters, parishioners, aunts, and sisters we need to learn to cover these men with fervent prayer and intercession. More so than any one else Christian leaders need people to be commited to pray for them.[5] As much as God may use clergy persons in your life, see them as humans who desperately need the grace of God to make it from day to day. Commit to pray for them, even those you don't suspect of having an ungodly sexual problem. Never assume that the clergy is exempt from temptations in this area. Reject the tendency to put your pastor or any others in spiritual leadership on a pedestal where only God belongs.

There are other practical things you personally can do to help your spiritual leader stay out of sexual trouble. First, don't be flirtatious or encourage him to be. Avoid talking about your marital sexual problems with male clergy. If you must go to a male, try to involve your husband as much as possible. A good alternative is to seek the counsel of a mature Christian woman. This way you avoid emotional entanglements with the pastor, which can easily happen if you only seek help from him.

Women should not be looked down upon. The old man who welcomed the priest and the concubine into his home saw no need to protect the woman from sexual abuse but he did protect the man. Oftentimes Bible scholars have interpreted passages pertaining to women incorrectly, placing women in lower or less respected positions than men. Even with all the push for equal rights for women, women are still often looked down upon and used as sex objects in our society. We need to understand that this is not a Biblical concept but a man made practice. God has always held women in high esteem and used them greatly and significantly throughout the Bible. God made women in His image and sees them as joint heirs of the grace of God (1 Peter 3:7).

In the same way, children are often looked down upon and not seen as the precious gifts God gives to us. While we are purchasing new choir robes, cushioned benches for the auditorium, or an air conditioned church bus, the church children and youth programs often have little or no funds. The nursery is often in some dark dingy room staffed with people who have been coerced to work or are ill-equipped to work there. Where these kinds of attitudes exist, children often get treated like "things" instead of people.

Sometimes women do share with the pastor, church leaders, or members in the congregation concerning various kinds of abusive situations in the home (spousal abuse, for example) and these leaders do not confront the husband. The wife is often told to be more submissive, more loving and encouraging, to read the Bible and pray more, to just be patient and wait for the Lord to work it all out. Unfortunately, without anything more, the problem either stays the same or escalates. *"If a man is caught in any trespass, you who are spiritual, restore such a one in a spirit of gentleness; each one looking to yourself, lest you too be tempted"* (Galatians 6:1)."

The church can make a difference. Now, let's go back to the priest and the concubine. This one man was outraged with the sexual abuse and murder of his concubine. He started a one man campaign to do something about it. It is a common trend in the Bible to see one person affecting a change for the good of the majority. Two examples: the daughters of Zelophehad appealed to Moses to change the law concerning women and property ownership (Numbers 26:33-27:7) and Esther, one woman, appealed to her husband the king, and saved the entire Jewish nation.

> My family went through hell after I found out my daughter was being molested by my husband. I had a lot of anger toward the church because that is where I turned and they knew very little about how to advise or help me and my family. After God took me through my ordeal, I made myself available to help my church become more aware of sex abuse and how they can be more effective. As a result, more hurting families are getting the help they need in all areas. –Ruby

If your church is not taking enough of an aggressive stand against sexual abuse, you can. Your actions might be the catalyst to get the entire church concerned and involved. After the nation of Israel was alerted to the horrendous sexual abuse and murder of the priest's concubine, the nation rallied together to make sure the offenders were punished and that such a crime would never happen again. "Hush, Hush..." can no longer be the way sexual abuse is dealt with in the church. Sexual abuse should be reported to the church leaders (unless they are the offenders) and discreetly but thoroughly investigated. The offender should be brought to justice and be made to come to terms with his actions.

Some churches have used 1 Corinthians 6:1 which says, *"Dare any of you, having a matter against another, go to law before the unrighteous and not before the saints?"* to justify inaction against abusers. But this passage is referring to civil suits against other members in the church, not criminal behavior. Romans 13:1-5 establishes the fact that civil government is instituted by God to punish criminal wrongdoing. Sexual abuse is a criminal violation of the law and should be reported to a law enforcement agency. Any legal proceedings are then in the hands of the law enforcement and judicial system.

Bringing someone to justice according to our laws appears harsh and understandably so when we are talking about a close family member. But remember that such laws were made a part of our system in the first place to try and protect the moral and ethical values of our families and our communities. It may be only then that the offender gets the help he needs.

> While he was in prison, I continued to visit a father who had incest relations with his daughter. Everyone else in his family had abandoned him. I eventually was able to lead him to the Lord and witness his repentance of his crime. It would have been easy for me to have forgotten about this man like everyone else, but somehow that is not what I believe God wanted me to do. I have a feeling there are a lot of men like him out there. –A pastor

Not only should the offender continue to receive spiritual support from the church, (especially if the family is too emotionally shattered to support him), but the victim's family should receive emotional and tangible help from the church as well. Help the wife find a job if the husband has to be removed from the home. Pay for counseling, if insurance will not cover it. Help in practical ways. In most places, secular counseling and support groups are the only avenue of help available for victims, offenders, and their families. The church should be there to supplement with spiritual and biblical input.

> I realize that no church in our community seemed to be helping sex offenders come to grips with their problems, nor helping men who haven't gone that far but are struggling with pornography, sex addictions, or other sexually deviant behavior. So I started one. We read through books, brought in experts to talk, but mostly supported one another. It helped the offender to know others are out there struggling in the same areas and we can be overcomers in Christ if we help one another.–John

The congregation can take steps for prevention. The nation of Israel devised a plan to see to it that this kind of hideous crime did not happen among them again. The church can do the same today. Education should be at least one part of each congregation's plan for prevention. Have a person who is knowledgeable on the subject to conduct a seminar or distribute materials. The more people are aware of the potential signs of abuse, the earlier the church can come to a family's aid and perhaps even prevent the crime from happening. Public acknowledgment of sex abuse puts offenders on notice and makes it more comfortable for a victim or the caretaker to report the abuse.

The church also needs to take precautions concerning the church nursery. As unseemly as it sounds, sexual abuse against children sometimes takes place right in the church. The church nursery, for example, is a prime target. Remember, Satan wants to start early destroying the lives of our little ones. What better way than to try to convince them early that the church people cannot be trusted, and that therefore God cannot be trusted with the rest of their lives? Pastor Bill Anderson offers some specific suggestions for keeping sexual abuse out of the nursery. [6].

- The nursery should have windows, be a clean airy place.

- Have a well trained staff and a good scheduled program. No one should work in the nursery alone, no teams from the same family.

- Only the parent should be allowed to drop off or pick up the child. Only an usher is to tell the parent if they need to come and see about a child.

- A single nursery worker should never be alone with the children.

- Screen nursery workers. Make a simple application that includes name, address, previous church membership, references, employer and name of immediate supervisor. Check with the church or other employers to see if there has been any problem. Also ask for a driver's license, social security number and a signature. This way you can check if there have been any previous convictions. If applicants refuse to divulge this kind of information, don't use them in the children's ministry; give them another job in the church. Conduct a personal interview and if you have doubts about a person, you have the right to turn him or her down.

THE PASTOR'S RESPONSE TO SEXUAL ABUSE

Pastors and church leaders need to become more aggressive in dealing with men and their inner conflicts, especially if these abusers are members or leaders of the church. They need to hold these men accountable for their behavior toward their family, and should exercise church discipline if they violate biblical principles.

A pastor needs to be prepared to handle sexual abuse. One pastor had to deal with sixty cases of child sexual abuse which occurred either inside the church building or at church functions. He wrote about the church's experience in *When Child Abuse Comes to the Church.* In his book, Pastor Bill Anderson says:

> "Like it or not, the pastor plays a critical role when child sexual abuse is suspected in the church or in a church family. The steps he takes will have far-reaching ramifications either for the good or bad, in the life of individuals, families, the church, and the community." [6]

In light of this great responsibility pastors should consider the following suggestions.

Become knowledgeable of the subject. It is better for a pastor to think through how to handle a sexual abuse situation before a family is sitting in the church office waiting for your advice. Have suggestions and a plan of action ready to help the family. If you have not become comfortably knowledgeable on the subject, do as Dr. Anderson suggests in his book and develop a network of ministries and organizations who can help you. [7]

States have different reporting requirements and various agencies and issue of privacy may be involved. As basics in your plan of action, know these things.

Do not ignore the victim and her family. In all your efforts to meet the reporting requirements, never forget that at the bottom of this murky pit is an innocent little child, usually a little girl who stands to suffer deep emotional scars. A pastor owes it to her not to ignore this serious situation. Many problems among adult women in the church today–marital difficulties, anger, bitterness, lack of trust in God and in others, controlling personalities–are the result of women believing that their own feelings and well-being have been disregarded. Don't let your church be one to minimize the victim's integrity. Also be careful not to make the non-offending caretaker responsible for the offender's action. In so doing, you would also be invalidating this person's feelings. Remember, as was mentioned earlier, a woman who has been sexually abused as a child will often marry an abuser. She has problems of her own to resolve. Consequently, a pastor may suddenly be in the midst of seeking help for, not one, but two scarred individuals. Through many prayers and resources, the pastor and the entire congregation can ensure that Satan looses two productive people for God's service–saved from a life of depression, detachment or self-abasement.

Notes

1. Dan Allender, *The Wounded Heart,* (Colorado Springs: Navpress, 1990), 15.
2. Ibid., 17.
3. Ibid., 19.
4. N. Carter, *Woman to Womn",* (Grand Rapids: Zondervan, 1996)
5. Rebecca. Osaigbovo, *Keys to Change: A Guide to Spiritual Growth* (Detroit: Dabar, 1996)
6. B. Anderson, When Child Abuse Comes to Church, (Minneapolis: Bethany House Publishers, 1992), 21.
7. Ibid., 24.
8. Ibid., 20.

EXERCISES

1. Are you willing to admit that you have been sexually abused? What steps do you need to take now?

2. If you have been abused, write out a prayer to God. Be sure (if you can) to include:

   • What you believe the sexual abuse(s) were. Be as specific as possible. Ask the Lord to reveal to you, in His own time, anything you might be blocking out. He knows how much you can handle and when

   • Mention the person(s) involved in the abuse, those who directly mistreated you and those whom you believe allowed this mistreatment. Confess your difficulty but desire to forgive these persons. Ask Him for His wisdom and power to do so. Also ask Him to make it plain to you if and when you may need to talk to these persons.

   Ask for the Lord's guidance in determining who you may need to talk to and where you may need to see help in dealing with the abuse. List any ideas He brings to mind.

3. If you think your child or someone you know is being sexually abused, look at the list below. What do you think you may need to do?

   ___ Pray.
   ___ Report it to the authorities.
   ___ Seek counsel.
   ___ Talk to the child.
   ___ Talk to the person you believe to be the abuser.
   ___ Gather as much information on the subject as you possibly can.

4. Evaluate any present program for sexually abused victims and their families in your church. How could ou start one or help someone else start one, if one does not exist?

Section Two

Satan's Sexual Attack
on Teen Age Girls

Chapter 9

Sex Education God's Way

If Satan has not successfully infiltrated the mind of our young girls and inflicted them with unhealthy attitudes and experiences during their early years, he certainly does not give up. As young girls move through their elementary, preteen, and adolescent years he continues to launch his malicious attacks. This is a time when girls are curious about their developing bodies, their emotions are swinging from one extreme to the other, and peer pressure begins to set in. The enemy sets up dangerous booby traps at every stage as girls move through these developmental years.

Satan attacks the mind. Satan is more subtle in his approach during this time of a girl's life. He puts less attention on directly assaulting her body and begins to work more directly on tainting her mind. His job is to plant incorrect ungodly thoughts that will cause her to make wrong choices and eventually lead her down a destructive path of sexual harm.

God wants believers to think about and dwell on what is *"true, honorable, right, pure, lovely, of good repute, excellent, and anything worthy of praise"* (Philippians 4:8). When our minds are set in this way it results in a life of contentment and peace (Romans 8:6). This is exactly what Satan does not want to happen. If he can capture our girls' minds and get them to concentrate on fleshly, worldly, sensual things, this will cause them to be distant from God.Therefore, Satan bombards them with materials and information–anything from explicit sex scenes on television and movies, to non-factual peer conversations, to seductive lyrics in music. He wants them thinking incorrectly, confused, and unlearned in the sexual area, so that they can make plenty of mistakes which will work havoc in the rest of their lives. Satan's damaging educational onslaught has to be countered by biblical teaching from godly Christian women.

Girls are more vulnerable. I realize that boys are also dealing with attacks on their sexuality; however, girls are more vulnerable to Satan's attacks. They are vulnerable because of the possibilities of pregnancy before marriage, the double standards that still exist (boys can be promiscuous but girls can't), because their reputations could be ruined (since there is a double standard), and because their emotional desire to be loved is often confused with sex. Girls usually attach more affection to sex than do boys, and therefore, when a boy moves on to make another score with someone else, *she* may be more emotionally or psychologically scarred.

MOTHERS NEED TO TEACH THEIR DAUGHTERS
Much of the sex education responsibility for our daughters falls in the lap of the mother. One of the most beautiful and insightful examples of a mother imparting godly principles and truth to her daughter is found in the book of Exodus. The mother-daughter team is Jochebed (Moses' mother) and her daughter Miriam. Now before you conclude that this is too far removed from mothers and daughters today, let me update you on what was happening during this particular time in Egypt.

Egypt was a world power, a very wealthy country. It held all the glitter, glamour, sights, and sounds anyone would desire. On the other hand, the Israelites' lifestyle was one of slavery, hard work and poverty, seemingly deserted by the God they claimed to know and to take care of them. A young Israelite girl would no doubt be attracted to the elegance of Egypt and come to the conclusion that the Egyptian way of life was better. Even if she knew that she could never be in Pharaoh's court, enjoying all the delicacies of this kind of world, in her heart she might secretly desire it, and resent God for keeping His people away from what seemed to be the good life. In this environment Jochebed had to teach her daughter to follow the ways of God, not the Egyptians, while the ways of the ungodly seemed so much easier and so much more attractive.

When Pharaoh declared that the Hebrew midwives were to kill all the male infants in Egypt at birth, the midwives risked their lives and disobeyed his edict. Keep in mind that the people of Israel had been in Egypt for 400 years at this point. Surely the Egyptian culture should have greatly influenced the people of God. But somehow the nation had keep their distinctiveness. The Hebrew mothers had taught their daughters for several generations that Egyptians do things one way, and that God's people did things another way. Jochebed had this task to fulfill with her daughter.

Does this sound familiar? As committed Christians, we still have the responsibility of teaching our daughters to obey God rather than men, people of the world who are not looking out for their best interest. We are still dedicated to teaching them not to follow ungodly principles that contradict the Word of God, to stand up against authorities that dictate non-Christian behavior. Today's mother has to accomplish all of this against a worldly backdrop that says, "Do it, do it, do it, and I promise it will satisfy." As a mother of this new generation, I go to God for words of hope, encouragement, and instruction for this great challenge. As usual, He does not disappoint me. We can learn from Jochebed who instilled godly principles in her daughter.

> The woman conceived and bore a son... she hid him for three months.... When she could hide him no longer, she got him a wicker basket... put the child into it, and set it among the reeds and by the bank of the Nile....His sister stood at a distance to find out what would happen to him....The daughter of Pharaoh came down to bathe.... She saw the basket...and...when she opened it, she saw the child....And she had pity on him....Then his sister said...."Shall I go and call a nurse for you....?" And Pharaoh's daughter said...."Go ahead." So the girl went and called the child's mother (Exodus 2:2-8).

Be a good example. Even though Jochebed's life history is only spelled out in about eight short verses in the Bible, we are able to glean that she is a woman of courage, wisdom, and faith. These characteristics are exemplified in her actions. Jochebed showed courage by going against the ungodly mandate to allow her son to be killed. She demonstrated wisdom (*chokmah*, which means intelligence, insight, or judgment that comes from God) by carrying out a plan that I believe was given to her by God. And when she placed that baby in the basket on the river and walked away, she demonstrated faith that God would take care of her child.

We see those same characteristics coming forth in Miriam, the daughter. Miriam showed courage and faith when she stood watch over her little brother, knowing that possibly an Egyptian soldier could come up behind her and kill her and her little brother. She demonstrated faith and wisdom, or quick insightful thinking (God directed) when she spoke up and asked Pharaoh's daughter if she could call a nurse, and then called her own mother.

I don't believe these mature, intelligent decisions just popped up into Miriam's mind just at the right time. These were characteristics and behaviors that she had witnessed in her mother. One way we teach our daughters is by our example. What is your daughter learning not just from your verbal instructions but from your lifestyle? Are you verbally or non-verbally saying, "Do as I say, not as I do"?

Obey God rather than man. Jochebed hid this baby for three months when those in authority said to kill it. She obeyed a higher authority and that was God. Does your daughter see you digging into the Word of God when you face a problem? Does she know that is the place to go for instructions and direction? Does she see you standing on the Word of God rather than the trends of our present society? Today there is plenty being said about what we should teach our girls; all of that should be secondary to what God's Word has to say.

> It was the logical thing to do. I was just starting college, my parents were visible leaders in the church, my boyfriend had deserted me–and I was pregnant. Getting an abortion seemed to be a quick easy way to take care of the problem. My mother and I were on the way to the abortion clinic. Half way there she turned the car around and said to me, "We don't do things this way in this family." Yes, getting pregnant was a mistake, but aborting the baby would have been an even bigger one. I'm glad my mother had the insight to see that. –Tasha

If we want our girls to love, respect, and obey God, we have to teach them God's Word.

> ..."And you shall love the Lord your God with all your heart and with all your soul and with all your might...." And these words which I'm commanding you today, shall be on your heart; and you shall teach them diligently to your sons (and daughters) and shall talk of them when you sit in your house and when you walk by the way and when you lie down and when you rise up. And you shall bind them as a sign on your hand and they shall be as frontals on your forehead. And you shall write them on the doorpost of your house and on your gates (Deuteronomy 6:5-9).

This will occur in our daughters' lives as we become personally involved with the daily affairs of our girls.

Teach, trust, and wait. There is no way Jochebed could have envisioned herself nursing her infant son in Pharaoh's court when she put that basket on the river. She had no idea of the fate of her daughter as Miriam stood a distance away watching over Moses alone. As far as we know, Jochebed committed everything in the hands of God.

Just because we teach our daughters the facts of life, tell about our past experiences, instruct them in the Word of God, and everything else we know to do to prepare them sexually, there are no guarantees that everything will turn out just fine. Or if we have prepared our daughters the wrong way, that is not a declaration that they are destined for a destructive lifestyle. We have to place all our parental instructions, past failures and mistakes all in the hands of God.

It takes faith and courage to teach our daughters God's way, just as it took Jochebed faith to teach her daughter by example. Your position may be unpopular and your children may be mistreated by the enemy through the meanness of ungodly children. But in the long run, Jochebed's obedience saved a life, one who dedicated himself to saving the lives of many others. Similarly, God wants to use our daughters for His work.

I had two daughters out of wedlock. Many men offered to live with me and help me out. This would have been an easy way to go. But when my girls were young I became a Christian and I sincerely committed myself to do things God's way. So I trusted Him to take care of me and my girls.

I did not want to see them hurt sexually the way I had been, so I'd talk to them constantly. You know that scripture in Deuteronomy 6:7, *"and you shall teach them (your children) diligently... talk of them (God's law) when you sit in your house and when you walk by the way and when you lie down and when you rise up."* Well, I talked to them when they got up and when they went to bed. Sometimes I'd wake them up in the middle of the night and tell them something that God had laid on my heart. I couldn't wait until in the morning; I might forget it. We prayed and read scriptures together, every morning and evening. I took them soul-winning with me. I took them to the hospitals. They went to prayer meetings with me. I kept them busy; they were in music lessons, swim lessons, and anything else I could get them in.

I told them all about my past mistakes. I talked to them about sex and how to stay out of trouble. I talked to them about themselves and what I could see in them and what I expected out of them. They were not two perfect little angels. In fact, one of them was kind of fast. But I talked to them, I talked to the Lord about them, and I did my best to live the Christian life in front of them. Both were virgins when they got married. God is faithful!
–Amy

KNOWING GOD'S WORD IN ORDER TO TEACH GOD'S WORD
Mothers can counter many of the ungodly messages being communicated by Satan to our daughters by the way in which we live, but we also need to study and know God's word in order to effectively and accurately teach.

In my elementary years I distinctly heard someone say, "Sex is not talked about in the Bible." I'm not sure why, but this statement stuck with me for quite a few years. I even found myself quoting it when the subject came up. I remember looking for the word "sex" in the Bible concordance. It confirmed what I believed: the word "sex" was not in the Bible. I concluded that the Bible does not talk about sex; therefore, I felt I had to go other places to get information on the subject. I gathered as much as I could from listening to older teenagers who talked often about their true or falsified sexual experiences. I paid attention when trashy magazines or novels were being read out loud on the back of the bus. I read and reread the little two page booklet given to us about menstruation in sixth grade. And I sat glued to the television on a regular basis, attempting to understand the sexual innuendoes on the screen. Satan used ignorance to start me down a path filled with misconceptions. He made sure I turned to other resources, not the Bible, for my sex education.

Many people today still reason the way I once did. The more I hear people today talk about sex, the more I realize their education is coming from present-day humanistic secular philosophies, the ungodly slant of the educational system, the electronic media, and talk shows, **NOT** God's Word.

In my early adolescent years, before I could get too far in my erroneous thinking, our church obtained a wise youth group director. When she first met with our group, she asked us to give her various topics we wanted to discuss. Of course, sex topped the list. We thought she would skip over that topic like so many other youth workers had done. Instead, she allowed us to spend several group sessions on the subject. We fired questions at her left and right. She did not condemn our natural curiosities or seem upset about our questions. She used the Bible, not a sex manual or biology book, to give us answers. For the first time, I understood the Bible extensively covered the topic of sex. I began to see the Bible and Christianity in a new light.

God's sex manual. The Bible is one of the best tools we can use to help girls understand their bodies and be informed about what God intended for them sexually. This should not surprise us. Remember, God created sex, sex organs, and the reproductive process. He made the female hormones and parts that require special care. It was all His idea and design.

It makes perfectly good sense when we buy an appliance and want to know how it works, or when we want to know what to do when it does not work, to check the manufacturer's manual. If we can't figure it out ourselves, we take it back to the manufacturer. If we want to know the best way for girls to understand their sexual inclinations, how their organs are to function, and the God-given purpose for their sexuality, God's manual, the Bible, is the best place to inquire. And God Himself (the manufacturer) is the best person to talk to about correct operation and any malfunctions.

TECHNICAL TERMS ABOUT SEX

As a teenager, one of the things that convinced me that the Bible did not talk about sex is that I could not find the word "sex" in the Bible. Now I understand that at times, the Bible uses different terms to define sex organs or functions. In order to understand what God is saying about sex, allow me to clarify a few terms.

Adultery - occurs when anyone has sexual intercourse with the spouse of another. Several scriptures speak strongly against this practice (Exodus 5:18; Deuteronomy 5:18; Matthew 5:28; 19:7-9).

Foreplay - A term describing the early part of sexual intercourse. A period of affection with caressing, kissing and enjoying the touching of each other's body. This prepares a couple for intercourse and makes reaching the pleasure of a sexual climax more likely. "Sporting" would be the biblical term for foreplay. In Genesis 26:8, Isaac and Rebekah were seen making sport with each other. By whatever they were engaging in, the king's servant knew they were not sister and brother, but husband and wife.

Fornication - any form of sexual intercourse between other than a husband and wife. This could be, like adultery, sex between a spouse and someone other than the spouse, or sex between two unmarried people. The Bible speaks against this practice (Acts 6:13, 18; 5:20; Galatians 5:19; Ephesians 5:3; Colossians 3:5).

Menstrual Cycle - The monthly discharge of tissue, blood, and fluid from the womb when conception has not taken place. It lasts from three to seven days, and may be uncomfortable. *"The manner of woman"* (Genesis 31:35) is one way it is referred to in Scripture. Some of the Old Testament laws refer to the menstrual cycle (Leviticus 12:2; 15:19; 18:19). Restrictions related to sex and other activities during this time were imposed basically for cleanliness purposes. There is no biblical indication that this process is unnatural or a curse on women. The menstrual cycle is all a part of God's reproductive plan for women.

Nakedness - The Bible forbids looking upon each other's nakedness other than a husband and wife. Passages in Leviticus provide an extensive list of those whose nakedness is not to be uncovered–father, mother, mother-in-law or father-in-law, sister or brother, daughter- or son-in-law, stepmother, aunts, uncles, nieces and nephews. This is not to imply that parents should never undress or bathe their children or that a doctor should not examine the genitals for medical reasons. The word uncovered (*Galah)* implies not only making stark naked, but also shaming a person. For example, Ham gazed upon his naked father and seemed to derive pleasure or amusement from what he saw and was severely punished. But his two brothers covered their father in a respectful way. They had to look in order to cover him, but they did so in a respectful way that did not disgrace or make fun of Noah *(Genesis 9:20-27).*

<u>Sex</u> - This means male or female. The sex of the baby tells us whether it is a boy or a girl. The Bible does not use the word "sex." God does, however, make a distinction between male and female. The word sex has also come to mean the act of sexual intercourse.

<u>Sexuality</u> - The qualities or attributes of males or females. Genesis 1:27 says that both male and female were made in God's image. In this chapter, He gives both specific universal instructions. In Genesis chapter 2, He explains specific responsibilities given to the man and to the woman. This pattern is repeated throughout Scripture.

<u>Sexual Intercourse</u> - Sex, coitus, or copulation, the most intimate of physical closeness between a man and a woman. The man's erect penis is inserted in the woman's vagina, with rocking and thrusting movements. Usually this causes a peak of sexual feeling called an orgasm. It results in the discharge of sperm in seminal fluid from the male and a wave-like contraction of muscles in the clitoris and vagina of the woman. It is highly pleasurable and unless preventive measures are taken, it may result in pregnancy. The Bible refers to sexual intercourse by using the words "came into" or "to know." Both refer to the sexual act described above.

<u>Virginity</u> - The state of a person who has not engaged in sexual intercourse. God desires singles to maintain virginity up until they are married (Deuteronomy 22:28-29; 1 Corinthians 7:36-38; Hebrews 13:4).

Today the term *second virginity* has been coined among Christians to mean a person who is no longer a virgin but has made the decision to no longer engage in sexual intercourse until marriage.

SEXUAL MATTERS IN THE SCRIPTURES
The following chart refers to some of the basic biblical teachings on some related subjects. But there are also lessons to be gleaned from character studies, in-depth studies of certain books, and other scriptural references.

SUBJECT	SCRIPTURES	BASIC TEACHING
Abortion	Jeremiah 1:5; Psalm 139:13-16; Exodus 20:13	The fetus is a human being; to kill it is murder.
Female sexuality	Genesis 1-2	God created two distinct sexes
Female's role in marriage	Genesis 2:18	To be man's helper and companion.
Homosexuality	Leviticus 18:22,20:13; I Kings 14:24; Romans 1:24, 26-27	It is an abomination to the Lord.
Incest	Leviticus 18:16-18; 20:11-21	It is prohibited
Lust	2 Timothy 2:22	Run away from ungodly desires (of all kinds)
Prostitution	Leviticus 19:29	Forbidden
Rape	Deuteronomy 22:25	Punishable by death
Sexual Intimacy	Genesis 2:24-25; 4:1; Proverbs 5:15-20; Song of Solomon 1:12-15; 3:1-5	Good and Holy; for procreation; for marriage only; for pleasure in marriage.

I was born into a Christian family which was very conservative and strict. We were instructed about God's love but I felt very little love from the members of my family and certainly no affection. I never remember my parents kissing, hugging or being warm toward one another. And nothing was ever said about sex.

I got my sex education mainly from kids at school who, I now know as an adult, were just as ignorant as I was. I wished my parents would have talked to me. I had so many questions.

My senior year in high school I became a Christian, decided to go away to college, and had my first sexual experience. I had sex with this boy I really liked. In my mind were going to get married, have children, and live happily ever after. When I was in his arms I always felt warm and loved. But I found out he was two timing me with another girl. His best friend told me my friend really liked me, but this girl would have sex with him everyday and he just couldn't give that up.

After this experience I had several sex partners. Once again sex seemed to be a way to be held and loved. I didn't necessarily want the sex or the boy oftentimes, just the attention and the affection. And if I were willing to give in sexually, it almost guaranteed I would get both.

After college I made a commitment to second virginity. For years I did not have intercourse, but I did engage in a lot of activities that were very close to it.

When I met my future husband we celebrated our engagement with a trip to the bedroom. I'm sure our sexual experiences before marriage have contributed to a lot of our marital difficulties.

I don't blame my parents for all my wrong choices, but I do wish they had talked to me more about sex and how to stay out of trouble. I've found out since I've been an adult that the reason they didn't was because of the guilt and shame they had about their sexual involvements before marriage. I can understand that, but I needed the wealth of their experience to help me channel my life in a different direction.

I am committed not to make the same mistake with my children. I'm working hard to build good relationships with them and we've already talked quite a bit about sex. My teenage girl and boy know a lot about my sexual involvements. I'm committed to seeing to it that they do not follow in my footsteps in this area. –Fay

It is important that we educate our girls before the world does. Let them hear the truth about sex from us before we have to reprogram a mind filled with wrong information. This is an extensive job because Satan–with those in the secular world as captive participants–is working hard to mentally enslave them at earlier ages with more and more damaging material. Most parents need practical help in communicating the technical facts and the practical truths to our girls. The next chapter will offer this kind of help.

Pray for your Daughter
from Head to Toe

Below is an example of how we can pray for your girls
from head to toe. Look up the Scriptures and design your own prayers
to fit the need of your daughter.

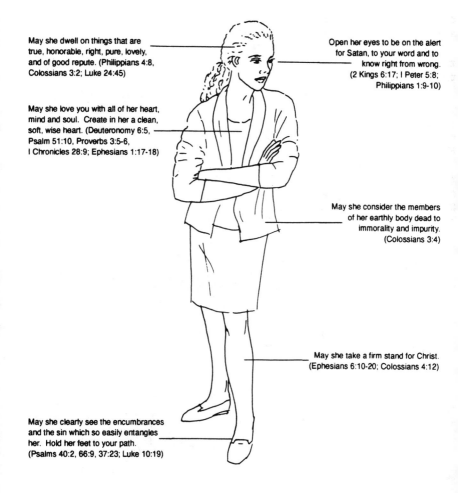

May she dwell on things that are true, honorable, right, pure, lovely, and of good repute. (Philippians 4:8, Colossians 3:2; Luke 24:45)

Open her eyes to be on the alert for Satan, to your word and to know right from wrong. (2 Kings 6:17; I Peter 5:8; Philippians 1:9-10)

May she love you with all of her heart, mind and soul. Create in her a clean, soft, wise heart. (Deuteronomy 6:5, Psalm 51:10, Proverbs 3:5-6, I Chronicles 28:9; Ephesians 1:17-18)

May she consider the members of her earthly body dead to immorality and impurity. (Colossians 3:4)

May she take a firm stand for Christ. (Ephesians 6:10-20; Colossians 4:12)

May she clearly see the encumbrances and the sin which so easily entangles her. Hold her feet to your path. (Psalms 40:2, 66:9, 37:23; Luke 10:19)

TALKING TO OUR GIRLS

Chapter 10

Talking To Our Girls About Sex

I'm sure I sounded like a parrot to my daughter when she was coming up. I used to say, "Keep your dress down. Keep your dress down." She got the message to keep her dress down, but I wonder if she also understood that her private parts were not dirty or bad. I never remember teaching her the positive side of her sexuality as a single person and the beauty of sex within marriage. –Kathy

I have worked in women's ministry for several years now. I am still surprised by how little women know about the sexual parts of their bodies, the basic information about the reproductive system's functions, and the essential information about intimacy between a man and a woman. Therefore, I should not be amazed that girls are even more uninformed and falling right into Satan's traps. It is important that we teach girls about sex so that they can have the truth to counter the lies Satan is prepared to tell them.

It's uncomfortable. Knowing what God's Word says about sex is one thing, but communicating those truths to our daughters so that they will not be snared by Satan's deceitful education is quite another. Parents usually are uncomfortable when talking about sex with their children. Misguided sex information or no sex education, however, can cause severe problems for young girls or even adult women.

I will never forget thinking as a little girl that babies came out of the place where people had a bowel movement. Every time I was constipated and it was painful to use the bathroom, I would think, "No way I'm ever going to have a baby." It wasn't until I took a biology class and the female anatomy was explained that I realized babies did not come out of the anus. I was so relieved. This one fact changed my entire perspective on having children.–Shelly

When I was in high school, I used to entertain my boyfriends in my bathrobe. I also dressed very seductively because I just thought that it was one way to get a boy to like you. No one ever explained to me that males get sexually excited from just looking at a girl dressed this way. I didn't realize any of this until after I was date raped. —Ilene

My period was irregular and I thought I was going through menopause and could no longer have a baby. I was shocked when I got pregnant. —Jo Ann

It's convicting. One of the biggest deterrents from a mother talking to her daughter about sex is of the mother's own personal failure to follow God's instructions in this area. Satan has a way of shaking the skeletons in our closets when we sit down and start to talk to our daughters about what their conduct should be. We feel like hypocrites telling our child to abstain from sex before marriage when our passions raged uncontrolled during our teen or young adult years.

To overcome this hurdle the first thing we must do is accept God's forgiveness for what has occurred in our past (I John 1:9). This verse only requires that we confess and He does the rest. Second, forgive yourself (Colossians 3:13). God views you as a forgiven person (Psalm 103:8-12). Next, ask Him to help you see yourself that way. Then make a commitment to live a clean life, if you have not already done so. Jesus told the woman caught in adultery to go and sin no more (John 8:11). We cannot expect our daughters to have high standards sexually and we do not. Also, *"Forgetting the past and press on for the prize"* (Philippians 3:13) does not mean we will never see the ungodly experiences in our mind again, but the sting, shame, and/ or anger will no longer be there. The prize is the time we have ahead to live for Him. And then, finally, believe God can take your past mistakes (the monsters) and transform them into a ministry for Him, even with your daughter. (Romans 8:28).[1]

It's confusing. You may know how to carry out the physical part of sex but you may not know all the technical terms, proper names for the body parts and how they all work together. Combine ignorance with your parental uneasiness and guilt from the past and it's understandable why mothers have a tendency to talk about everything else except sex. Hopefully, the following chart will help you know if you are on target with your daughter's sex education or if you need to play catch-up. The additional information at the end of the chapter will equip you with good resources to help you talk to your daughter.

WHAT OUR GIRLS SHOULD KNOW AT EACH STAGE OF DEVELOPMENT

BEFORE BIRTH

- I know what God's word has to say about sexuality. (Genesis 1-2)

- I have read and I am well informed about sex education for my children at each stage of their development.

- I have personally examined my attitudes toward sexuality. (Psalm139:23-24)

- I have examined my feelings about my past sexual activities.

- I have no skeletons in the closet in the sexual area that have not been brought before the Lord for His examination, instruction, and compassion. (Psalm 62:8)

- I have sought counseling (if the Lord leads in this way) for persistent negative thoughts about past activities concerning my sexuality and past sexual activities.

- As far as I know right now, I will not pass on any unrealistic fears to my daughter but will keep listening to the Lord for further enlightenment.

INFANCY

- I continue to pray for God to reveal any sexual hang ups I need to face and to strengthen me to deal with them.

- I talk positively to my daughter about her sexuality. (Psalm 139:13-14)

- I know what the correct names for sex organs are and I use them to refer to her sexual organs.

TODDLERS/PRESCHOOL YEARS

- I have read the Bible to my child and from there have shown her positive aspects about the body God created. I use Bible stories to communicate God's desire and design for sex. (Deuteronomy 11:19)

- I have read books and materials to inform me about what is going to happen with my daughter sexually at this stage. (Proverbs 11:14)

- I have a children's book that will help me explain any questions from my child or situations that may arise.

- I realize this is the stage my child may began to do some genital exploration and I am dealing with it in a positive constructive way. (Matthew 18:2-18)

- I have communicated clearly concerning my child that her private parts are not to be constantly played with and are to stay private.

- She has been told not to allow anyone to attempt to touch, kiss, or hug her in a way that is offensive or hurtful to her. I question her about this and keep the lines of communication open.

- My daughter knows that her female body is specially made by God with specific functions. I have communicated in such a way that my child can understand the reproductive process.

- She understands the physical differences between boys and girls (Genesis 1:27), and I have emphasized the special privileges of being a girl.
- I patiently and cautiously potty train my daughter, realizing that harshness or impatience at this stage could damage her thinking later on in the sexual areas. (Galatians 5:22-23)

ELEMENTARY SCHOOL YEARS
- I have discussed the reproductive organs (this time in more detail) with my daughter again and re-emphasized the goodness of the body and the uniqueness of God's design. (I Corinthians 6:19-20)

- She understands intercourse and that it is something God reserves for the husband and wife in marriage. (Genesis 2:23-25)

- My child has some basic understanding of issues she may hear about at school or on television, like teen pregnancy, AIDS, or homosexuality. She knows what the Bible has to say about these matters and knows that several messages in her world will be contrary to what the Bible says. (I John 2:15-17)

PRE-TEEN YEARS.

Include everything from elementary years but add the following:

- My daughter knows the changes that will occur in her body as she becomes a woman. I realize her menstrual cycle could start at this age. She knows about it and is prepared to handle it.

- My daughter is also aware of the changes that will occur in a boy's body as he becomes a man.

ADOLESCENCE

- My daughter sees her female body, its sexual functions and purposes as a unique plan and gift from God.

- She is aware of what the Bible says and the conflicting messages the world communicates concerning things such as sex before marriage, homosexuality, masturbation, pregnancy, abortion, lust, fantasies and contraceptives. But she also knows the biblical view on these issues.

- My daughter is well informed about the changes occurring in her body as a teenager. She knows more about hormonal changes and more details about the reproductive system.

- She also knows the sexual processes the male teenager undergoes and is more informed about his organs and sexual thinking.

- I have prepared my daughter to develop friendships with the opposite sex and have talked to her about dating (if you allow it).

GENERALLY

- I keep the conversation centered on God, His creation, and wonderful unique plans for our sexuality.

- I have been and continue to be prayerful for my daughter in each stage of her development. (More on these prayers in Chapter 11.)

- I don't use graphic terms or materials to explain my points.

- I stay calm when my daughter asks questions and either tell her as much as I know or I get resources for her to answer her own questions.

- I feel that I have done an adequate job in preparing my daughter sexually for what she has to face in this over-sexed society.

- I show respect for the opposite sex when I talk to my daughter about these matters.

If you can answer yes to each of the above guidelines, then give yourself an "A".

HELPFUL SUGGESTIONS IN COMMUNICATING TO YOUR DAUGHTER ABOUT SEX

Start early. As stated previously, ideally one should start early talking to children about sexual matters. Use natural opportunities through the years to discuss reproduction (like your pregnancy or the pregnacy of someone you know), sexuality, and sexual organs. Using animals as examples can be informative, but we do not want our girls thinking that our sexual relationships are the same as animals. Otherwise, we could have problems later on when we have to explain that we are people created to follow God's instructions, not dogs in heat!

Be positive. A grandmother was changing her granddaughter's diaper and she began to talk to the baby. "Oh look at this little belly button and behind it is a little womb that may carry a little baby for your husband one day." She is communicating three things to this little girl. (1) She is being positive about one of the roles God has given us as women. (2) She is calling the sexual parts by the proper name. (3) She is giving a moral message that husband, wife, and babies all go together. If she and the parents continue to talk to this little girl in this way it will help contribute to her emotional and sexual well-being.

Explain sexual intercourse. Talk to your child early about intercourse between kindergarten and second grade–before she hears about it from someone other than you.[2] If she gets the idea from television, a magazine, or one of her playmates, it may not be correct and the child may get the wrong idea about sex.

God has a special gift for new husbands and wives too. It is called sex... When a husband and wife are alone, there is no need to cover their bodies. They enjoy touching each other and holding each other close. When a husband and wife lie close together, he can fit his penis into her vagina. His semen flows inside her and their bodies feel good all over.

This is the way that babies are made. A husband can't make a baby by himself, and neither can a wife. But God has made their bodies so that they *fit perfectly* together. And together they can make a baby. Husbands and wives want to be alone during sex because then they are thinking only of each other.

God's rules say that only people who are married to each other may have sex. It is God's way of making families strong.[3]

The biblical and moral aspects of her sex education are up to you. Remember, the sex information your daughter is getting from other places probably does not include giving her the moral or Christian aspects of sex. This part is solely up to you. I will discuss more about how to instill this aspect in our daughters in the next chapter.

If you are a little late. If your daughter is older and you have not communicated about sex before, it is NEVER too late to start. Follow these suggestions to begin:

- Work out as many of your past issues as you can. Get help if necessary and make a clean commitment to live a pure life before your daughter. (Also see Chapter 9 for more suggestions.)

- Be confident that your daughter wants to hear from you. A 1983 study revealed that the majority of teens preferred to discuss sex matters with their parents, rather than peers or other adults.[4]

- Tell her about an incident that happened when you were growing up. Children love to hear about things their parents did when they were younger. Use this incident to admit to her the wrong way you may have handled a situation.

- Explain what you wished that you had done or said about sex education. Children can be very forgiving and you may be helping to erase some previous misconceptions the child has picked up from you.

- It may be appropriate, depending on her age, to have materials on hand explaining her body parts and how they function. Read some of the materials through with her and give her an opportunity to ask questions. She may be unusually quiet if this is the first time you have brought up the subject of sex. But don't take the silence as an indication to stop. She is probably taking in a lot more than you think. (Also make use of some of the resources listed at the end of the book.)

- Once the door has been cracked, continue to talk periodically to your child about sexual matters, even though she may not have questions or comments. If you find a good magazine article or happen to see a good television program, use these as opportunities to ask her what she thinks and to reinforce your points and God's principles.

- Remember, the whole point is to stop Satan from gaining victory over our daughters in all areas of their lives, especially this one. He will attempt to steal them at any stage where we give up and let go. When we accept God's challenge to move past our failures and our fears, we are not only assuring that God has a stronghold on our daughters' lives, but we are also claiming God's victory in our own lives as well.

ADDITIONAL INFORMATION

The following are subjects we need to include in our sex education talks with our girls. There are definitely ways in which the enemy gets in and causes confusion and sexual problems with our teens. Because these topics are briefly handled here, you will need to read additional books and information to educate yourself more about these subjects and how to relate them to your children.

Masturbation. We have already discussed genital exploration in chapters 2 and 3. Hopefully, you have not shamed or punished your daughter for this practice and she thinks positively about her sex organs. But, as already stated, when a child is in school, other interests should preoccupy her hands. If your daughter persists in this practice through elementary school, or starts during adolescence, it is considered masturbation–stimulating one's genitals for the purpose of sexual satisfaction or orgasm.

There are varying opinions on masturbation, even in the Christian community. Some believe it is a sin because it is outside of the sexual act in marriage. Others say it is not a sin, but is not a good idea. Still others defend it and say it is a way of relieving sexual tension.

This issue canot be settled by pointing to one scripture in the Bible because there is none that specifically addresses masturbation. The Bible does, however, refer to *nocturnal emissions* often called "wet dreams." This starts in adolescence once a young man's penis is developed enough to release sperm. It is a natural way for a man to release tension. A girl's sexual desires do not build up physically like a boy's. Her needs are more emotional; she has a need to be loved which, during the teen years, should be met by family relationships and healthy, non-sexual friendships. Both of these are ways God has given to naturally give those who are not married sexual release.[5]

Masturbation, on the other hand, is another way to experience sexual tension release. When girls read sensuous romance novels or think up erotic fantasies, these may draw her into sexual stimulation through masturbation. The problem is that she is attempting to get her need for love met through lustful thoughts and fantasies, rather than real love relationships. The Bible says we are not to lust: *'Do not commit adultery.' But I tell you that anyone who looks at a woman* [man] *lustfully has already committed adultery with her* [him] *in his* [her] *heart (Matthew 5:27-28).* [6]

We need to help our daughters understand that once a woman develops a practice of masturbation, it may be habit-forming. Also, this is not a good practice because it intensifies a girl's desire to become sexually active. It focuses totally on self, and it is an escape from reality. Paul says that we are not to be in this kind of rut: *"All things are lawful for me, but not all things are profitable... I will not be mastered by anything"* (I Corinthians 6:12).

Pornography. Pornography comes from the Greek word *proneia* , which means to sell. It was first applied to prostitutes who used their bodies for money.[7] Today, pornography refers to all types of sexually explicit material. Many of our children are exposed to pornography at early ages from someone who brought a book to school or by viewing erotic material on television or videos, even if initially by accident.

I was visiting a home once and happened to glance in the direction of the television when the channels were being changed. I was shocked to see the very explicit sex scenes on a cable station. Thank God my children were not with me, but I wondered how many times the same thing may have happened to them as they visited the homes of relatives or friends.

As Christians, we should not be looking at or permitting our kids to look at pornographic materials. They usually show, not a loving married couple, but an immoral sex act, violence involved with sex, and/or sexual perversions. Pornography also usually depicts women in a degrading way, as mere sex objects for men. We are to fill our minds with good things (Philippians 4:8-9).

We should tell our girls about the possibility of pornographic material being present at school, in the homes of their friends, or in adult romantic novels. We should explain that sex as depicted in these sources is not the way God intended for men and women to relate to each other. Explain that sex is not entertainment designed to make people laugh or stare. It is a special gift God has given to married people.

If you discover that your daughter has pornographic or other sexually arousing material, be understanding as this is a natural curiosity for girls. Reassure your daughter that it is okay to be interested in sex, but make it clear that this is not an acceptable, appropriate way to learn about sex. More sex education with appropriate diagrams may help satisfy her curiosities. So might open discussions with her about sex and sexuality.

I, in fact, strongly urge you to talk to your daughter about sexual arousal and sexual feelings. Explain, first of all, that these kinds of feelings are given to us by God. We are not to view them as bad or wish we did not have them. Tell her about your own feelings. Let her know that certain things can cause these feelings to occur–things like reading novels with descriptions of couples having sex, articles in magazines about sex, or watching videos, movies or television programs with sexy scenes. Let her know that arousing herself this way frustrates the order of things as God intended.

You can also explain sexual feelings from a physiological perspective. By understanding what is happening to her physically–that her body is naturally producing some of these feelings–your daughter may be more likely to learn to live with and control sexual urges when they do surface.

Explain that women are sexually aroused during certain times within their menstrual cycle, and that at those times they feel more driven to have sex. God has built these sexual feelings into a woman's cycle so that she will then greatly desire sex, get pregnant, and bear children. Sexual arousal is God's way of insuring that people continue His most important unit in the world, the family. But tell her that this is also when young girls usually get pregnant and this is not a part of God's plan and this is the reason she needs to stay away from sexually explicit materials.

Contraceptives. Another highly debatable issue is whether or not we should tell our girls about contraceptives. One view is that if we do tell them, it is the same as saying, "Don't, but here's something to use if you do," which is a confusing double message. Others point to the statistics which show that girls who don't know about contraceptives are more likely to become pregnant or to contract sexually transmitted diseases.

Hopefully, before you have gotten to the point of discussing contraceptives, you will have already seriously discussed premarital sex, sexually transmitted diseases, and pregnancy with your daughter. You have let her know what the Bible has to say and the consequences. If you choose to go beyond this and desire to explain contraceptives. St. Clair and Jones give a way for a Christian to go about it: (1) remind her about what God says about sex before marriage and express your own desire for her to remain a virgin until marriage; (2) tell her sex does not just happen–people make that decision, and if she chooses that way, it is sin. God wants her to live a life of purity; (3) tell her that if she chooses to violate God's principles that she will hurt herself more by not using any protection. So I'm going to tell you a little bit about contraceptives. [8]

From a practical point, this is a great approach. But I am not completely comfortable with it from a spiritual perspective. As Christians, we need to approach this subject with our teenage girls with the gripping fact that there are consequences to sin. As parents, we want to shield our children from as much as possible; however, they do make choices. When we have made our position clear and have plainly shared with them what the Bible has to say about sexual immorality, they must still make the final decisions. Those decisions will affect them one way or the other, and in some cases, for the rest of their lives. Even without other consequences, sexual immorality left uncorrected will affect their relationship with God. Without the mercy of God, sin left unchecked will build up and bring judgement to somebody, even if it is down the line of our family tree. Offering contraceptives may be our way to temporarily tamper with God's consequences.

Although I give room for different opinions, I personaly would not tell my daughters about contraceptives to help them avoid the consequences of sin. Yet I do think I have an obligation to be satisfied that the information they receive about contraception is accurate and complete. Going over the facts with my daughter myself would give me that assurance.

God is able to give wisdom to each of us. As we seek Him for His will, He can help us sort through our motives for talking to our children about contraceptives. He can also help us know how to approach the subject if that is what we decide to do.

Be knowledgeable of the different kinds of contraceptives or have a booklet on hand that explains each. Be sure you make it clear that none of these methods are 100 percent foolproof. There is still a risk of pregnancy or disease.

NOTES

1. John Nieder, *What You Need to Tell Your Child About Sex.* (Nashville Thomas Nelson, 1988), 33-34.
2. Staton & Brenna Jones, *How and When to Tell Your Child About Sex,* (Colorado Springs: Navpress, 1993), 117-119.
3. Carol Nystrom, *Before I was Born,* (Colorado Springs: Navpress), 1995, 25.
4. Josh McDowell, *How to Help Yor Child Say 'No',* (Waco: Word, Inc., 1987), 17-18.
5. Barry St. Clair and Bill Jones, *Sex: Desiring the Best,* (Wheaton: Tyndale, 1993), 103-104.
6. Ibid., 105-106.
7. Rick Stedmen, *Pure Joy,* (Chicago:Moody Press, 1993), 87.
8. St. Clair and Jones, *Sex: Desiring the Best,* 240-241.

Chapter 11

Ungodly Sex Education in Schools

Once our girls leave our homes to enter school, they will most likely be exposed to sex education in the public school. This chapter provides a brief history of the development of these programs and some present trends and concerns related to them.

By way of sex education, Satan has definitely found his way into the schools and he is teaching anti-biblical ideals to our girls. Even if your daughter is in private school or is being home-schooled, you should still read this chapter with great interest. Children who go to public school most likely live in your community or attend your church. They will probably interact with your children. Therefore, you should know what they are being taught in public school and how it might be persuading your child's thinking, now and in the future.

In Proverbs we are told to *"Watch over our heart* (mind, in Hebrew, heart and mind are used interchangeably) *with all diligence* (Proverbs 4:23). When our girls are too young or too immature to watch over their own minds, it is the parent's responsibility.

THE FACTS ABOUT PUBLIC SCHOOL EDUCATION

History. In the early 1970's, sex education classes became popular. Today, depending on what state you live in and what curriculum the public schools use, your child could be exposed to a sex education course as early as kindergarten or as late as high school. The motivating force behind introducing sex education courses in the schools was an attempt to control teen pregnancy and disease rates. Therefore, the focus of most of the classes has been contraceptive information and distribution.

About seven years before sex education was ushered into public schools, prayer (in 1963) was ushered out. According to one educator's view, with that turn of events in 1963, we escorted into our school premarital sex, sexually transmitted diseases, pregnancies, abortions, increased divorced rates, and a rise in violent crimes among teens.[1]

By 1993, sex education courses were mandatory in seventeen states and recommended in thirty others. An increasing number of cities in the United States had a condom distribution program in the schools. Between 1988 and 1993, the number of school-based clinics grew from five to 325. These clinics are supposed to promote "good health," but in most cases they make referrals for abortions and push contraceptives and safe sex.[2]

If the goal of sex education classes in the public schools was to bring down the rate of girls getting pregnant as teenagers, the success of these programs has been disappointing. During a three-year span at Adams High School, in Commerce, Colorado (the first to hand out condoms to students), the teen birth rate rose by 31 percent over a three year period. In addition, between 1970 and 1987, teen pregnancies in this country have increased from 300,000 to 750,000 a year. [3]

Problems. I am not implying that no sex education is needed in the schools. But what needs to be addressed is how the subject is approached and which children are receiving what information. One way Satan infiltrates the minds of our girls is to give them explicit information for which they may not be ready. Young elementary students do not need to know details about various kinds of sex, how to use condoms, or how homosexuals have sex. We need to ask whether the sex education programs are effective in helping students stay away from sexual trouble. The main questions Christians should ask are, "Is the program against Christian morals and principles?" and "Does it sway them in the direction of non-Christian values?" The answers to these questions may determine the kind of choices the students make when confronted with sexual challenges.

> The women in my family were very influential in my life. My grandmother lived with us along with her daughter. My mother was married but divorced when I was just a little girl. All three of these women talked about what was wrong with men and how women were better off without them. I concluded early in life that I didn't want to have anything to do with men. Our health teacher invited a lesbian to come in and talk to us about her lifestyle as a part of our sex education class. From that point on I decided that was the kind of lifestyle that I wanted. –Lee

THE VALUE-FREE APPROACH
A major problem with many sex education programs is their value-free approach. Consequently, the results they espouse to achieve are frustrated

from the beginning. The teen pregnancy rate, for example, has not gone down but up.

What is it? Value-free sex education is still the number one way sex education is taught in the public schools. The value-free approach tries not to push anyone's morals on the students. It teaches the physical nature of sex without guidelines. There is no explanation or guidance as to when or why a person should or should not have sex. The value-free approach is the reason that some sex education curriculums now include teaching small children and teens about homosexuality as an alternative lifestyle. This approach to sex education causes confusion among our girls, especially if the information given is contrary to what the parents are teaching at home. Value-free sex education also might encourage your daughter to participate in sexual activities highly objectionable to you as a parent.

Below are examples of what is being taught in some schools. They are from Josh McDowell's book, *The Myths Of Sex Education*. Before he list the examples, McDowell gives his readers this warning:

WARNING: Sections of this chapter will be extremely offensive to you–and they should be. However, we felt these sections need to be included to alert you. We want you to gain a true picture of the information, especially some of its language and instructions, being disseminated among our children in the name of "value free, morally neutral sex education."

- Norfolk, Virginia middle school, a coed class of eighth-graders were given these two pamphlets, "Proper Use of Condoms" and "Safer Sex." This information encourages creativity in sexual activity and offers safe sex ideas such as, "mutual masturbation, showering together, visual fantasies, using your own sex toys, anal intercourse with condom and oral sex."

- Some educators encourage condom use by providing students with cards on Valentines day which have a bright red condom attached and the printed message says, "Love Carefully;" having the students use cucumbers to practice how to roll a condom on, and they suggest carrying a condom for a friend and be ready to help them out if they need to.

- Some students in high school and college are receiving a "safer sex" kit. This kit includes a brochure which gives suggestions as to how to enjoy sex without having to worry about sexual diseases, free condoms, and some kits include the controversial morning-after pill. [4]

Think about your thirteen-year-old (or even nineteen-year-old) impressionable daughter receiving this kind of information! What makes this kind of material even more damaging is that it is extensive and meticulous. It is doubtful that a teenage couple will go through the ten steps of how to properly put a condom on properly in the heat of the moment in the back seat of a car. It is foolish to think you can give adolescents information about the pros and cons of sexual activity and expect them to come to logical, healthy decisions. Some adults are not even capable of doing so.

> I would hear my girlfriends talk about having sex with their boyfriends but I was always afraid. My father would kill me if I got pregnant. But then when I was a freshman, our sex ed class explained all about birth control and how not to get pregnant if you had sex. Then I felt okay about trying it. –Josie

Say no...but. At best, some sex education programs give our girls and boys a mixed message: "Don't have sex, but if you do, use a condom." There are even programs which strongly advocate abstinence but which also include birth-control and disease-prevention components. However, the abstinence message is undermined if you are also showing girls how to use condoms. [5]

> I kept saying no to my boyfriend about having sex. But he kept pressuring me. I told him I didn't want to get pregnant. In his sex ed class they gave out free condoms. He also had this booklet about how I wouldn't get pregnant. That night when we were out he explained all this to me. Then he asked, "What's your excuse now?" I didn't have one so that night I lost my virginity. That's not really what I wanted, but I thought if I kept saying no he would dump me. After that, it seemed like he just wanted to have sex all the time. We never went anywhere or did anything else. And then he dumped me anyway. –Helen

ABSTINENCE AND OTHER ALTERNATIVES
It is true that Satan uses factors other than sex education classes to steer our girls to wrong choices regarding sex. However, it has been proven that a different kind of sex education can make a difference in the moral choices girls make.

Abstinence programs. So what is this different kind of sex education? Abstinence-based programs. Yes! Curriculums designed to discuss and stress the emotional problems of teenage sexual activity–not just the physical or psychological problems–have shown the most success in reducing teenage pregnancy and other related problems. These programs give girls solid reasons why they should wait for sex, and involve parents in the sex education process and in the decisions their daughter might have to make.

Girls are asking for information that will tell them to abstain and how. There are currently at least thirty-eight abstinence-based curriculums available. They encourage abstinence by teaching teens life skills that enable them to resist peer pressure. In a 1990 study of 1000 sexually active girls under age sixteen, participants were asked on what topic they would most like more information. As high as 84 percent of the girls said they would like to know how to say "no" to sex without hurting the other person's feelings.[7] Our children do not want to know how to have sex safely; they want to know how not to have sex at all! Likewise, Jim Coughlin, the author of the Project Respect curriculum for high schoolers, has said, "The most common thing we hear from kids is, 'Why hasn't anyone told us this before?'"[8]

> As an early teenager, I had every intention of saving myself sexually until marriage. I escaped much of the sexual pressures of the teenage years. In fact, those pressures when I grew up were not as great as they are today. Later my friends, especially one of my girlfriends, would chide me and ask, "What are you saving yourself for? It's not dessert!" How sick it all sounds now, that someone would compare something as precious as the core of my femininity to a chocolate pudding!

> Well, I did give in, since I was the only girl I knew my age who hadn't already "done it." I started to feel like a freak. That was when all my troubles began.

> I wish I had someone to tell me, even as I reached young adulthood, "You don't have to do it." I wish they had been telling the boys as I grew up, "You don't have to do it, even if your body makes you think you do." But no one did. When I was a teenager, it was only the girl who got the dirty look if she became pregnant. The girl got the baby and the shame.

> As I approached early adulthood, even the church seemed to look away as young people made that transition. It was as if the attitude was that God no longer requires purity once you reach a certain age. How I wish I had stronger teaching and encouragement! I would have saved myself many regrets and heartache.

> By the way, the girl who didn't understand what I was saving? She is now a lesbian. She was even more confused than I. I thank God that He spared me even more pain and sorrow. –Julie

Abstinence curriculums have proven successful in deterring teenage sexual activity. The evidence has been seen in two popular programs: Sex Respect and Teen-Aid. Both teach the emotional and physical dangers of premarital sex and teach abstinence as the healthiest lifestyle.

Abstinence-based programs are also beginning to show that they have a positive effect on the prevention of teenage pregnancy. One Teen-Aid program in California is credited with decreasing pregnancies from 147 to twenty at a junior high school after only two years of use. The program incorporated materials that discussed commitment and family, as well as sexuality.[9]

Five years ago, an abstinence-only approach was almost non-existent in schools. Today, thousands of parents, teachers, professional lobbyists and politicians–many of whom are Christians–are attempting to get this material into the public schools.

WHAT PARENTS CAN DO

Even though abstinence-based programs are growing in popularity, they are not in all the schools and there are some things parents need to do.

Pray. It may have been taken it out of the public schools, but we still have the freedom to pray in our homes. Prayer is still, by far, the most powerful force at a parent's disposal to keep Satan from tainting the minds of our daughters. *"The effective prayer of a righteous man [woman] can accomplish much"* (James 5:16).

> I talked to my daughter's teacher about the sex education classes and materials. After I looked them over, I did not approve of my daughter learning the material. I went to the principal and complained, but he did not say he would make any changes. He just thanked me for my concern. My husband is not a Christian so when I talked about taking my daughter out of the class, he did not agree. I tried to talk to other parents but no one seemed interested in getting involved. So every day at fourth period when my daughter had sex education classes, I sat in my house and prayed during that entire period. My daughter never wavered from her biblical beliefs that sex should stay within marriage.When all else fails, pray!
> –Maggie

Know what your child is learning. A parent should know what their children are being taught in schools. Most of the time, teachers welcome inquiries. Yet most parents do not take the time to find out. Connie Marsh in her book, *Decent Exposure,* gives several excellent suggestions as to how to evaluate the sex education program in your child's school and what to do if you are not pleased with it. Here are a few:

- What is the character, tone, and general orientation of the program?
- Is chastity presented as something positive?
- Is the innocence of the young protected?
- Is the instruction given on a sex-separate basis?
- How does the program handle the problems associated with promiscuity, contraception, and abortion?
- What kinds of values are implicit or explicit in the program?
- Is the idea that "all values are just choices" the dominant theme?
- Are there a lot of "unfinished statement" exercises, such as "I would like to have sex with somebody who...?" [11]

With these questions in mind, look at the student's and teacher's books used in the program. Consider making a copy of the chapters. That will enable you to know exactly what your daughter is being taught, and you will be able to talk to her at home about the moral aspects of the material.

Push for parental consent laws. In some schools, a teenager can get a pass to leave school to have an abortion and return to school, without her parent's knowledge. If the fear of having to face mom and dad with a pregnancy is taken away, and girls know they do not have to face the consequences, they are more likely to have sex.

If you do not think that parental involvement in the sex education and decision-making with teens is helping to diminish the sexual crisis among our teens, think again. Every state in the country that has passed a parental consent law for abortion has seen a marked drop in the abortion rate among teens and in teenage pregnancy. [12]

Teach her at home. A girl who is being taught sex education at home and is taught early, is better equipped to counter Satan's lies because truth is already instilled in her. In the previous chapter, we have already provided suggestions as to how to teach sex education to your child.

THE CHURCH'S INVOLVEMENT IN SEX EDUCATION
Teaching only one side. Unfortunately, the church has often contributed to misconceptions and contrary opinions in the sexual area. Too often pastors, youth leaders, and church school teachers have fervently quoted parts of the Bible that forbid sexual activity without ever discussing when and how God approves of sexual activity. Some church leaders have even

taught that sex is only for procreation and not for pleasure. Others have implied that people are closer to God when they are not engaging in sexual activity.

> When I have sex with my wife the only way I can enjoy it is to shut my mind off about God. –A pastor

Come out of the dark ages. For too long the church also has promulgated the myth that if you talk about sex, kids will do it; if you say nothing, they will stay innocent until marriage. That might have worked during the days of the Dick Van Dyke Show twenty-five years ago when the husband and the wife slept in separate twin beds. But we now live in a culture in which sex without moral values is being taught in the public schools and sexual innuendoes hit the television screen about every fifteen minutes. Sexually explicit billboards litter the highway, sexy magazines are common at the checkout stands in grocery stores, and even the greeting cards in the department stores have sensuous messages. The negative messages are all around us. The church must counter Satan's destructive sex information onslaught with God's truth.

Sponsor helpful programs. Parents do not always feel comfortable or have the know-how to talk about or teach sex education. Here are a few ways the church might be able to help:

> Our church sponsored a small group for mothers and pre-teen daughters. We worked through a Christian sex education book together that explained the physical changes that were going to take place in my daughter's body as she approached the teen years. This really helped me and my daughter open up about sex. I learned a lot that I didn't know. I think more churches should do this. They think parents are talking to their children, but most really are not. –Denise

I had the privilege of hearing A.C. Green, one NBA basketball player, speak at a church in Milwaukee. He and his girlfriend have a ministry encouraging young people to stay virgins or to reclaim a second virginity. When Green gave his testimony about his conversion to Christ and his commitment to stay a virgin until marriage, it was spell-binding. When he gave the challenge for the young people to come forward and make a commitment to virginity, the altar was filled. The A.C. Green rally opened the door for my daughter and me to talk about some sexual areas. At the end of our conversation, she asked for a chastity ring. It is a symbol to remind her that she is married and committed to Jesus Christ. The ring is worn on her left hand where the wedding ring will go. With it, she made a commitment to stay pure until marriage. The church needs to sponsor more programs like this to help parents open the door to more dialogue about sex.

Help parents get abstinence curriculums in schools. The church can also get involved to ensure that schools use an appropriate sex education curriculum. Public schools need a good abstinence sex education program. Several members of the church can help rally around such causes. There may not be much one parent can do against a school or a school system. But you will see more and quicker results if you get several parents to rally behind an issue.

Organize and bring your requests to the principal and move on to the school board if necessary. Josh McDowell's book, *The Myths of Sex Education* is an excellent tool for parents or a church congregation to use to present the facts before a school principal or school board. It lays out the problems with value-free education, the rising statistics of sexual activities among our kids, and lists the various abstinence programs and their effectiveness.

An accurate biblical sex education for our girls is a tall order, but it has to be met if we are going to defeat Satan's destructive information and keep him from destroying their minds. In the next three chapters, you will learn more about what God wants us to teach our girls in the teen years.

NOTES

1. Kunjufu, Jawanza, *Hip-Hop vs. MAAT*, (Chicago: African-American Images, 1993), 99-106.
2. Marian Wallace, *Sex Education: Failing to Make the Grade,* (Family Voice, September 1993), 4.
3. Josh McDowell, *The Myths of Sex Education,* (Nashville: Thomas Nelson Inc., 1990), 81.
4. Ibid., 94-99.
5. Andres Tapia, *Abstinence: the Radical Alternative",* (Christianity Today, February 8, 1993), 28.
6. Wallace, *Sex Education, 5.*
7. Ibid., 8.
8. Tapia, *Sex Education, 28.*
9. Ibid., 28.
10. Ibid., 25.
11. Connie Marshner, *Decent Exposure,* (Brentwood: Wolgemuth and Hyatt, 1988, 41.
12. Ibid., 9.

EXERCISES

1. Where did you receive your sex education? List the pros and cons of it.
2. What is your sex education plan for your daughter? If you have never talked with your daughter about sex, look at your calendar and set a date for when you are going to begin.
3. When you think about sexuality and your own sexual history, do you have hang-ups that need to be cleared up? What specifically are you planning to do?
4. Think of some ways the church can help teach girls about sex. Plan to present these ideas to the youth group leader or your pastor. Be prepared to help implement the ideas.
5. Do you know what is going on in your public school system pertaining to sex education? Ask a local teacher or principal. Is there some way your church can get involved in helping to put abstinence-based curriculums into the public schools?

SATAN IS OUT TO DESTROY TEENS

Chapter 12

Teen Girls Are Hungry For Love

God understands that raising teenage girls in today's society is no picnic. Keep in mind, however, this complicated stage of development called adolescence is *His* unique design. Even with all its challenge, it is still a part of God's plan to develop our young women into the vessels of glory and blessing He designed them to be. He has not left adults alone to wonder what to do with these girls. Nor did He intend for decisions to be made and conclusions drawn about this time of life–or any other–without His divine input and guidance. When we take matters into our own hands, we allow Satan to damage the lives of our young girls in ways that seem beyond repair.

In these chapters about adolescent girls, I also will talk considerably about parents. People sometimes take one of two extreme positions about parenting their children. Either they had nothing to do with the way the child turned out or they blame themselves for everything. Both extremes are wrong.

Parents do set the stage with their input or lack of input into a child's life. When our children live in our homes, parents do have the task of guiding them through the perils of this life. We should constantly ask ourselves, "Am I clinging as tightly as I possibly can to the God who put these children into my care? Do I daily seek His mind and heart, through His word, for decisions I make pertaining to my daughter?" Yet, on the other hand, there is a point when our children have to make their own choices.

I taught a women's class on the book of Proverbs. After the class, many made comments like these: "I wish I had read and studied Proverbs when I was raising my children, or better yet, before I got married." One woman said tearfully, "I needed this book as a teenager. I could have kept myself away from a lot of heartache if someone had taught me these principles."

God's word is a faithful lamp to our feet and ample light for our path. Parents continually cry, "I don't know what in the world to do with this girl!" God responds, "Read the Bible. It's all in there." The Holy Spirit has been given as our counselor to take the word of God and make it applicable and practical for today. His Word will help us avoid mistakes with our teenage girls. It is also able to restore the broken pieces of the lives that have already been shattered.

Let's look at the historical account of Amnon and Tamar, two young people who got themselves into sexual trouble (2 Samuel 13:1-19). I will be referring to various parts of this bibical account of Ammon's obsession and subsequent rape of Tamar throughout these next few chapters. Since we will engage in such a close study of the scriptures, I suggest you take the time now to pull out your favorite version of the Bible and read the entire nineteen verses. This incident happened years ago, but it is interesting to note that Satan's strategy has not changed.

SEEKING LOVE IN WRONG WAYS

"...Absalom the son of David had a beautiful sister whose name was Tamar, and Amnon the son of David loved her" (2 Samuel 13:4). Amnon was King David's son. The text does not tell us how old he was specifically, but from his behavior I believe we can safely assume that he was either a teenager or in his young adult years. Being the son of one of the wealthiest kings in Biblical history, we can also presume that he probably had every material thing a young person could desire. Yet, Amnon seemed to lack one important thing–love.This love should have come from his family unit, but somehow it was missing.

Business and disobedience. During this time in biblical history, King David was busy building Israel into a gigantic world power, exercising his wise leadership and courageous battling abilities. He made plans for one of the most exquisite worship centers in the entire known world, which included establishing clergy administration, worship services, and writing worship songs.

In spite of David's positive achievements, he unfortunately still possessed areas of weakness. David was called "a man after God's own heart." But he did not obtain his title because of perfection and sinlessness. Some of his disobedient acts affected the well-being of the rest of his family. One of David's classic sins helped to set the stage for Amnon's and Tamar's awful sexual encounter.

First of all, David practiced polygamy. God gave Israel's kings specific instructions in the law. One stated, "Do not multiply wives or horses" (Deuteronomy 17:16). David violated this command and collected several wives and concubines. In fact, Tamar and Absalom (brother and sister) would never have existed had David adhered to this law and stopped marrying after his first wife. Tamar and Absalom were children from David's third marriage. (Amnon was his first-born by his first wife.)

Secondly, most of David's wives had children. There is no way David could have been personally involved with each of these women and their children in addition to his kingly responsibilities. It appears that David's children grew up with very little guidance and instruction from their godly father. Perhaps David only came to see about them upon request, illness, or an emergency. It is not uncommon for men in biblical history to accomplish great things for God, yet neglect their families.

Finally, David's classic downfall in his life occurred with Bathsheba, Uriah's wife. David committed adultery with her and she became pregnant. David had Uriah (her husband) killed, then took Bathsheba as his wife. This happened at the height of David's kingly career. Was it boredom? Was it too much wealth? Too many women? A mid-life crisis? What compelled David to answer his lustful desires for Bathsheba by having her sent to his bedroom chambers? The little boy who conquered the giant Goliath, and won many battles against powerful enemy nations stood helpless against the burning passions within himself for another man's wife.

After David's sexual sin with Bathsheba, the dominoes in his life began to fall. God specifically told David after the adulterous situation with Bathsheba, *"I will raise up evil against you from your own household..."* (2 Samuel 12:11). David's child by Bathsheba died, war broke out, and AMNON RAPED TAMAR! Distressing events continued until David's death.

Amnon might have looked to his mother, Ahinoam (2 Samuel 3:2), for the loving parental relationship he needed. But she was just one wife in the long line of women in David's palace. With more than one wife in the household, it is likely that jealousy prevailed. I can imagine David's wives spent most of their time beautifying themselves, just in case David came along and wanted to spend a night of romance with them. Amnon did not seem to get his need for love met by his mother.

This scenario in the book of Samuel played out ages ago. However, it sounds like twentieth century parenting to me. Many of today's parents are too busy to adequately spend time with their children and are not paying attention to God's instructions in the Bible. Many times they are busy attempting to buy themselves and their children everything they never had growing up, only to neglect giving their children the one thing they really need and want–love.

Girls want intimate love, not sex. Lack of intimate love and affection is the major reason young people are having sex. Josh McDowell, originator of the "Why Wait" campaign for teenagers sponsored an essay, called "Write Your Heart Out." Teens were to answer the question, "Why do people in your age group become sexually active?" The number one answer: "I'm searching for a father's love."

When I was only fourteen...I dated an eighteen-year-old boy. After a month...of dating, he told me...he loved me..., had to "have" me.... If I loved him, I would have sex with him.... If I couldn't, he couldn't control his desire for me and would have to break up with me.

What did I think at fourteen...? I knew sex was wrong.... I didn't want to lose my virginity.... I so desired to have a man love me.... I finally gave in. I felt so guilty.... I can remember sobbing in my bed at night after I'd come home from being with my boyfriend. I wanted so much to have my virginity back...yet it was gone, forever....I began to feel...lonely inside.... There was no one I could turn to. Certainly not my father, who would really "hate" me if he ever knew what an awful thing I had done.

After two years I broke up with my boyfriend, but soon had another...went through the same cycle with him...and another....

I'm 27 now.... I felt lonely tonight.... I realized... what I was lonely for was a "daddy." To be able to call him up when I hurt and hear him say he understands and to listen to me.... I never had that with my dad.

... My life has been a search for my daddy's love. And in Jesus, I am found and I am loved. Forever.[1]

I was hard pressed to find a teenage girl or woman who could tell me about a positive healthy relationship she had with her father, one which kept her from going outside the family for the warm loving relationship she craved. This is very sad. Mothers get a lot of praise and attention from their children and a mother's role in her daughter's life is extremely important. However, if you are a mother raising your daughter alone, make sure there are at least one or two men in your daughter's life who give her some special attention. It doesn't have to be a long-term and committed situation. But your daughter does need a father figure who will occasionally make her feel special and perhaps be there to offer godly, fatherly advice.

I remember an older man at my home church when I was growing up. He always had a smile for me when I walked in the door. Maybe he smiled at the other kids too, but he always made me feel special. If I walked across the basement to give a glass of water to my grandmother, he had a compliment for that. And he always added, "You are going to a be a fine young lady when you grow up." His admiration and encouragement was a significant part of my growing up years –Pearl

Even though the relationship between a father and his daughter is special, and that relationship fills a unique need within our girls, the love, attention, and affection of *both* parents is especially important in the teenage years. As you can see from this chart, the time when our girls need to be embraced and assured of our love is the same time that teens are the most rebellious and contrary. The parents' physical warmth and affirmation lessen considerably or are non-existent toward the teenage girl then. This period is also the time when most teens become interested in the opposite sex. Imagine, then, what will happen when a young girl who has been devoid of physical affection or verbal approval for years meets a smooth-talking boy who has lots of caressing, touching and positive things to whisper in her ear.

NEEDS IN GIRLS, INFANCY TO ADOLESCENCE

GIRLS AGE	AFFECTION	AFFIRMATION	AFFECTION/ AFFIRMATION FROM PARENTS	AFFECTION/ AFFIRMATION GIVEN FROM OTHERS
Infancy thru Elementary years	Great	Great	Lots of hugs and kisses	Family friends and church
Pre-adolescence	Great	Great	Less affection/more verbal conflict	Less
Adolescence	Very Great	Very Great	Less or none at all/more verbal conflict	Boy Friend

Touching. Often when girls start to develop physically, fathers may be hesitant to hug. As mentioned earlier, it is not uncommon for a parent to have arousal feelings for his own child. If you are a father reading this, let me remind you that the arousal feelings are not sin. But if you continue to play with these thoughts in your mind, or make any kind of suggestions or advances toward your daughter, you are now dealing with sinful behavior. These are indications that perhaps you should talk to your wife and maybe a knowledgeable person about your urges. This is especially true if you are a child abuse victim or have a history of sexual struggles.

Parents should not allow the fear of child sexual abuse to keep them from being affectionate with their daughters. A hug does not always have to be a bear hug for a long time. Physical affection can be given to her by holding her hand at meal times during prayer, by placing your hand on her shoulder to pray with her, touching her shoulders while she does her homework, or by a kiss on her cheek each time she leaves the house. Any of these forms of affection will communicate love and caring to your daughter.

What is intimate love? Our girls are not hungry for sex, but intimacy. "Intimacy is the gradual growth in understanding of another person by listening, discussing, sharing, being mutually involved. Intimacy can occur in may areas: emotional, social, spiritual, and physical. Thus you can become intimate with a person and not have physical contact." [2] Going back to the Amnon and Tamar story, we will later see that Tamar had true feelings of intimacy toward her brother, but Amnon only wanted sex.

When God said that we are made in His image and likeness, He not only meant we were different from animals, having the ability to think and relate to God, this passage is also saying that, like Him, we have a desire for closeness and intimacy with another person. All human beings are born with this desire.[3] Our need for intimacy should be met initially by our parents. Then we learn to give and receive it from others. When parents are not attempting to understand their daughters–listening to them, discussing and sharing with them, the daughters usually go outside the family unit to get their needs met, through dating or other social phenomena. (More on dating in a later chapter.)

The lack of intimacy from relatives and friends. It used to be that the extended family or caring persons in the church compensated when parents were absent or incapable of providing their children with the intimacy and affirmation they needed. Today, however, many families do not live close to relatives and there is not a cohesive bond in our neighborhoods and churches. Very few children live in the same house all their growing up years. Older adults who used to stay home in the neighborhood are now out to work or afraid to open their doors. This puts more responsibility on the parents to provide the nurturing environment for their children.

Amnon was apparently missing this same kind of cohesiveness in his family. Otherwise, he might not have been obsessed with the desire to have sex with Tamar. Many studies indicate that those adolescents who feel alienated from their families are more prone toward sexual involvement. [4]

Evaluating our home environment. Now that you understand your child's need for intimacy, ask yourself a few questions to see where you may be lacking in providing this kind of intimacy in your home:

- What is the spiritual climate in this home? Is the Lord building the home (Psalm 127)? Is He respected as the head of the home and is His love controlling the members of the family (2 Corinthians 5:14)? Do we realize Satan is attempting to destroy our family and, therefore, keep prayer and God's Word prevalent to protect it?

- Are my children open and expressive? Do they share with us their deepest feelings, ask questions seek advise, talk about personal or embarrassing topics?

- Do the parents in this home realize they are not perfect, but strive to work on areas that are broken and in need of fixing? Are they open with their children about this process (Romans 8:12-13)?

- What kind of verbal exchange goes on in this house? Is it loving and assuring? Do I hear "I love you," "Thank you," and "I appreciate you" regularly? Is this house full of anger, strife, and name-calling, with everyone taking it for granted that love is here somewhere? Is this house silent, with very little exchange at all, either good or bad (Colossians 3:8-9)?

- Is this home clean, organized, and run somewhat on a predictable timetable? Are there places and times set aside when the whole family can do things and discuss things together (I Corinthians 14:33)?

- What kind of marriage exists in this home? Does the man love his wife sacrificially? Does he take on his God-given role as provider and spiritual leader in the home? Does the wife respect her husband? Does she manage her <u>household</u> well? As well as she manages her career (if applicable) or her other activities (I Peter 3:1-2)

- Is this a home which makes memories? Has it had warm moments, family outings—even difficult times when the family had to pull together?

Improving the intimacy in our homes. If, after going over the above list, you realize there is work to be done in creating a better intimate environment in your home, here are some suggestions to get you started.

- Ask God to help you know where to start. Your home may be like a monopoly game turned upside down in the wind. You don't even know where to begin to pick up the pieces. The most important thing is that you do start. God wants families to be healthy. He will give us wisdom and strength.

- Commit yourself to spend time in God's Word and in prayer on a regular basis on behalf of your family. Pray specifically about the things you noticed in the evaluation that need to be straightened out.

- Spend time with each of the children before they go to bed at night. This is good talk time, prayer time, and Bible reading time. If you start this practice early, it is easier to do later.

- Don't scold children for accidents or mistakes; let them know that you understand. This makes it easier for them to come to you about other things.

- If you have personal issues or problems that need to be resolved, get help. Your inner conflicts can and often do upset the climate in your home.

- Make it a point to make positive, appreciative, and encouraging statements to your child, not always, "You didn't," or "Didn't I tell you...?" Don't call your daughter names or tell her she will never amount to anything.

- Take a couple of days out of your regular routine to clean and organize your house. Read a book or go to a seminar on how to keep it that way. Make sure there is a place in your house where you all can spend time together that is warm and cozy.

- Get help with your marriage if you are having problems. If your husband won't go for counseling, you go alone. An improvement in 50 percent of the marriage is better than no improvement at all.

- Plan some activities for you to do together as a family. Be committed to carrying them out.

My parents yell and scream at each other all the time. It never seems to fail whenever they get like that, they start to holler at us. Then I find something to yell at my two brothers about. When we start fighting, our parents start yelling at us. Our house is crazy. I can't wait until I get my driver's license, I'm never going to be at home. –Jane

Most of the books and materials I've read pertaining to girls and sexuality devote a considerable amount of space to talking about marriage, home environment, and parenting skills. One might ask, "What does this have to do with my daughter's sexual activity?" A whole lot! Yes, other factors do contribute to the paths your daughter chooses. However, if we do not strive to have godly attitudes in our family relationships, we open the door for Satan to destroy, not only our homes, but the lives of our children as well. Our daughters especially will seek stability through other means, including sexual relationships.

NOTES
1. Josh McDowell, *How to Help Your Child Say 'No' to Sexual Pressure,* (Waco, Texas: Word Books, 1987), 33-34.
2. Rick Steadman, *Pure Joy.* (Chicago: Moody Press, 1993), 173.
3. Berry and Carol St. Clair, *Talking With Your Kids About Love, Sex, and Dating,.* (Wheaton, Ill.: Victor Books, 1993), 19.
4. Josh McDowell, *How to Help Your Child,* 33-34.

Chapter 13

Clearing Up The Love/Lust Confusion

In the previous chapter, we saw how important intimate love is in keeping our daughters from building unhealthy relationships outside the home. Another place Satan attacks and causes problems among our girls is confusion about the differences between lust and love. What is lust? What is love? And how can we teach our girls the difference?

SATAN CAUSES CONFUSION ABOUT LUST AND LOVE

Returning to the historical account of Amnon and Tamar, we see that confusion over love and lust was even a problem in ancient times. Amnon was supposedly in love with Tamar. But his actions clearly demonstrated lust (2 Samuel 13:2). The word "love" in verse 2 is *ahab* in the original Hebrew language. It denotes a strong emotional attachment for and a desire to possess or be in the presence of the loved object. It is used in Scripture to mean sensual love within God's laws of marriage.

In verse 4 Amnon says, "I love Tamar," but what he should have said is, "I lust after Tamar." Obviously, the sensual movie in Amnon's mind, starring himself and Tamar in a steamy bedroom scene, no longer brought him satisfaction. His body desperately wanted to experience sex with Tamar. His daily concentration on her made him ill.

Lust defined. Lust is a strong, greedy appetite, which longs for something or someone. Very few young people understand the difference between love and lust. The following "Love/Lust Test" is based on a chart in a book by Berry St. Clair and Bill Jones called *Sex: Desiring the Best.* [1.]

THE LOVE/LUST TEST

LUST	LOVE
"I can't understand why you wait to have sex. I want it now."	"I respect your stand on wanting sexual purity; I wouldn't want to violate that in any way."
"You see, I have needs."	"I have needs but I will control myself."
"Don't you want to satisfy my needs?"	"I realize if we have sex before marriage, it will mess us both up emotionally, mentally, spiritually and maybe even physically."
"You keep saying no and it's getting me upset."	"I can wait 'til we are married. I'm glad you are not an easy mark."
"You better not even look at another man."	"It's OK. with me if you have other male friends."
"I just know you are going to please me."	"I realize once we get married, it may take time for us to grow in the sexual area."
"I like you. You like me. Lets get it on; what else is there to discuss"	"I'm really in prayer about our relationship. I like you a lot but I want what God thinks is best for both of us."
"You better tell me about all the other men in your life".	"Share what you need to and when you feel comfortable."
"Thanks for the jollies baby, so long..."	"When I say I love you, that means I'm willing to marry you and be committed for a life time."
"I just love sex."	"I'm attracted to all of you, not just your body."

As we move through the account of Amnon and Tamar's tragedy, you will begin to see more clearly that Amnon's response to Tamar was strikingly similar to the statements above that are exemplary of lust. Love seeks to please the other; lust seeks to satisfy itself.

Jesus offered a solution for the lust problem: *"Pluck out your eye and cut off your hand."* Sounds pretty drastic. If we took this passage literally, every single one of us would be walking around without eyes and hands. But in Matthew 5:27-30, Jesus clearly communicated important information to us about lust.

> You have heard that it was said, 'You shall not commit adultery,' but I say to you, that everyone who looks on a woman to lust for her has committed adultery with her already in his heart. And if your right eye makes you stumble, tear it out, and throw it from you; for it is better for you that one of the parts of your body perish, than for your whole body to be thrown into hell. And if your right hand make you stumble, cut it off, and throw it from you; for it is better for you that one of the parts of the body perish, than for your whole body to go into hell.

The main points of this passage are these:

- Lust in the mind is just as bad as the act itself. Some have attempted to twist this verse around to mean, "I might as well carry out the sin, since I have thought it." But that would mean one more sin, with consequences for both.

- Lusting leads to the behavior pictured in the mind.

- To avoid lusting, drastic measures will have to be taken.

- If we don't deal with lust, there could be eternal consequences. Lust problems will not keep an individual out of heaven if we are trusting Christ and Christ alone for our salvation. Even believers, however, are required to give an account for deeds done in the body during our time here on earth. Our rewards will be based on these acts.

- To abandon the lust problem, one may have to abandon activities that have become habits and may be difficult to part with. We may need to stop watching, reading or listening to sexually explicit material–anything that encourages sexual arousal or makes one think about having sex. The culprits could be soap operas, "R" rated movies, sexually explicit magazines, or music. There is an added benefit to eliminating these materials: Once we begin to realize and admit the impact of sexually-loaded materials on us as adults, we will begin to more clearly observe and understand the impact it is having on our children.

I teach sixth grade and have done so for nine years.... We took our fifth and sixth graders on a field trip.... During the trip, one of my students let me listen to a tape.... I was so disgusted with what I heard. And these were good kids from good homes! I...was appalled to learn that their parents didn't care that they listened to this stuff.... I can't tell you how many parents don't even know what their early adolescents are listening to. [2]

SATAN DEVALUES VIRGINITY

"And Amnon was so frustrated because of his sister Tamar that he made himself ill, for she was a virgin, and it seemed hard for Amnon to do anything to her" (2 Samuel 13:2). Amnon may not have had explicit audio and video tapes as we do today, but apparently he had a lustful tape in his mind that he played over and over about Tamar. He was so desirous of Tamar that not having her made him physically ill. (Let's not interpret from this statement that if one does not have sexual release, he will make himself sick.)

Virginity in biblical times. Amnon definitely felt the protective parameters around Tamar. The ancient Hebrews hid and separated the young women away, as a way of protecting them and as a public declaration of their great value. This did not occur with the young men; the women were considered special.

The root word for *virgin*, in fact, means to hide and separate. A virgin (*bethulah* or *almah* in Hebrew) in the Bible means a person who has not been touched sexually; they are hidden away or separated out.

I own an everyday jacket that I take my morning walks in and I put it on to make quick runs to the store. I leave it on a hook by the kitchen and I don't care if the kids knock it down or even if it gets dirty. But then I have a coat I wear on Sundays and on special occasions. My husband gave it to me as a special gift. The way I handle my coat and my jacket are very different. I would never leave my special coat on the hook near the kitchen. I make sure it's stored in a special place. My kids know not to come near me with anything that might soil it. In the same way, in biblical times virginity was seen as something very special and it was treated that way. The public respected it and the girls saw it in the same light. Girls were honored, and treated with the utmost respect because of their chastity. Over the years, Satan has seen to it that virginity has become devalued. That, in fact, is the whole point of bombarding our society with sexual preoccupation and lustful things. Girls today are put down, made to feel immature, and stupid for not giving up this precious gift. Make no mistake about it. This is all being done by evil design and the foundation lies not in the physical world, but in the spiritual.

SATAN BOMBARDS YOUNG PEOPLE WITH LIES

...Amnon had a friend whose name was Jonadab, the son of Shimeah, David's brother; and Jonadab was a very shrewd man. And he said to him, "O son to the king, why are you so depressed morning after morning? Will you not tell me?" Then Amnon said to him, "I am in love with Tamar, the sister of my brother Absalom." Jonadab then said to him, "Lie down on your bed and pretend to be ill; when your father comes to see you say to him, Please let my sister Tamer come...."(2 Samuel 13:3-5).

Amnon thought his hands were tied. According to the law, all crimes of unchastity were regarded as grievous offenses against God, affecting the whole Israelite community. If a man had sex with a virgin he was obligated to marry her (Deuteronomy 22:28-29). But his lustful feelings also involved incest. Tamar was Amnon's step-sister. The punishment for having sex with a sister or stepsister was death (Leviticus 18). The pressures of the law and the general social disdain for sex before marriage indicated to Amnon that he could not act on his desires.... Ah, but in enters Jonadab. Up until his meeting with his cousin Jonadab, Amnon had chosen to abide by God's laws. Unfortunately, Jonadab was smart in the wrong things. He helped Amnon devise a plan to seduce Tamar, following the wayward path of Satan and in disregard of God's laws.

It is interesting to note that when Amnon was eventually killed for raping Tamar, Jonadab, the prompter, was not in the assassination line-up. The schemer and accomplice to the crime got off free. Today, Jonadab takes on many forms–a sexually active teen, a drug dealer, a violent rap song, a sexually explicit video, a pornography magazine, a sexual movie– anything or anyone to cause a child to discard her moral upbringing and follow the enticing way of the world. Jonadab represents all the contrary outside forces–Satan's spiritual chess pieces, used to influence our girls against God's principles in Scripture. Because the world cooperates, girls can now be unreservedly taught, mainly through the media, how to disregard God's plan for sex–all in the name of family programming!

PARENTS CAN BE BLIND TO SATAN'S PLANS

"So Amnon lay down and pretended to be ill; when the king came to see him, Amnon said to the king 'Please let my sister Tamar come and make me a couple of cakes in my sight, that I may eat from her hand.' Then David sent to the house for Tamar saying, 'Go now to your brother Amnon's house, and prepare food for him.' So Tamar went to her brother Amnon's house... (1 Samuel 6:8).

If there was ever a time when a parent needed to be made aware of Satan's deceptive plans, it was when David walked into his son's room.

Be connected with God. When Amnon raped Tamar, Satan ruined three young lives in one fatal stroke. Tamar was raped, cast away in anguish for the rest of her life. Amnon eventually was killed by Tamar's brother, Absalom, who sought to avenge the rape of his sister.Absalom never forgave David for not taking action in this whole matter, and eventually attempted to take over David's throne. David's army captain, Joab, killed Absalom during the revolt. How different this picture could have been had David been in tune to God! Satan's plan could have been revealed.

Parents cannot be everywhere every minute with their children. But God can. He knows what they are up to and can let us know what to do. It is essential for a parent to be constantly on one accord with God and in prayer. We could save our children and ourselves much heartache by averting trouble before it starts.

> One Sunday an assistant Vacation Bible School teacher called and asked if my children could attend a get-together at her house for the children who had attended VBS. All week I did not call her back; something inside kept saying, "No, this is not a good idea." But her children were begging me, my children were begging me, people in the church were saying how much this young woman had changed by working with the VBS and other projects in the church. So I agreed, against my better judgment. Later I found out she showed the children "R" rated movies. She only stopped when the children said they did not want to see them. I was outraged! The nudging I felt was from the Holy Spirit. I should have listened. He was telling me "No! This is not a safe, good environment for your children. Believe me, this lesson taught me to listen and be more in tune to what God is trying to tell me. –Jill

Be observant. Obviously David did not think rape was on Amnon's mind when he sent in his precious beautiful daughter to nurse her brother back to health. He was totally unaware of what could happen in this kind of situation. Not only was David not aware of Satan's plan, he was totally unaware of the struggles going on within his son. An ungodly cousin could see that something was frustrating Amnon, but his own father was apparently too busy running the country to make these important observations. On the other hand, maybe he did notice and suspected his son's problem, but chose to ignore what he saw.

Because parents are sometimes too lenient, too busy, or just unwilling to deal with certain problems, they will often make excuses for their children's behavior. The following is a list of behaviors that may alert you to some problematic issues related to your child's sexual experience.[2] Even though her behavior may not suggest it, your daughter may need you the most when she's acting this way.

WARNING SIGNS OF POTENTIAL SEXUAL ACTIVITY
- [ ] emotionally pulls away from family
- [ ] resists family values
- [ ] family struggles relationally
- [ ] dissatisfaction with how much freedom is allowed
- [ ] becomes friends with kids you've never heard of
- [ ] ceases to bring friends home
- [ ] becomes defensive about friends
- [ ] makes unusual phone calls
- [ ] careless about curfew but always has a good excuse
- [ ] becomes excessively selfish
- [ ] begins to exhibit negative personality changes
- [ ] lies and searches for loopholes
- [ ] receives grades that are much lower than usual
- [ ] absence from school or tardiness without your knowledge
- [ ] change in dress or appearance
- [ ] increased isolation
- [ ] gets fired from after school job
- [ ] stays out all night
- [ ] drops participation in sports or extracurricular activities
- [ ] deep depression
- [ ] smoking
- [ ] extreme weight loss or gain
- [ ] expulsion from school
- [ ] hostility towards adults or authority figures
- [ ] mention of suicide or runs away
- [ ] seductive, promiscuous behavior

NOTES

1. Barry St. Clair and Bill Jones, *Sex: Desiring God's Best,* (Wheaton: Victor Books, 1993), 53-54.
2. Victoria Johnson and Mike Murphy, *Parenting Streetwise Kids*, (Elgin Ill: D. C. Cook, 1995), 121.

LET'S LOOK OUT FOR OUR LITTLE ONES

Chapter 14

Stopping Generational Curses

In the early part of my childhood, my father committed adultery several times on my mother. My mother was one of the sweetest women in the world and very passive. For years she put up with this treatment. I knew about my father's activities and harbored a lot of anger because I thought my mother should do something about it. When I was a teenager, it expressed itself in my rebellion. My mother taught me that sex before marriage was wrong, but I wouldn't listen. I was pregnant with my first child when I got married at a young age.

Not long into the marriage, I realized that I had married someone just like my father. He had other women and left me home with the baby. Well, I wasn't passive like my mother, I started going out too and got involved with another man (I'll call him Odis, but this is not his real name). I really loved Odis, but I kept going back to my no-good husband. In the meantime, Odis married someone else. I finally divorced my husband and married someone else as well.

But Odis and I stayed in contact with each other. He eventually divorced his wife and we began to spend time together again. This time together produced a child. Finally, I told Odis I wanted to be faithful to my new husband. We stayed in touch for the sake of the child but no longer had an intimate relationship.

The moment I held my daughter (the one Odis had fathered) in my arms, I knew I didn't want her to experience all the pain in the relationships I had gone through, so I began to pray.–Ermma

***

I attribute my making it to the altar as a virgin to my mother. When I was about three years old, she told me the story about the white wedding dress. She explained the significance of the white dress and how it was a privilege to wear one. She painted such a beautiful picture for me that from that point on I determined that was what I wanted.

After I started school, if a boy peeked under my dress or wrote me a nasty note, I went straight home to tell Mama about it. I didn't want anything to keep me from my white wedding dress. My mother would drop whatever she had in her hand and would take me off into her room and listen to what I had to say, no matter how silly and insignificant. She wouldn't just inattentively listen, but she would actively ask questions, "Now what happened? And what did he say?...and what did you say?" These little talks throughout grade school helped me to know that Mama was the place to come whenever I had problems or questions.

As I got older my mother would explain to me some of her own failures. Sometimes with tears in her eyes, she would tell me how she regretted things she had done as a teenager and young adult. I know some parents fear sharing these kinds of experiences with their children, but for me it worked. I wanted no part of that kind of sexual action in my relationships. She was eighteen when everything started with her.

I was pressured in relationships. Especially in college. Everybody told me that I needed experience. I remember feeling like maybe I did. But I went home and talked to Mama about it first. She told me, "That's how everything started with me." As soon as Mama said that, I knew, pressure or no pressure, experience or not, I didn't want to go through the pain and hurt my mother had experienced.

I used to explain to boys I went out with who pressured me sexually, "I want to wear a white dress when I get married. I do not want to have sex before marriage. And I want someone who understands that and respects it." If they kept pressuring me, I knew I needed to look elsewhere for the relationship I wanted.

When I finally met my husband, I still felt kind of bad about not having any experience. After we were engaged I explained to him very hesitantly, "Well I don't have any experience" as if that would make a big difference in our relationship. But he only said, "I'm a virgin too, and I don't have any experience either." I could hardly believe it. Not only had God kept me pure, but he had blessed me with a man who also had kept himself pure. And I got to wear the white wedding dress.

When we got married the first couple of weeks took some time for us to adjust sexually. Things were slow going. Satan tried to run that game on both of us, "You should have gotten some experience." But after those

first few weeks, this area of our marriage has been growing and developing beautifully. Mama was right; it was definitely worth the wait.
–Ermma's Daughter

When I heard the stories of this mother and daughter, it brought tears to my eyes. What a testimony of the power and grace of God. I've talked to so many women who have discovered that the sexual problems they have experienced have been a problem for several generations in their family. And, like a snowball, with each generation the problem seemed to get worse.

Could it be that Satan knows the weak sexual areas of a particular family and starts the ball rolling to keep it going from generation to generation?

My mother had me at fifteen years old. Fifteen years later I had my daughter–in the same month and almost the same day. We also had similar experiences in the way we got pregnant. What is so interesting about this is that my mother didn't raise me. I was raised in a foster home and didn't find this out until I was older. –Gloria

Now let's go back to Amnon and Tamar. God has a storehouse of information on the account of their experience–even about generational sexual problems.

STOP THE BALL FROM ROLLING

David could have stopped the ball from rolling. David's sons seemed to share his sexual weakness for women. Amnon raped Tamar, and his uncontrolled desires cost him his life. Absalom had sex with his father's concubines. And Solomon–need we even mention his problems with women? His downfall caused a serious division and a spiritual decline in the entire nation of Israel. The outcome of Amnon's and Tamar's story might have been different if David, rather than Jonadab, had noticed Amnon's distressful face. David could have sat down right then with his son and discussed sexual lust and the devastating consequences. David, on the heels of the adulterous situation with Bathsheba, had a wealth of knowledge to share on the subject. He could have spared his son the same agony he experienced, and even saved Amnon's life. Observe the similarities of David's and Amnon's sexual sins.

DAVID	AMNON
Sexually lusted over a forbidden woman.	Sexually lusted over a forbidden young girl.
Had plenty to time to think about what he was planning to do.	Had plenty of time to think about what he was planning to do.
Schemed to have his sin with Bathsheba covered up.	Schemed to get Tamar to his bedroom.
Ordered Bathsheba to come to his home and have sex with him.	Forced Tamar to his bedroom.
Had to be forced to admit his sin.	Never admitted his sin.
Regretted his actions afterwards	Was repulsed by the whole situation afterwards.
Suffered negative consequences of his sin.	Was killed because of his sin.

LIKE FATHER, LIKE SON

Most scholars believe Psalm 51 is David's prayer of remorse and repentance after his sin with Bathsheba.

> Wash away all my iniquity and cleanse me from sin. For I know my transgressions, and my sin is always before me. Against you, you only, have I sinned and done what is evil in your sight, so that you are proved right when you speak....Cleanse me with hyssop, and I will be clean; wash me, and I will be whiter than snow. Let me hear joy and gladness; let the bones you have crushed rejoice. Hide your face from my sins and blot out all my iniquity.
> (Psalms 51: 2-4; 7-9)

It is obvious that David was deeply grieved about his sexual weakness and the detrimental consequences of his sin. God forgave him and continued to bless his kingdom. But wouldn't it have been great if David had taken his repentant actions one step further and concluded that he needed to talk to his children?

David's children probably knew about his sin with Bathsheba, but did they know about the remorse in David's heart afterwards? Instead, the incident with Bathsheba probably communicated several ungodly messages to his children: "If you see something you want, get it, using any means necessary–lies, murder, or schemes." "Don't bother to talk to God about your problems, even when you see that you are in the middle of a mess; work it out yourself." David could have openly discussed his sin with his children and warned them about the deceptiveness of giving into lustful indulgences, making clear to them the consequences of disobeying God.

GENERATIONAL CURSES

When a common sin or weakness seems to run in a family, it is called a *generational curse*. This concept is based on the verse in Exodus and various other places in the Old Testament: *"The sins of the fathers do fall on the children, visiting the iniquity of the fathers on the children, on the third and fourth generation of those who hate Me"* (Exodus 20:5).

David and his sons are a perfect example of this verse. Was David's past behavior instrumental in his son's downfall? Is there any way he could have stopped his weaknesses from being inflicted upon his sons?

Neil Anderson, in his book, *"The Way of Escape",* answers some of these questions:

> Are succeeding generations guilty for the sins of their parents? Absolutely not! .... Everyone will account for his own sin. But we are all affected by the sins of others. Children are not guilty <u>for</u> their parents' sins, but <u>because</u> their parents sinned, judgment will fall upon them and their household.... Once a father has set himself against God,...*it* (h*is rebellion against God) is likely to be passed to the next generation.* [emphasis mine]

> Do we inherit a specific bent toward sin from our parents?.... Is this transmission genetic, environmental or spiritual?.... Yes...all three!.... We are genetically predisposed to certain strengths and weaknesses. However, genetics cannot be blamed for all bad choices.... It has been clearly shown that some people are genetically predisposed to alcoholism. Yet no one is born an alcoholic. People become alcoholics by drinking irresponsibly.

> ...Environmental factors also contribute to sinful behavior.... If you were raised in a home where...sexual promiscuity was modeled, you would certainly be influenced in this direction. Unless parents deal with their sins, they...set up the next generation to repeat their moral failures.... [1]

Neil Anderson goes on to say that we cannot deal passively with our "unholy inheritances." It is essential to take a position in Christ in His power to renounce the sins of our ancestors, and in so doing, to keep these sins from passing on to us and our children. In Leviticus 26:40, we are told to confess our sins and the sin or our forefathers. If we cover up their wrongdoing, we allow the cycle of bondage to continue. *"No matter what our ancestors have done, if we repent and believe in Christ, God rescues us from the dominion of darkness and brings us into the kingdom of His dear son"* (Colossians 1:13)." [2]

It is essential that we deal with sexual sin that may have been passed down to us by our ancestors so that the same behavior will not repeat itself in our children. "Many...come from family backgrounds where witchcraft, root working, and mysticism were accepted practice. These occultist beliefs may be mixed with their Christian faith."[3]

BREAKING GENERATIONAL BONDAGES

Know what you are dealing with. How do we break generational curses? Find out as much as you can about the sexual behaviors of especially the women in your family. Go as far back as possible. When we were younger, our grandmothers, great aunts, and other relatives may have concealed family secrets. But often when we are adults, they may be more open–even about their mistakes.

See if there are any patterns. For example, in one family, all the women on one side of the family may have broken up with their husbands at one point and had adulterous relationships. In another, several of the family members may have been affected by incest or some other sexual dysfunction. If you can see a pattern like these in your family, even if you are only able to go back two or three generations, you are probably dealing with a generational curse. Ermma, the mother whose story we read at the beginning of the chapter may not have realized it at the time, but she was dealing with a generational curse in her family. Her father had been an adulterer, and she engaged in sex before marriage and was an adulterer. But at the birth of her daughter, she began to break the cycle. Let's look at some of the things she did and how God used them to break the curse.

She prayed. At the time Ermma's daughter was born, Ermma was a Christian but was not in a close relationship with the Lord. Ermma did, however, believe in the power of prayer and at that point began to pray for her daughter. Ermma admits, "Not only did prayer help my daughter, but God began to deal with me. As my daughter grew up physically, I began to grow spiritually."Prayer is an effective tool to prevent Satan from severely hurting our girls. But in order for us to be effective intercessors on behalf of our daughters, God may have to do some cleaning up in our own lives. Rebecca Osaigbovo, author of *Chosen Vessels* and seminar speaker, teaches women how to become a "house of prayer." This includes having a heart and desire to effect change in our daughters and being sensitive to the Holy Spirit's leading and direction in our lives. The theme of Mrs. Osaig-bovo's book is based on 2 Chronicles 7:14: "[If] *My people who are called*

*by My name humble themselves and pray, and seek My face and turn from
their wicked ways, then I will hear from heaven, will forgive their sin, and
will heal their land."*

In to order effectively deal with the ungodliness in the lives of our girls
(and those around her who may be negatively affecting her behavior), we
may need to turn from behaviors in our own lives that are not like Christ.
We can accomplish this by talking with God, then allowing Him to talk back
to us as we study His Word. The next step is to follow through with His
strength and do what He asks us to do on a daily basis. [4]

She presented sexuality and virginity in positive ways. "Just don't
do it. You'll cause yourself a lot of problems if you do." "You don't want
to get pregnant, do you?" "All men are dogs and out for one thing." These
kinds of comments seem powerful, but usually carry little weight. But when
we latch on to a *principle* that is in the Word of God–is God's idea or
solution, and is empowered by God–we can rest assured that He will help
us bring it to pass.

Virginity was God's idea. God presents it in the Bible as though it is
a precious diamond to be held up and admired. Not like a basketball that is
being fought over and has to be held on to as tight as possible! When Ermma
painted the picture of a white wedding dress for her daughter, she gave her
something positive to anticipate. She did not arm her for tackle, with the
attitude "I dare you to try and get it." Instead, she reinforced her virginity
the way God does: she presented it as something to be proud of, something
precious and valuable.

As our daughters grow older and we begin to talk to them more
specifically about marriage, this same godly principle about the precious-
ness of sex needs to be explained to our daughters. Explain that God
intended sex to be used to unify a couple after marriage to enhance their
relationship. Tell them that it is a sacred part of God's plan as the couple
comes together in every way–spiritually, emotionally, and physically.
When sex is taken outside of this context, it cannot be fully enjoyed and
God cannot enter in and help make this relationship glorifying to Himself.
Sex was intended to blossom as the relationship grows through good times
and bad times. Reinforce in your daughter's mind that regardless of the
pressure and media hype, sex relations God's way are the best guarantee of
a fantastic sex life.

In all of our communications about sex, these two principles just
discussed are often missing. The world is busy concentrating on avoiding
babies and diseases. We do need to talk about the consequences of sex

outside of marriage, but Christians (and the rest of the world) should be concentrating on and making sure our girls understand God's original intentions and see the positive godly side of sex.

She developed a relationship with her daughter in the early years. When Ermma's daughter would come home and announce, "Mamma we've got to have a talk," Ermma would drop everything, take her daughter to another room, listen, and ask questions. This seems insignificant but it says to a child early, "Your concerns are important to me, I'm interested in you, you can come to me at any time with anything and I'll be there for you." Ermma's habit carried over into her daughter's college years, when her daughter was away from home and really felt the sexual pressure. She had listened to her boyfriend's appeals and her girlfriend's reasoning but in the back of her mind she had to talk to mama.

She faced her own past shortcomings. In Ermma's story we see the benefit of coming to grips with past sin in our lives. Sometimes mothers will try and justify their behavior and rationalize it away, but the best way to deal with it and make sure it does not continue is to call it what is was and confess it to God.

She was honest with her daughter about her past. This is a difficult one for many mothers. We think our past behavior will give our daughters an excuse to follow in our footsteps. ("Well you did it, so who are you to tell me what to do?") Usually this happens when a mother waits to tell her daughter about her sexual mistakes only after her daughter is already in a state of rebellion. Communicate honestly and do it early.

Through the combination of prayer, close open relationships with our daughters and a clear focus on God's intentions, we can keep sexual sins from continuing on to our daughters and future generations.

NOTES
1. Neil Anderson, *The Way of Escape.* (Eugene, OR: Harvest House Publishers, 1994), 93-94.
2. Ibid., 93-94.
3. Clarence Walker, *Bibical Counseling with African Americans.* (Grand Rapids: Zondervan, 1995), 57.
4. Rebecca Osaigbovo, *Chosen Vessel.* (Detroit: Dabar Services 1992), 85-123.

Chapter 15

Practical Help for our Teenage Girls

More than 50 percent of our teenagers become sexually active by the time they finish high school, and 60 to 80 percent during college. It is time to really think through what is happening in our homes, churches, and society with our girls. It is time to put a stop to Satan's action in this area.

CLOSE THE DOOR ON SEXUAL OPPORTUNITIES

Do we leave too many doors of opportunity open for teenagers to engage in premature sexual activity today? Let's return again to God's lesson through Amnon and Tamar. Amnon ordered everyone out of his bed chamber so that he could be alone with Tamar. *"Have everyone go out from me. So everyone went out from him."* (2 Samuel 13:9). This was the perfect opportunity for the sexual act to occur. No one questioned him. Everyone let him have his way.

Know what's going on in your home . Did you know young people no longer have sex in the back seat of cars? The new place to have sex is in their parents' home, between three and five o'clock in the afternoon, when both parents are often at work. This is also the common time for children to watch offensive television or videos, call the porno line, and engage in drug experimentation. Your child may have abided by your house rules up to now, but remember Satan's "peer pressure plant" may appear at this time. Remember how Jonadab negatively effected Amnon? This person often operates in a form that will give your daughter the courage to override your restrictions--a cute boy, or a close girlfriend.

Whether your child is five or fifteen, you or some responsible adult should be around to check on her if she is home alone. She should be fully aware that a responsible adult may walk in any time. After you have done all you know to do, then ask the Lord to make you alert to whenever you may need to immediately go home and check things out.

For the sake of the child, I also challenge parents to reconsider the amount of time they are spending outside of the home. ALL the child rearing years are essential from infancy to eighteen. Our youth need parental care and attention, even when it appears that they are grown up enough to tend to themselves. I urge parents to seek God's direction about how much time He wants them to spend at work and on career development. Do not make these decisions based on personal desires or gain, but on what GOD wants for the children.

Seek God's help and direction if you are a single parent. If you are a single parent, it may be especially difficult to keep an eye on and spend time with your children. God knows and understands the difficult plight of single parents and the economic struggles usually involved. Seriously pray about this matter and wait for God's answer. One mother describes below how she desperately wanted more time with her children. God provided a solution, as He will for you.

> My husband died with cancer, leaving me two teenagers and two grade school children to raise. I knew I would have to work, but my constant request was, "Lord, work it out so I can spend more time with my children." Now, more than ever, I felt like they need me around.
>
> Not long after my husband's death the Lord gave me a job in the school system. My daytime hours are the same as the children, and I have vacations and summers off when they are at home. It worked out perfectly. I took a cut in pay, but I budget tight and we can make it. Being with my children is more important that having a lot of the material luxuries. I believe God worked it all out. –Monica

Josh McDowell in his book, *How to Help your Child Say 'No' to Sexual Pressure,* makes this suggestion to single parents:

> Allow the child's other parent to continue to interact with the child, unless that parent is abusive or morally harmful for the child. This may be especially beneficial in keeping your daughters away from sexually dangerous situations. A boy may be less likely to pressure a girl into doing something she knows is wrong, if he knows her father may show up at the scene. It may even help knowing that the girl has a strong relationship with her father, whose values about sex before marriage she embraces. Finally, as McDowell suggests, be a good example for your child by demonstrating sexual purity. Make a vow of purity along with her and work together at doing what is honoring and pleasing to God.[1]

Think seriously about single dating. Another opportunity for sexual contact to begin or take place is on a single date. In light of society's sexual pressure, miseducation, and life-threatening sexually transmitted diseases, is it still wise to allow our daughters to go out on single dates (or even double dates with their peers)? You may answer "no" to this question, but what are the alternatives?

This is one area the church could really give parents some help. Every church in the country needs to hire a full-time youth pastor, one who is able to conduct informative, creative, fun activities for the youth. When we restrict children from all secular activities (dances, proms, and dates) and then tell them, "Stay home and clean your room," we give them a picture of the Christian life as restrictive, boring, and unappealing.

I asked several people about effective youth ministries in their churches—ones that are helping parents educate teens about sex, that offer attractive youth activities, and that are seeing a significant rate of young girls (and boys) in their church make the decision to stay sexually pure. So far, unfortunately, I have not found such a ministry. We need to pray and do what we can as parents to develop this.

Family time is another alternative to single dating, if such a thing still exists within the family. At one time, when a teen became interested in a person of the opposite sex, that person was naturally drawn into the family's activities. The whole family got to know the person around the dinner table, at church, and family outings. Unfortunately many young dating couples spend most of their time together in front of the television, or watching videos, alone. Some are even allowed to entertain their guests in the bedroom. Opportunities. Opportunities. Opportunities.

Help your daughter develop friendships. Start early teaching your daughter how to be hospitable and to develop friendships with both males and females. The parent should be the model in this area. Then, when the teen years come, your child is not all alone, void of any relationships with her peers, having only a boyfriend with whom to go places and do things. Some families make it a point to interact with other families particularly for the social interaction of their children. They get together regularly, for dinner or other outings. Some have even planned vacations together. This gives the children opportunity to develop friendships with other children in their peer group. It reinforces spiritual values taught in both families, and it helps our girls realize that there are more ways to have fun than single dating. The book of Proverbs is full of passages about friendship. Do a study with your daughter. Talk to her about her about the positive and negative aspects of friendship.

Keep your daughter active. Be willing to sacrifice some of your time to haul groups of girls or girls and boys to fun activities such as amusement parks, plays, or other social and sports functions. If there is not a youth group functioning in your church, many times our girls tend to date and have a boyfriend because there seems to be nothing else to do.

> Early on I could see that Earlene was going to be quite popular with the boys. From an early age she always had a boy hanging around and she called him her boyfriend. One thing I did was to keep her busy in activities. Throughout her elementary and high school years she was in dance, sports, and anything else I could involve her in. She enjoyed these activities and had very little time to hang out with the boys.–Nancy

Nancy has the right idea. Remember when I talked about children and excessive genital exploration? One of the suggestions was to keep them occupied so that their hands are not busy on their bodies. This suggestion applies to preteens and teens. Give them something to do with their hands, keep them active. In the early years, expose them to all kind of sports, games, and cultural activities. Then, when they become teenagers, they will be accustomed to participating in these kinds of things.

Teach your daughter that her body was made for some type of physical exercise. Many girls (and mothers, too) have weight problems because they don't do any kind of physical activity. You and your daughter could begin exercising or take up some kind of sports activity together. Go biking, walking, learn to play tennis, or have an aggressive game of basketball. Many schools today do not offer home economics classes, so girls often lack basic homemaking skills such as cooking or sewing. We may have to take the time to think creatively about how to get our children involved in good, healthy activities. If we don't provide these kind of things for our daughters, we'll probably find them "playing doctor" with their boyfriend for amusement.

Give dating guidelines. If you do decide to allow your daughter to date, make sure you give her the facts and the guidelines: Early dating and early steady boyfriends often lead to early sex. Most girls start dating around fifteen or sixteen. However, when to date should depend on whether the girl is showing signs of maturity, responsibility, honesty, and respect for dating limitations.

Discuss the guidelines with your daughter before you allow her to date. Discuss when and who to date, curfews, and calling back home. Make sure your daughter only dates Christians, and make sure that you meet the young man before the first date. Remind her that no physical involvement should take place if it cannot be expressed toward a brother in Christ in public. I would even recommend writing down your guidelines and discussing the consequences if certain things do not happen as agreed upon. It's better to work as much out as possible beforehand than to have to deal with a messy situation later on.

Group dates are suggested first. Give positive affirmation about the persons your daughter chooses to date. Don't just put her friends down or you will have to deal with rebellion. Even if your daughter thinks she's in love with one particular guy, encourage her to build a friendship. Do a study on Proverbs 7 and apply these verses to a man who is enticing a woman. (Refer to chapter 17 for more help with this). Help your daughter make wise choices.

Giving our girls "no" reasons.

Some girls eventually give in sexually because they run out of reasons to say no. Now, let's return once again to Amnon and Tamar. When Amnon first attempted to have sex with Tamar, she had her "no" reasons ready. There are lessons here for our daughters today.

> "Come, lie with me, my sister." But she answered him, "No, my brother, do not violate me, for such a thing is not done in Israel; do not do this disgraceful thing! As for me, where could I get rid of my reproach. And as for you, you will be like one of the fools in Isreal. Now therefore, please speak to the King, for he will not withhold me from you." However, he would not listen to her since he was stronger that she, he violated her and lay with her (2 Samuel 13:11-14).

Tamar said "NO!" to Amnon for several reasons:

"No! Because it will violate me." The original root of the Hebrew word _violate_ here means to "look down upon." Tamar was asking Amnon not to perceive her as a cheap, loose woman. In the congregation of Israel, women were respected and not forced to have sex with a man. Tamar was the daughter of the king; surely she carried herself with dignity and honor.

"No! Because such a thing is not done in Israel." In the Old Testament, the nation of Israel represented God. The pagan nations performed all kinds of illicit sex acts in the name of their gods. The true and living God required sexual purity. This is part of what distinguished His people from the rest of the world.

Christians represent God in the world today and God desires the same purity for those who call on His name. Today, one of the least mentioned reasons for not having sex is that to do so is disobedient to what God wants.

Today we care only about what we want and we do what God wants only if it fits into our plans. This kind of attitude caused big problems in biblical times and it still does today.

"No! Because it is disgraceful." Disgrace is the opposite of love, mercy, and kindness. To force someone to have sex using physical or emotional coercion is not merciful, loving, or kind. It is lustful, mean, and harsh.

"No! Because where will I go to get rid of my shame?" Smart girl. Tamar realized that once her virginity was gone, shame and guilt would set in. This kind of stain seems as though it will never wash out. The original root word of "shame" means to "pull off or expose." God forgives the girl who gives away her virginity, has an abortion, or bears a child before marriage. But, like a sore with the scab pulled away and laid bare, sometimes the wound takes a long time to heal.

"No! Because it will prove that you are a fool, wicked, or stupid." Tamar saw that she was not getting anywhere with reasons that pertained to her, so she began to appeal to Amnon's reputation and legal consequences. As stated earlier, to have sex with a sister or stepsister meant death. Amnon thought he was above God's laws and for two years he did get away with what he did. Eventually, though, Tamar's brother killed him.

Just think about it. Most teens know the facts about AIDS, sexually transmitted diseases, and pregnancy. But they continue to have sex anyway. Like Amnon, their actions are foolish indeed.

"No! Because we can wait until we are married." Amnon had fantasized and lusted for Tamar so much in his mind that he could not stop his sexual urges and reasonably talk about wedding plans. The momentum seemed impossible to stop once Tamar was so close to him. So it is with our children today. If they are really committed to waiting until marriage to engage in sex, the X-rated movies in the mind will have to go. See chapter 7 about how to help our girls deal with sexual urges.

We can teach our daughters to respond appropriately to sexual pressures as Tamar did. It's okay to say "No" today. Just as Tamar had been taught all the right reasons to resist Amnon's advances, so we can teach our daughters. The following are more "no" reasons to sex outside marriage:

"No! Because it takes away from building a friendship." Teenagers ought to be making friends with people of the opposite sex, not choosing marriage partners at that age, or playing marriage. The probability of a teen marrying the person she dated in high school is slim. The "goingsteady" relationships may cause bad habits. The two persons get close, then find out something they don't like about the other. Or maybe they see someone else they like better. They break off the relationship and start up another. This could develop a mindset for divorce. "Once I get married, if I don't like you any more or I see someone better. 'So long.'"

When sex between teens enters the picture, matters get even more complicated. Sex usually becomes the center of the relationship. The individuals no longer concentrate on getting to know each other above the waist. Now all the concentration is below.

"No!" Because I don't want my future marriage relationship hampered." There are several consequences of premature sexual activities. Some are physical. Haman Cross in his book, *The Wild Thing* outlines many of these physical ramifications. But even if a person never experiences any physical consequences, they will likely experience the emotional ones. Insecurity, guilty feelings of being used, distrust, lack of commitment for fear of being abandoned–these are just a few. When one has sex before marriage, one can bring this emotional baggage into marriage.

"No!" Because Jesus is right here watching us, and I don't want to displease Him." Even as Christians, we often fail to mention Christ's presence in our lives. Christians are the temple of the holy Spirit. I had a youth director who constantly reminded our youth group. "Wherever you go, you take Jesus with you. If He were there in bodily form, would you be comfortable with where He is and what He is observing?"

"No!" Because I want to save my virginity as a special gift to my husband." This reason enforces to your daughter how special she is. Each time she used this one, she will become more and more excited about presenting this special package to her husband!

Your daughter will at times feel that she is all alone in trying to remain sexually pure. Try to lovingly provide her with opportunities to meet other girls who have chosen the road of abstinence. Such young women do exist. The following excerpts are from an article, entitled "Prom Night Sex: Just Say No," written by a teenager who chose to stay sexually pure.

There is a saying that "everybody's doing it." I really don't believe that. Maybe everybody is thinking and talking about it, but everybody is definitely not doing it!

One day I was reading a booklet entitled "101 Ways to Make Love Without Doin' It!.... It says...you can show love by trusting one another, having a picnic together, going out to dinner, holding one another close and giving each other sexy looks. You can even respect each other and tell one another that you love them.... If that person is just out for sex...then maybe it's time to find another...date.

Virgin is not a bad word! If you made the decision not to have sex, it's a decision you can be proud of!...Not having sex...doesn't make you a wimp or a geek or a nerd or any other weird thing. Not having sex simply means you haven't had sex. " [2]

"No!" Because I don't have to." That's right – period!

EXPOSING THE GLORIFIED SEX MYTH
After having his sexual fantasy fulfilled, Amnon gave a response to Tamar. Typical for many teenagers, he did not want her any more.

> "Then Amnon hated her with a very great hatred; the hatred with which he hated her was greater than the love with he had loved her. And Amnon said to her, "Get up and go away" But she said to him, "No, because this wrong in sending me away is greater than the other that you have done to me." Yet he would not listen to her... "Now throw woman out, away from me, and lock the door behind her" (2 Samuel 13:15-17).

ANYTHING PURSUED OUTSIDE OF GOD'S WILL NEVER DE-LIVER THE SATISFACTION WE IMAGINE. This is one of Satan's oldest and cleverest tricks. He puts you on the ladder to whatever is your heart's desire. With each step he encourages and makes promises of ultimate fulfillment. He gives several rewards and incentives along the way to keep you climbing. Then you get to the top, only to discover this is not what you really wanted and needed after all. You want to retrace your steps. You see that following God was the best route after all. But then Satan does a cruel thing. He knocks the ladder from under you. He sits back and laughs, "Yes I got you here and you are stuck. No way out."

Amnon's greatest desire was to seduce Tamar. Satan gave him the plan, opportunity, and desire. Amnon took the entire package. But Satan could not deliver the satisfaction. He never can. It is not in his power to do so. It is not even his desire. Satan's job is to constantly lure us away from God's perfect plan for our lives then leave us scrambling. He never feels obligated to help us pick up the broken pieces of his destruction. The only one who obligates Himself to do that is God. *"And we know that God causes all things to work together for good, to those who love God and to those who are called according to His purpose"* (Romans 8:28). The truth is that God would rather that we never had broken pieces to pick up in the first place. When we follow Him and His ways, we avoid much brokenness.

Once we as parents and other adults truly understand God's reasons for saying no to premarital sex, we can begin to teach our children. We can be part of God's plan of action against all of Satan's modern day tactics by teaching them, first of all, that most of what they see on TV is hype. Teach them that there is no ultimate physical experience. People end up thinking something is wrong with them when their sex lives don't match the media hype. Tell them that sex is not done to combat boredom or to cap off a nice evening out. Teach them God's principles as though they apply today as strongly as they did in David's day. Remind them that the consequences of ignoring His precepts are the same, if not worse.

NOTES

1. Josh McDowell, *How to Help Your Child Say "No" to Sexual Passions*, (Waco: Word 1987), 64-65.

2. Aretha Frison, *"Prom Night Sex: Just Say NO,"* <u>The D-Town Collaboration</u>, Advanced Studies Journalism, 1995, 1.

IT'S FIXABLE

Chapter 16

Broken Teens and Other Dilemmas

> Jenny had her sixteenth birthday party last month. She's a pretty girl....She is an honor roll student, plays the flute in the school band, and is an active member of the youth group at church.
>
> Jenny has been dating Brad for several months. Both teenagers are from middle-class families. There are no remarkable problems in their lives. Actually, their futures look quite bright. However, this afternoon there was a frightening shadow cast on Jenny–and on Brad for that matter. Jenny found out she is pregnant.
>
> While lying across her bed this evening, tears stream down Jenny's face. Panic, loneliness, and confusion filled her heart. What will she do? How can she tell her parents? Will Brad still love her? Who will help her? Why, oh, why has this happened to her? [1]

J enny is not alone. One out of four girls get pregnant in the United States each year–more than a million young ladies. Most of us would pay any amount of money if it would guarantee that no harm or danger would interfere in our child's life. No matter how hard we pray, Satan may find a loophole and try to take full advantage. It is better to think ahead and be prepared for his interference, knowing that we can have the victory.

As Tamar left Amnon's bedroom chambers she responded to her calamity in several ways.

> "And Tamar put ashes on her head, and tore her long-sleeved garment which was on her; and she put her hand on her head and went away crying aloud as she went.... So Tamar remained and was desolate in her brother Absalom's house (2 Samuel 13:19-20).

She put ashes on her head. Whenever the Israelites put ashes on their heads, it symbolized grief, pain, and disgrace.

She tore her long-sleeved garment. Verse 18 explains why: "Now she had on a long-sleeved garment; for in this manner the virgin daughters of the king dressed themselves in robes." Long sleeves were a symbol of virginity. As her virginity had been torn from her, Tamar tore her sleeves. She placed her hands on her head, a symbol that great trouble had come upon her.

She went away wailing. Some translations say "crying bitterly."

She remained desolate for the rest of her days. She was a violated virgin in Israel. The word desolate means ruined or wasted. A person is without joy, hopeless, devastated, or in despair.

Tamar said to Amnon, as she tried to dissuade him from raping her, "Where could I take my shame?" Can you hear hundreds of girls asking this same question down through the centuries? Teenage girls today do not put ashes on their heads or tear their sleeves. Maybe we do not hear their bitter wailing. Rather they seem to be going on with life after their first sexual encounter as if nothing has happened. But believe me, the pain that they carry today is the same as what Tamar experienced centuries ago. It manifests itself in bitter faces, rebellious attitudes, violent behavior, self destruction through over- or undereating, sex additions, harmful relationships, and/or hopelessness and despair about their present experiences and future.

SITUATIONS THAT MAY SEEM HARD TO FIX

Hopefully your home is a balance of "Let's not have that happen here, but if it does, I hope and pray you will find your way home to talk to me about it." This is hard for a parent to do. But if in those early years we establish a foundation of high standards in our home in an atmosphere where fears and failures can be voiced, when we get to the teen years, we will be able to work with our children through difficult problems.

Prayer is the number one solution. I pray that by the time you have teens, you will know how not only to tell God about your struggles, but you will be able to listen to what He has to tell you about what you need to do. Each person responds to a crisis differently. With one child you may need to take a firm stand; with another the need may be for more love and understanding. You may need to make changes or adjustments. Some things in your household or your daily schedule may need to change. The Lord is where we need to turn in every crisis.

Below are some situations related to sexuality or sexual activity that you may face while nurturing teenage girls or young adult women. This information can give perspective on how to initially approach these problems. The explanations are not extensive, but available resources are listed at the end of this chapter. If faced with any of these difficulties, it is strongly urged that you seek further counsel.

Lost virginity. To detect loss of virginity, look for changes in your daughter's behavior–signs of depression, extreme anger or hostility, or even talk of suicide. For some girls, this transition may appear to be no big deal, but for others it may be emotionally devastating. Both types need to be observed closely.

Listen to her. Don't become so buried in denial that you miss what your daughter might be indirectly telling you. Pray and ask God to help you determine a course of action. Be as helpful as possible to her, not condemning. Remember that your goal is to help pick up the broken emotional pieces and get her back on the right track. You may need to go over your household rules or dating guidelines. Be careful not to simply add more limitations.

If you can, walk through what happened and help her understand where she could have made different choices. If you discern that your daughter is being pressured by an older or aggressive boy, you may need to talk to both of them. In addition, you both may need to seek counsel especially if there are major changes in your daughter's personality or she seems to be in a state of rebellion. Work together to find God's solutions. This can be an opportunity for you to become a prayer partner with your daughter.

Pregnancy. Every 2.1 minutes in America, a teenage girl gets pregnant.[2] It is, therefore, not unrealistic or unwise to prepare yourself and your daughter for this possibility.

Make sure your daughter understands that she can get pregnant without having intercourse. Also let her know the signs of pregnancy, the need for prenatal care, and how unwise it would be to hide the reality from you, or to decide on a quick abortion.

If, in spite of your teaching, your daughter does announce to you that she is pregnant, give her a sincere hug and reassure her of your love and commitment to her. Then, if at all possible, before you say anything else, get alone and deal with your feelings. Go to God and unload any feeling of anger, hurt, disappointment, or bitterness you may be experiencing. Apologize if you already have said something harmful or damaging. Forgive her. Let her know that the Lord forgives her and will still look out for her and the child.

Figure out what you and your child's alternatives are. Will she keep the baby? If so, how will she complete school, support the child, and what are the parameters for how much you will help?

Finally, find a support base for you and your daughter. This will be a difficult time for both of you. Call on friends and organizations to provide as much encouragement, information, and love as you can get.

Abortion. Biblically, abortion is wrong. Society debates about when a fetus actually becomes a human being. God's Word says it happens the moment the sperm hits the egg: "For Thou didst form my inward parts; Thou didst weave me in my mother's womb" (Psalm 139:13). From that point on, God begins to relate to this being as a person with a future. To abort is to destroy God-given life. Your daughter and you need to understand this because many girls (and parents) will say, "I didn't think it was a baby."

Unfortunately, many Christian girls have quiet, quick abortions because they cannot bear the embarrassment their pregnancy would cause them and their parents. In their haste to get rid of the problem, sometimes parents and the girl do not think about the emotional trauma that follows an abortion. There might be grief, anxiety, sadness, shame, hopelessness, sorrow, lowered self-esteem, hostility, insomnia or even suicidal behavior. Chemical abuse, sexual addictions, isolation, and eating disorders sometimes result. Sometimes the pain does not surface for years. On the other hand, some girls immediately conclude that they are "bad" for what they have done, that they can't ever do anything right, and so set themselves up to be constant failures.[3]

Nancy Michels, in *Helping Women Recover from Abortion* outlines nine steps of healing following an abortion. My prayer is that your daughter or loved one will never have to use this information. But, if you do, I highly recommend reading the entire book. For now, remember that Satan uses abortion and other painful experiences related to female sexuality to keep women from walking and serving in the wholeness that God intended. Do your best to help your daughter work through her post-abortion emotions.

Date rape. Sexual assault occurs when a woman knows her offender and has consented to go out with him. She has not consented to having sex with him, but he forces her anyway. Statistics tell us that one in five college-aged women have been, or will be raped. Women, (at least 90 percent) believe, at least in part, that they are to blame, 75 percent of those same women suffer from loss of self-esteem, recurring nightmares, and sometimes debilitating depression, suicidal thoughts, and self-hatred.

Let's help our girls understand that men CAN control their sex drives. They can say "no". Girls need to communicate verbally their standards with boys they date, stay out of dangerous situations as much as possible (wild parties, dating strangers, entertaining male company alone in his or your apartment, secluded areas), and see group dating as an alternative to single dates. Often another man will be able to identify a guy who may be "bad news." Gather information about what to do in a sexual assault situation and talk it over with your daughter.

Finally, if rape does happen, teach your girls not to be passive, feel responsible, or try and hide the incident but to report it to authorities, and go to a hospital immediately. Do not shower or attempt to clean up, you could be destroying valuable evidence. Then, make use of any appropriate and available counseling.

Rape is something the church seems to ignore. But the Bible exhorts us to "Open your mouth...for the rights of the unfortunate.... And defend the rights of the afflicted and needy (Proverbs 31:8-9). Often rape victims feel powerless and unsure where to turn for help. Christians need to become more aware of this crime and reach out to those who are hurting.

Lesbianism. According to the Bible, the homosexual lifestyle is wrong. In several places (Leviticus 18:22; 20:13; Romans 1:26-27), God condemns people for following through on their sexual urges toward the same sex. Our society is doing its best to convince our girls that they should be able to choose this lifestyle. We should teach our children to respect the homosexual person, but to acknowledge that the lifestyle is sinful and not pleasing in God's sight.

Many girls show tomboyish behavior growing up. Don't reinforce such activity, draw attention to, or encourage it by teasing your daughter or by suggesting that such behavior leads to lesbianism. Instead, regularly reinforce her female sexuality and tell her what God says about it.

It is also not uncommon for girls to feel affectionate toward other girls. This does not mean that they are lesbian. All people, in fact, do feel some affection for their same sex. While that fact may be somewhat confusing to a child, your role is to continue to model what is proper affection to be shown to her same sex. Of course, reassure her that she is not lesbian whenever she seems concerned. It is equally important, especially in the marriage, to model for her what is proper love and affection for a husband. With prayer and exposure to healthy, heterosexual relationships, your daughter should develop in a godly manner.[4]

Mothers and other females need to be careful not to male bash–especially in the presence of young girls. In so doing, you might be setting the stage for girls to hate men and turn to other women for their intimacy needs.

If you believe your daughter is moving in this direction, seek counsel. There are several resources available to Christians on the subject. Try to keep the lines of communication open between you and your child so that she will talk to you about any fears or anxieties she may have about her sexuality.

Cohabitation. Unmarried couples living together is a widely accepted practice in our society. Cohabitation has increased 600 percent since the 1960's. Many secular educators encourage this practice because they feel it is a way for people to find out all about those they may consider marrying. Statistics show that persons living together before marriage will most likely divorce and have less satisfaction in marriage.[5]

Of course, Christians should not engage in this practice because when an unmarried, unrelated male and female live together, the arrangement usually includes sex. This kind of lifestyle will hinder our relationship with the Lord.

Some young women, even Christians, succumb to cohabitation because they think it will lead to marriage. However, this is not always the case. Many women will find themselves trapped in a live-in situation with a man who is very content not to marry.

God can help us know what to do. *"Now when King David heard of all these matters, he was very angry.... Now it came about after two full years..."* (2 Samuel 13:21,23). Once David knew about the rape of Tamar, Amnon's sexual problems, and Absalom's anger, he DID NOTHING! He did get upset, but he chose not to punish Amnon, force him to marry Tamar, help her deal with her pain, or attempt to bring the two brothers to the table of reconciliation. He ignored the whole ugly scene and went on as usual with his kingly responsibilities. Maybe he did not address Amnon's violent act because rape was punishable by death in Israel and he could not bear to sentence his own son to die (Deuteronomy 22:25).

However, his lack of action caused Tamar to remain alone and in her shame for the rest of her days, Amnon to be killed, and Absalom to orchestrate a major rebellion against the king. Even if David did not know what to do, the difficulties were not beyond God. Just as God had given David step-by-step battle plans, He could have given David step-by-step plans to put his household back together.

We cannot afford to turn our heads and look the other way like David did. We must act on behalf of our children and teach them to combat the plans of the enemy. God will show us how.

EXERCISES

1. Develop a strategy for teaching your child the difference between love and sex. Think of things someone might say, especially to your daughter, in a lustful situation. Teach her what to say in response.

2. Think of things or situations which sexually arouse you, then think how your child might respond to these same things, if exposed. Decide if your child needs to form new habits to avoid ungodly sexual thoughts or behavior, and how much you can do to help her develop these habits.

3. Count the number of sexually explicit items in one TV show or a music videotape each day for one week. Use this information as a teaching tool. How will you use it? How can you change your child's exposure to it?

4. Share an incident from your past where you mistook love for lust. Show how God saved you from doing so or rectified the situation. Pray about what to share and how much to share with your daughter.

5. Set aside time each day or week to spend with your daughter to share important thoughts and answer questions.

6. Show your child what would be inappropriate touching. Tell her what to do if someone touches her in this manner. Reassure her that in all situations, you will be there to help her and listen to her.

7. Even though she is a teenager, make it a point to give your daughter a hug every day.

NOTES

1. Barry and Carol St. Clair, *Talking With Your Kids About Love, Sex, and Dating*, (Wheaton, Ill.: Victor Books, 1993), 154.
2. Nancy Michels, *Helping Women Recover From Abortion*, (Minneapolis: Bethany House Publishers, 1988), 36.
3. Andy Landis, *Andy Landis: A Survivor's Story,* "Christian Single," March 1995, 11-12.
4. Jones, *How and When To Tell Your Child About Sex*, 247-250.
5. Ibid., 245-246.

Section Three

Satan's Sexual Attack
on The Single Woman

Chapter 17

The Enemy's Plan for the Single Woman

My mother was fourteen when she had me. She gave me to my grand-mother to raise, and then she went to live with her father in Chicago. My grandparents had separated when she was a little girl. I adored Granny. All of her children were grown, so it was just me, her, and the chickens she raised on a small farm. Two of her sons lived close by and they came everyday to do the chores which left me and granny a lot of time to sit around and talk. Granny never finished grade school but she could read and write. She taught me about things in the Bible, about cooking and keeping house, and warned me about a "life of sin."

I could tell she was very hurt over what my mother had done, but she never talked bad about her. Each night we would kneel by the bed and pray. Granny would pray for my daily activities and my future. She'd ask the heavenly Father to keep and watch over me wherever I went.

We lived a very simple lifestyle; church on Sunday, prayer meeting on Wednesday, market on Saturday, and choir rehearsal on Saturday night. I went to school everyday and on special holidays all the family got together for a big dinner. Life for me was uncomplicated until Granny died. It was the summer after I finished the seventh grade. My mother whom I never knew came to the funeral. She was wearing a skin-tight suit and a big fancy hat. This was the kind of outfit Granny had always told me not to wear because it made a man's heart beat too fast and sometimes do crazy things to a woman.

My relatives begged her not to, but she insisted on taking me back to Chicago with her. She never had much to say to me, but she saw to it that I had what I needed each day. I knew how to cook, do my own hair, and basically take care of myself, so my mother let me. She enrolled me in one of those big city high schools. Going from a country school to a large high school in Chicago was a shock to me. I remember being very afraid as I went out that first morning for school. A woman who also lived in the same apartment building was sitting on the porch. She must have seen the terror-stricken look on my face. "Hey Marie, don't worry, it's going to be alright." That's all she said, but that was all I needed to remind me of Granny's prayers. I could almost her praying that morning, "God keep watch over this baby wherever she goes." That had been Granny's daily prayer and it was enough to assure me that God was with me.

I started to attend a church down the block from my mother's apartment. There I met several woman like my grandmother, who prayed for me and encouraged me. My mother continued to live her wayward lifestyle, but all through high school I continued to followed my Christian convictions. Obviously, the first thirteen years of praying and teaching from my grandmother was enough to instill in me that I didn't want to live "the life of sin." Finally, I married a committed Christian man who also attended my church. We settled down to raise our children like my grandmother raised me. Yes, I've lived in Chicago, for over fifty years now, but Chicago, thank God, and thank Granny, never lived in me. –Marie

The single life of a woman. It comes in all shapes, sizes, and backgrounds. Your single life experience may be or might have been like Marie's –simple and pure–not without its share of problems, but still victorious. Or your story may be more like Bernadine's in chapter 19–immoral, stormy, and inconsistent. It is challenging to address single women because there is such a variety of them, all with different needs. There is the young single woman who has never married and has no children. Also included are the never married older single women with no children, divorced women with young children, divorced women with grown children, young widows with small children, and older widows with grown children. Finally, there are women who are married but living single because their husbands are incarcerated or even missing.

But what brings all of these women under one word of reference is that they are presently without a mate. Satan has a special destructive dart pointed at these women–not because they do not have a mate, not because they are without spiritual covering, not because they are half a person in need of the other half, not because they are often lonely, not because of sexual temptation–but because he knows a Spirit-filled godly single woman can do significant damage to his kingdom. So he tries to see to it, either early or later, that most of the women who reach this station in life **DO NOT** get close to God or use this phase of their lives to do God's bidding. Satan does his best to keep women depressed, angry, bitter at God, and thinking marriage will solve all their problems. He entangles a woman's life with damaging relationships, sexual temptations, doubts about her future, and whatever else he can hurl her way to trip her up.

Paul said it is good for people to stay single so they can do the maximum for the kingdom of God (1 Corinthians 7:26). A single woman does not have to work at harmonizing her aspirations around her husband's goals (which can take years with a lot of conflict, trial and error). She can spend time with the Lord, develop her career and ministry, and any other endeavors she chooses.

Even in the church, we have often missed the boat with singles. Instead of encouraging them and telling them how desperately they are needed to work unhindered for the Lord, we often chide and tease them about getting married. ("Yes, I'm praying for you a husband.") We may see their single state as something that needs to be hastily moved through and on to the so-called good life–marriage. One reason that so many people are miserable in their marriages is that they did not allow God to work with them, use them fully, and bring them to a place of appreciating their singleness. Many singles do not witness His power in their lives at this stage of development.

As usual, God's Word offers help and guidance to single women. He also provides them with insight into Satan's deceptions. Before we look at God's solutions, let's look a little closer at how Satan tries to enslave the single women.

JUST BEYOND THE TEEN YEARS

A young woman leaving home for the first time to be on her own may be so anxious to get out from under parental wings that she gives little thought to Satan's temptations awaiting her.

> As I watched my parents drive away from my college dorm, a part of me said, "Yes! I'm finally on my own." But as I turned around and saw a group of guys staring at me like a piece of fresh meat, I thought, "Oh no, am I really ready for all this?" The next four years of my promiscuous behavior in college proved that I was not. –Pam

When a child is playing in the back yard, a parent can still swing open the back door, keep an eye on what's going on, and control her activities if necessary. But when a child goes down the street and around the block, she feels more comfortable trying a few things she would not dare do in the parents' backyard.

When a young woman turns eighteen, she is legally in the driver's seat of her own life. At this age she can move into her own apartment, get an abortion (earlier in some states) get married, live with a man outside of marriage, drink, vote–all without parental approval or interference. I can see Satan licking his chops. Whatever he could not destroy in the turbulent teen years, he sets out to accomplish in these young adult years.

If high school was Satan's back yard, college is definitely his playground. At college, even in supervised dorms, there are ample opportunities for Satan to sexually entice young women. Sex before marriage is the socially acceptable norm on the campus. Contraceptives, abortions and medical attention for sexually transmitted diseases are all readily available.

Even when a young woman does not go to college, she faces similar temptations. A new job, a first apartment, and independent responsibilities all bring fresh appeal.

> I had it all planned. I was going to stay with my Aunt who lived about three hundred miles away from the place where I grew up. I would work during the day and take night classes. But after a few months, things were not working out, and I had to move out. Living in an apartment alone in a big city scared me to death. I met a young man and it was so comforting to have him around. I ended up allowing him to live with me, and that's when so many of my troubles began. Things were fine until I got pregnant. This signaled to him a long-term commitment that he was not ready for. As the pregnancy progressed I became ill. I grew more financially and emotionally dependent on him. All of this responsibility was not what he bargained for in this relationship. He became physically abusive and finally abandoned me after the birth of our son. –Jean

Preparing our daughters for life on their own. The "school of hard knocks" is going to teach our daughters many lessons. Once they are out of our homes, it is inevitable that they will face Satan and his sexual temptations, maybe even more than when they were under our care. We can teach them to make the Word of God personal to their circumstances. Take your daughter through passages in the Bible and show her how to look for similar situations in her life. An example is provided below using Proverbs 7. The lesson about the immoral woman has been rephrased and expanded upon to provide a lesson about the immoral man.

> My daughter pay attention to what I have to say, see it as valuable, and a life saver.
>
> Keep God's Word close at hand and put it in your heart. Pay close attention to God's guidelines and principles of behavior. Keep God's Word with you and desire to converse with God, like you would your closest friend.

God's guidance will keep you from a seducing, smooth-talking man who may say he loves you and cares about you, but really has only one thing on his mind, conquering you sexually.

I've seen too many like him. And many girls who pay no attention to God's Word have been tripped up by him. He looks good. He has a nice car, a good job, and doesn't mind wining and dining you. He knows how to show a woman a good time.

A girl can be taken with him very quickly because he's a smooth talker. He knows how to kiss ever so gently on that first date. He exerts no pressure. He knows how to play you into his hands. He is experienced ineventually getting what he wants.

He even says, "I'm a Christian, too" when you tell him about your commitment to Christ. He may take you to his church, raise his hands in praise as you raise yours, and squeeze your hand ever so tightly as the minister prays.

But all the while he's pursuing you for only one thing. After he has you emotionally attached to him, then he will take you to his cozy little place. It's clean. Nicely decorated. A built-in stereo plays soft sensuous music as you both sink down into his nice soft carpet. After a few kisses and caresses he shows you to his king-size waterbed and entices you to ride the waves until morning. He puts on his answering machine and turns off the ringer. He assures you of his undivided attention, no one will interrupt. It's just the two of you all alone.

He knows where to touch, what erotic buttons to push. He will talk you out of all your excuses. You'll keep saying no but he knows how to make your body say yes until he has conquered. Another notch on his waterbed. You did not realize when you took that first ride in his car, accepted that first dinner invitation, and allowed him that first kiss, that it would lead to this. You thought you were strong enough, Christian enough, to refrain.

Then when all your resistance is gone and you are willing to be with him and give him what he wants–any time, any place, for any reason–he'll be gone. You will watch him drive by with another young woman to conquer at his side. So listen my daughter; don't close your ears. Take it from one who knows. He will break your heart like he has done many others. He's conquered the strongest, most committed Christian girls. You see, you must understand this man is not his own, the master schemer Satan is controlling him. And Satan's goal is to be sure women do not desire to walk close to the Lord. So he plants as many smooth-talking, good looking decoys as he can. Sometimes they even say they are Christians. Their job is to keep you falling sexually or feeling so guilty that you will never want to get close to God.

- Be honest with your daughter about some of your experiences while on your own. If you never went away to college or lived away from your family, find a young adult who has and would be willing to talk to your daughter about her experience. Be sure she is a committed Christian interested in giving your daughter some good spiritual advice.

- If your daughter is going away to college or leaving the city, help her locate a good Bible believing local church, or a Christian campus group. Make the contact yourself if necessary. Perhaps meet the pastor and encourage the church's involvement with your child. Although your daughter will ultimately make her own decisions, this is the time and place you must be aggressive. You must know that Satan is real; he is out there waiting to destroy your daughter's future.

- Respect your daughter's decisions about career choices, leaving home, male and female friends, and living arrangements–even if she seems to be making some wrong ones. Let her know you disagree with her, but try to keep the lines of communication open.

- If your daughter is in a good relationship with someone right out of high school and wants to get married, don't immediately say no. Pray and seek the Lord earnestly. This might be the best thing to help her avoid sexual problems. America is the only country in the world that insists that our children go to college, get a career, and have enough money to manage a household before the parents approve of a marriage. Is this putting too much sexual pressure and temptation on our children? The Lord may have the parents of this young couple to help support them through school until they can support themselves. Be open to God's leading and direction, not merely what our culture dictates.

WATCHING THE BIOLOGICAL CLOCK

After a certain age, single women who have never been married often start to watch the biological clock. A virgin who is waiting until marriage may begin rethinking some of her earlier firm convictions, especially if she is past the age when most women are no longer virgins. She may have experienced several men's rejection because she failed to give into their sexual advances. Now she might begin to feel desperate or panicky and decide the next time a good man comes into her life that she feel will make a good husband, she'll hang on to him regardless of what it takes.

There were four of us that were very close in college. All three of my friends had gotten married. I had been in all three weddings. At the last wedding, one of my friends pulled me aside and told me if I was ever going to get married I had better rethink my idea of waiting until I got married to have sex. "Men want to sample the goods," she said jokingly. When I went home that night to my empty apartment and crawled into my bed alone, her words kept echoing back to me. Maybe I had been a fool all these years. I had met some pretty nice guys and we had gotten very close. But when they realized I was not going to allow them to spend the night in my apartment unless we were married, they always found an excuse not to continue the relationship. It seems I had been hurt so many times because of my convictions.–Julie

SUDDENLY SINGLE AGAIN

Today, a number of illness and diseases are claiming the lives of even younger men. For a number of reasons, it is not uncommon today to find women without a spouse because of death. Often there are still young children in the home, and a woman finds herself facing daily challenges of single motherhood while working through a time of grief.

It is not uncommon for a widowed woman to be intensely lonely. After all, your companion of many years is now gone. Perhaps some of your obstacles or new emotions are those related to overcoming the fear of being alone, or of developing new male friendships, or of being viewed differently by your friends now that you do not have a husband. Perhaps your status in life has changed, and you wonder how you are going to make it financially. You wonder if the cloud of sadness will go away and if your life will ever have clarity again.

If any one had told me that at the young age of thirtynine I would be single again, I would not have believed it. However, my husband of seventeen years was found with terminal cancer and just seven months later I was a widow.

I did not spend a lot of my early years dating and in committed relationships with other men. My late husband and I met and developed a close friendship quickly. So for me to be without him and now available to other men seem strange and extremely uncomfortable.

I found myself being very cautious. I never would allow any men inside my house when I was alone. I would always talk to them on the porch. I felt I had to be very careful not to allow myself to get into any compromising situations. I also set up little rules in my head, for example, only meet men in public places, never go to a man's house or apartment, no touching.

At first I had no thought of developing a new relationship. I assured my children that it would be just me and them for a long while. However, four months later I begin to have the urge to get to know other men, at least on a friendship level. I realized I longed for male conversations. But relating to single men was scary to me. The Lord and I had developed such a close relationship since my husband's illness and death. I didn't want anything to come between our relationship. And I definitely did not want to mess up sexually. –Jasmine

Absence because of divorce. A major killer of marriages in this country is divorce. In fact, in the last fifty years, the divorce rate in America has risen more than 700 percent, and divorce claims about 50 percent of all U.S. marriages.

Like newly widowed women, divorced women face a barrage of new circumstances. In addition to the daily experience of the single life, the divorced woman may also have feelings of failure or rejection and a plummeting self-esteem. If the marriage dissolved mainly because of an unfaithful spouse, a wife may question, "What could I have done differently? Am I not attractive? Why did my husband leave me for another woman?" During these times a woman may be tempted to engage in sexual behavior just to feel that a man still appreciates her and thinks she is sexually attractive.

When I walked down that aisle to get married, I envisioned my husband and me growing old together and still loving each other like we did at that moment. What I didn't envision was, fifteen years and two children later, finding him in the arms of another woman. We were Christians. We got premarital counseling. We initially worked hard at our relationship and at being good parents. Then as we reached the mid-life years it was as if something snapped. Sure, there were problems before that, but nothing like this. My husband seemed discontent about everything. He was like a caged bird wanting out. After I caught him with another woman, I let him out of his cage. As of this day he has never looked back. –Faye

THE SINGLE PARENT
Whether left alone because of a husband's death or divorce, a mother who has children to raise without a mate can be overwhelmed by the responsibility. God never intended for this 'humongous' task of rearing a child to be done without two parents. A single mother is often so exhausted,

mentally, physically, and spiritually, that she welcomes help and support anywhere she can get it. Consequently, the state of single parenthood can open a huge door for Satan to come in and take advantage of a vulnerable woman. Since finances are often a concern for a woman who is divorced, this is especially true of the single parent. Satan is standing by, prepared with a willing man who wants to help mom meet her financial and social needs, but without the commitment of marriage.

Single mothers who have never been married face the same practical issues as mothers who are divorced or widowed. When it comes to financial temptations, the never-married single may be even more vulnerable to Satan's traps. In addition to possibly having hurts and wounds related to their past sexual lives, they are more likely than once-married parents to have financial hardships.

> I never thought I would allow a man to live with me but it happened so gradually. I met this guy on my job. At first he would just occasionally buy me lunch. I really appreciated it. Those bologna sandwiches I brought to work each day started tasting like cardboard after a while. We talked a lot and, of course, my financial struggles came up often. He had a good job and so he began to buy little things for me and the kids. At first I felt uncomfortable with it but I needed the help so badly. So when he started to make sexual advances, I felt obligated to give in. Then when he lost his job and was about to lose his place, I felt like this was my chance to help him out. He moved into my apartment and he has been there ever since.
> –Sue

From the stories and statistics, it is not difficult to see the vulnerable areas in the lives of single women. Satan knows every one of them and strategically launches his attack according to every woman's weaknesses. But God tells us how to protect ourselves and how to avoid the destructive path Satan wants single women to follow. Most of all I believe God wants the single woman to appreciate His gift of singleness and the time He has given her without a mate. She can use this time to help other single women who are being destroyed daily because they are victims of Satan's malicious plans. The next two chapters explain how this can be done.

NOTES

1. Zig Ziglar, *Courtship After Marriage*, (New York: Ballantine Books, 1992), 42-43.

Chapter 18

Without a Mate But Not Alone

Growing up in the south with four brothers who were big eaters, I've been chubby ever since I can remember. In junior high, I had a lot of male and female friends but no boys really took a special interest in me. I assumed it was because I was fat. In my last couple of years of high school I began to lose weight. After that I had a couple of boyfriends. But once I put the weight back on again I was everybody's friend again I had concluded that as long I was overweight I would never have a boyfriend.

Then, in college I met this guy. Turner just seemed to like me for me. I had never been involved with anyone sexually. My weight seemed to protect me from anyone ever wanting to get that close. But Turner didn't let this stop him. I was in love and thought he and I were on a one-way street to the altar. But Turner decided to transfer to a another school and finish his degree in something our college didn't offer. I was all prepared to go with him. But he insisted that I stay and finish. He promised to write, but once he left I never heard from again.

Soon I discovered there were plenty of guys who didn't mind having sex with a fat girl. I hopped in and out of bed with anyone who was willing. It seemed like a way to fill the hole in my heart that Turner had left. But after several years, I realized that the hole remained. No amount of sex was going to fill it. I was still fat and very alone. – Sylvia

Satan says to the single woman,"You are alone. Experience how horrible it can be to be alone. Hear the empty hollow walls of your humble little home. Feel the empty space next to you as you lie in your bed. Taste how sickening it is." And it's true. Feeling all alone can sometimes make us think that life itself is being squeezed out of us. God, however, wants the single women to know that she may be without a mate but she is never alone.

ASSURANCE OF GOD'S PRESENCE

The angel of the Lord. In theology, the term <u>theophany</u> is used to describe the angel of the Lord that appeared at different times in the Old Testament. He would come in the form of a man and converse person-to-person with an Old Testament personality. Whenever the Bible specifically refers to "the angel of the Lord," and not simply "an angel," most scholars believe this particular angel is Jesus Christ Himself.

The first time a theophany ever occurred in the Old Testament was when the angel of the Lord came and spoke to Hagar. He did not just appear to her once, but twice. First she was a second wife, being mistreated, and then she was a single parent. We find the story of Hagar in Genesis chapters 16 and 22. As God speaks to her, I believe He is also speaking to other women who find themselves facing the challenges of life without a mate.

> "And after Abram had lived ten years in the land of Canaan, Abram's wife Sarai took Hagar the Egyptian, her maid, and gave her to her husband Abram as his wife.... She conceived; and when she saw that she had conceived her mistress was despised in her sight.... So Sarai treated her harshly, and she fled from her presence" –Genesis 16:3-6.

Hagar's story is like that of a victim. Webster defines a victim as "one whose adverse circumstances have been thrust upon them." Hagar seemed to have no choices in her situation. Abram and Sarai most likely picked up Hagar in Egypt when Abram fled to Egypt to escape the famine in Canaan. Hagar was probably a part of Pharaoh's gift pack when Abram left town. When she left Egypt, Hagar might have been just a child or a very young girl. So here is this young girl yanked from her home and maybe even her parents and the fine high-class living in Egypt. She was taken as a servant to a man and his wife who lived out in the middle of nowhere in a tent.

After ten years, Hagar seemed to have served Sarai well and probably saw her as a mother figure. Obviously, Sarai thought highly of Hagar because when Sarai had not borne the child God promised, Hagar was the servant girl she chose to have one for her. This was not God's way, however, but a custom of that time to allow one of the servants to bear a child for the mistress if the mistress could not have her own.

Once again Hagar had no choice in this matter. She obeyed her mistress, had sex with Abram and became pregnant. Hagar's pregnancy seemed to cause strife between the two women, which resulted in Hagar running away. As she headed back home to Egypt, she was confronted by the angel of the Lord.

Now the angel of the Lord found her by a spring of water in the wilderness.... And he said, "Hagar, Sarai's maid, where have you come from and where are you going?" And she said, "I am fleeing from the presence of my mistress Sarai." Then the angel of the Lord said to her, "Return to your mistress, and submit yourself to her authority.... I will greatly multiply your descendants so that they shall be too many to count.... You are with child and you shall bear a son; and you shall call his name Ishmael, because the Lord has given heed to your affliction...." Then she called the name of the Lord who spoke to her, "Thou are a God who sees," for she said, "Have I even remained alive here after seeing Him?"...So Hagar bore Abram a son; and Abram called the name of his son, whom Hagar bore, Ishmael (Genesis 16:7-15).

"Now the Angel of the Lord found her...." I like that. So many times I've heard people say, "I found the Lord." But in reality hasn't the Lord, since the day of our birth, been attempting to get our attention? So it was with Hagar. Here was this slave girl, being visited by the King of Kings and the Lord of Lords. Some may say that was because of her association with Abram (Abraham), but other places in Scripture demonstrate that God talks to women even when they have no association with great men. I believe the angel came because He cared. Jesus is an advocate, helper and friend to those who are helpless and at times treated unfairly.

It is interesting that the first thing Jesus said to Hagar was, *"Where have you come from and where are you going?"* Keep in mind that Jesus already knew the answer to both questions, but He wanted Hagar to think it over. Hagar had an answer for Him. In essence she said, "I'm getting away from my troubles." Hagar's solution to her problems was to go back home to Egypt.

Jesus offered Hagar another alternative. He challenged her to face the difficult situation, to go back to Sarai and continue to submit to her authority. Then, He told her she would bear a son, Ishmael, who would be a "wild donkey of a man" (Genesis 16:12). A wild donkey was an admired and valuable animal in that day.

God is with us. Jesus also assured Hagar of God's presence and told her that God knew all about her struggles. God pre-named Hagar's son Ishmael, which means *God hears*. This would remind Hagar each time she called her son's name, that God was attentive to her cries. The place in which God met Hagar was also given a symbolic name, "Beer-Lahai-Roi" meaning, "the Living One who sees me." Hagar met the angel of the Lord. He let her know that God was always present, observing, and listening.

Hagar must have had some knowledge of God and his ways because she knew she should have been dead after this encounter with God She was amazed that she still lived. Abram's talks with God were perhaps well known in his household. He might have gathered his family and servants around periodically to teach them about God and what he had experienced.

But that day at the well, Hagar met God for herself. Abram's God became her personal God, for He had spoken to her in the same way as He did her master. She now had a story to tell.

Hagar also had a choice to make. Would she follow God and His instructions or would she continue on her homeward path back to Egypt? She chose to obey God. She went back to Sarai, Ishmael was born, and everyone lived happily ever after.... Not quite.

> Now Sarai saw the son of Hagar the Egyptian, whom she had borne to Abraham, mocking. Therefore she said to Abraham, "Drive out this maid and her son, for the son of this maid shall not be an heir with my son Isaac.... So Abraham rose early in the morning, and took bread and a skin of water, and gave them to Hagar, putting them on her shoulder, and gave her the boy and sent her away. And she departed, and wandered about in the wilderness of Beersheba. And the water in the skin was used up, and she left the boy under one of the bushes. Then she went and sat down opposite him.... Do not let me see the boy die.... And lifted up her voice and wept. And God heard the lad crying; and the Angel of God called to Hagar from heaven, and said to her, "What is the matter with you, Hagar? Do not fear, for God has heard the voice of the lad where he is. Arise, lift up the lad and hold him by the hand; for I will make a great nation of him." Then God opened her eyes and she saw a well of water; and she went and filled the skin with water. and gave the lad a drink. And God was with the lad, and he grew; and he lived in the wilderness, and became an archer. And he lived in the wilderness of Paran; and his mother took a wife for him from the land of Egypt (Genesis 21:9-21).

God is patient. We can see from this passage that Hagar found herself in the same predicament about twelve years later. This time she was permanently kicked out of Abraham's house. Hagar ended up in the wilderness, but this time she was not alone; She was a single parent with a son depending on her for protection and survival. The water supply was depleted and Hagar didn't know what to do, so she remembered Ishmael's name, "God hears," and cried out to the Lord, right? She remembered this place where she met the angel and was confident God would meet her again, right? Wrong. Hagar put the boy under a bush and said, "I know he's going to die, just don't let me see it happen." God is always so patient, so kind, and so understanding–even when we forget about Him and ignore His presence.

God is faithful. God took the initiative and responded to the cries of Ishmael, not the prayers of Hagar. I imagine His words to be gentle and soft.

He said to Hagar, "What's the matter with you?" In other words: "Don't you remember the promise given in the wilderness years ago? I told you about your son's future and assured you of My presence and care. Get up Hagar. Pick up your son. The provision (the well) is right here and has been all the time. You just need to open your eyes." The passage goes on to tell us that Ishmael did grow up and that he took a wife. Once again, the faithfulness of God prevailed.

EXPERIENCE THE PRESENCE AND CARE OF GOD

Take time to think. Sometimes a single woman may want to submit to God's care, but she may not know how. First, she would start by making time periodically to take inventory of where she is going and where she has been. The first thing Jesus said to Hagar was, "think about your past and your future." For the single mother, this is important because lacking the support of the other parent, it is quite easy to get caught up in the rat race of working, household responsibilities, children's activities–not taking time to rest, let alone reflect. This is one way the enemy gets in with anxieties, loneliness, frustrations, or cause us to fear.

Gordon McDonald in, *Ordering Your Private World* refers to the Sabbath rest. He says the Sabbath should be a time for Christians to review past actions, to think through and evaluate which way God would have us to proceed, and to renew commitments based on what God is showing us.

McDonald suggests a daily devotional, a weekly extended time with the Lord (a whole day if possible or a few uninterrupted hours each week), and a once or twice a year personal retreat. Some women may feel they don't have the time. But if you break it down to only ten minutes a day, one hour a week, and one weekend a year, this is not much time. Ask God to help you find that time to still yourself before Him. You will find yourself more refreshed and ready to face each new day.[1]

As you approach your periods of reflection before God, the following are some principles to help focus on trusting and submitting to His care:

- Hope in God. Hagar received specific details about her future from the angel of the Lord. Most Christians do not get a full color picture of what is
  up ahead. Instead, we have God's promises like the one in Jeremiah
  29:11: "I know the plans I have for you, declares the Lord,...not for calamity...to give you a future and a hope." You may not know all the details of
  God's plan for your life, but He does. And God does not just sit back and
  watch our lives unravel. He is always actively engaged in each activity, desiring to guide and cushion our every step.

- <u>Realize God knows all about your troubles</u>. The angel told Hagar, "The Lord has given heed to your affliction." Simply, He knows. In the gospel of Matthew we are told that God is aware of the sparrow when he falls (Matthew 10:29). At first, when I read that verse I would picture a baby bird falling out of a tree during a storm and God taking care of it. In reality, this is referring to every time a sparrow hops. God is aware of that tiny space in each hop between the sparrow's foot and the ground. How is that for knowing detail! God is just that acquainted with every nook and cranny of our lives. He cares about every little detail.

- <u>Know that God sees you where you are</u>. Hagar called God, "Thou art the one who sees." God not only knows everything but He sees everything. A speaker once said, "If we were to make a movie of all our past actions and thoughts, that is one movie we wouldn't want anyone to see." But God has seen the movie, and He still loves us. This also could be a good thing to remember when we are fighting sexual temptation. God is right there watching our every move. He is also willing to help us resist, if we ask Him.

- <u>He is always there for us</u>. We may forget about God, but he never forgets about us. When Hagar got kicked out of Abraham's home, she forgot about God's protective care and availability. If God seems far away, guess who moved. When the Lord says He will never leave us or forsake us, He means it, and He has the power to make good on His promises. When we say, "I'm going to stay close to you Lord," some of us need to add the clause, "as long as You are doing what I think is best for me." When God does not provide a single woman with a mate right away, it's easy to think God is withholding something good from her that she really needs. But that is Satan's lie. *No good thing will He withhold from those who walk uprightly* (Psalms 84:11).

When I was a little girl my mother was always telling me, "Slow down sister Sally (I always thought I had to do everything quickly). It will come to you." I'm sure she had no idea that those would be the words that would stick with me as I went through my single years. I was determined to enjoy my single life and let God give me a husband in His own time. (Little did I know how long HIS time would be.) I started my own business and between that and church I didn't have a lot of time to spare for social things and dating. It took God fifty-two years to bring a good Christian man into my life for me to marry. We were both established in life by this time and many of the financial pressures, child raising days, and wondering what to do with our lives was over. So we basically just enjoy each other's company. It's great. It was well worth the wait. –Deanna

- <u>God will open up our eyes to see His provision if we ask Him</u>. The well for Hagar and Ishmael was there all the time. But in the midst of Hagar's lack of faith and distress, she did not see it. All our needs are taken care of, we need only to ask God to open our eyes and allow us to see where and how.

- <u>God keeps His promises</u>. God had told Hagar years before that Ishmael would be a wild donkey of a man, not that he would die in his teenage years. If Hagar had remembered and believed God's promises, she could have faced this trial with confidence. Instead, it caused her a great amount of distress and worry.   Historical accounts of people like Hagar remind us of the faithfulness of God. And when single people are lonely or greatly in need, those are definitely the times to reflect on what God has done for others in similar circumstances.

I've been a single parent for almost eight years now At first when the baby was born, I continued in my wild, rebellious lifestyle. I'd find someone who was willing to keep my baby on Friday nights, and every weekend I was out there doing my thing–drinking, partying, laying up with some man. But as my daughter grew up, I could see her watching me and she began to ask questions. Where was I going? Who was this guy or that guy? And could she wear a dress like me when she got older? (I dressed to kill on Friday nights.) The more I thought about it, the more I didn't want my daughter following in my footsteps. I had received Christ while at junior high camp years ago, but strayed away. One Sunday I got up and went to church. It just so happened (I knew God planned it) that the minister preached on the prodigal son. I went forward and rededicted my life to Christ. It has not been easy. Sometimes when I am alone on Friday nights, Satan tries to tell me I was better off out in the streets and laying up with a man. And I've fallen from time to time. But I know following after Jesus and allowing Him to minister to my needs is the way to go. As I look at my daughter, I know I'm sowing the right kind of seeds. –Jo Ann

THE ENEMY'S PLAN FOR SINGLE WOMEN

Chapter 19

The Single Woman With a Tainted Past

My mother was a substance abuser. Whatever got and kept her on a high, she used it. I was the oldest girl so I remember doing anything to take care of my younger brothers and sister. I stole out of grocery stores to get food. I made up lies and begged people on the street for money. I even allowed men to have sex with me if it meant the difference between a meal and going to bed hungry. My mother always had men in and out of our home. So when I got a boyfriend in junior high, he moved in with us. My mother was very immoral and didn't care. By the time I was a sophomore in high school I had two kids of my own to care for and my boyfriend was a drug dealer. We were coming home from a night club one night and someone walked up to him and shot him in the head, point blank.

Somewhere in all this turbulence I met a Christian young man who led me to the Lord. Once I started reading the Bible, I realized how messed up my life was. But bit by bit God began to pick up the pieces of my life and make me into a new person. He still has a way to go but I'm confident of His love for me and His commitment to make me like His Son. I'm counting on Him.–Bernadine

There is one thing I never tire of and that is a story about someone being healed. The very idea of something all twisted, turned, and messed up being divinely touched by God, straightened out, and restored carries power. Whenever I read about such an incident in the Bible or hear about one, it renews my faith in what God can do. It motivates me to take my problems to Him no matter how impossible they may seem.

I can understand why Satan hates public testimonies about healing and restoration. I can just imagine his little demons covering their ears when someone stands up and says, "Let me tell you what God has done for me." I believe Satan calls special meetings to sabotage personal testimonies. He doesn't want the word to get out about what God can do when you turn it all over to Him.

Bernadine has a powerful testimony demonstrating the ability of God. Her first healing step was a meeting with Jesus. When God turned to Eve and said, "What is this that you have done?" (Genesis 3:13), it started a wonderful trend of the Divine One conversing with women. And God has been personally addressing women ever since. One such occurrence is the woman at the well found in the book of John.

JESUS HEALS A WOMAN WITH A TAINTED PAST

This incident with the woman Jesus met at the well is often used as an evangelistic tool to teach people how to share their faith. I agree. This is an ideal passage to convey those principles. God is also, however, using this passage to relate a serious, affectionate message to single or married women with a sexually damaged past.

Jesus initiated the conversation

There came a woman of Samaria.... Jesus said to her..."Give Me a drink...." The Samaritan woman therefore said to Him, "How is it that You, being a Jew, ask me for a drink since I am a Samaritan woman? For Jews have no dealing with Samaritans" (John 4:7-9).

Jesus began talking to this woman with an immoral lifestyle. This was even before the woman recognized who He was, repented, and became a changed person. Jesus initiated the conversation. She was not looking for Him, like the woman with the hemorrhage, or the woman with the demonic daughter (Matthew 9:20-22; 15:22-28). She came to draw water from the well. She was not looking for healing. As far as she knew, He did not even know she was wounded.

The woman, in fact, came to the well at a time when she thought no one would be there. This is a woman with a corrupt past. She had five husbands and was considered immoral. She did not want to endure the stares and ridicule of the other women in the city. This was a woman with layers of guilt and pounds of shame. When she saw Jesus sitting there she probably dropped her head, hoping He would not notice her.

But He was there specifically to see her, to set her free of the bondage of her sinful lifestyle and shame. She probably never would have said anything to Him at all–because of the facts, her past sins, her Samaritan background, and her position as a woman. (During Jesus' day Jewish rabbis did not ordinarily speak to women.) Jesus knew that in order to talk to this kind of woman, He would have to take the initiative, and for Him that was not a problem at all.

It is amazing how often Jesus breaks into our personal worlds and speaks to us–especially when we are engaged in activities that are not pleasing to Him. We may turn our backs on Him but He never turns His back on us.

I'll never forget the day I came home after my first abortion. It was my second year in college and I could not believe I had allowed myself to get into such a mess. The first day on campus I met a guy. I really didn't even like him. But I liked the attention he gave me. Maybe I was homesick. Maybe I saw an opportunity to finally experience what my friends had always said I was missing out on; I don't know. But before the week was out, we were in bed together.

That was the start of a promiscuous lifestyle in college. I let Satan convince me that once I started, I could not stop. I can't even remember how many sexual partners I have had. It's only by the grace of God that I did not contract a disease or AIDS. But I did get pregnant that second year of school. I never told the father of the baby. I just decided to take care of everything myself. And I did. I had an abortion that was quick, with very few discomforts.

The abortion procedure had gone so well physically that I didn't expect the rush of emotion when I got back to my room. The doctor had given me valium in case I experienced any pain. The pills were large and I remember attempting to commit suicide by swallowing them one by one. But they kept getting caught in my throat and one by one I had to run to the bathroom and choke them up. I lived on the second floor and there were bushes outside my window, so jumping would not even have hurt me. I did have a razor but the sight of blood always scared me so I knew I was too chicken to kill myself that way. I remember lying on my bed thinking, "I can't even kill myself. I can't do anything right."

It's hard to describe, but all of a sudden I began to sense the presence of the Lord. Although I was a Christian, ever since I found out I was pregnant I refused to talk to the Lord or read the Bible because I didn't want Him to talk me out of having an abortion. I felt I couldn't bear the embarrassment of it, nor face letting go of my career goals and becoming a single parent. But Jesus came anyway. In spite of my rejection. In spite of my past sins. It was like I could sense Him walking around my room, filling it with love and forgiveness. I didn't see any visions or hear any voices. But I knew God was speaking to me, telling me that He forgave me, telling me everything was going to be all right, to pick up and go on with my life.

I remember tears rolling down my face. I could not believe after what I had done that God accepted me and loved me in spite of myself. I couldn't believe that He would even speak to me again. I didn't even turn to Him. He came to me. And I'll be ever grateful that He did. –Wilma

Jesus identified Himself

Jesus answered and said to her, "If you knew the gift of God, and who it is who says to you, 'Give Me a drink,' you would have asked Him, and He would have given you living water....Whoever drinks of the water that I shall give him shall never thirst; but the water that I shall give him shall become in him a well of water springing up to eternal life.... I who speak to you am He" (John 4:10, 14, 26).

Three times Jesus had to identify himself to this woman. Sometimes Jesus has to speak several times and identify Himself with women who have been sexually active before marriage and who have led a sinful lifestyle before they can truly hear and understand who He is. But notice that Jesus is not irritated or hurried with the Samaritan woman and He does not mind repeating Himself until He is heard. He is the same with any woman who has a past filled with shameful activities.

Satan will say to the woman with an ungodly past, "You might as well run with me now. God is through with you. You are washed up with Him." He tries to make it difficult to hear the truth of God. But God will talk and keep on talking until you hear. In fact, He will make a special trip the long way around, if necessary, because He is looking specifically for you–as He did for the Samaritan woman. He deliberately and aggressively opens the conversation and keeps it going until you are open to hear the truth. However, we still must keep in mind that He gives us a choice whether to respond to Him or not. Jesus is a perfect gentleman and will never force Himself upon us.

Jesus told her what she needed.

..."If you knew the gift of God, and who it is who says to you, Give Me a drink, you would have asked him, and He would have given you living water...." She said to Him, "Sir,... Where then do you get that living water? You are not greater than our father Jacob, are You, who gave us the well, and drank of it himself....?" Jesus answered,..."Everyone who drinks of this water shall thirst again; but whoever drinks of the water that I shall give him shall never thirst; but the...well...springing up to eternal life." The woman said..."Sir give me this water, so I will not be thirsty, nor come all the way here to draw" (John 4:10-15)

Jesus was saying to this woman, "You need Me." She immediately began to tell Jesus that He had nothing with which to draw water. And what about Jacob? She didn't understand that He did not need a cup. And yes, someone far greater than Jacob sat in her presence. She was discussing the physical requirements of getting her thirst quenched, but Jesus was talking about the spiritual requirements of getting her soul's longings quenched. So it is with so many women today.

> In my early twenties I remember specifically struggling as a single person. In the afternoons I'd come home. I had worked hard and usually I was tired. My day had been full of different experiences and as I started up the steps, I would begin to murmur, "I have to go into this empty apartment again. I wish I had a husband to share my day with." I'd noticed over a period of time this daily habit picked up more bitterness and resentment. On one particular afternoon, I was doing my daily murmuring ritual coming up the stairs, I opened the door and it was as if Jesus said, "I'm here. I can share your day. Tell me all about it."

> After that coming home became a joy instead of a daily dread. Those first few minutes I came into the apartment before dinner and before the noise of my roommates, I would enjoy the silence and tell Jesus all about my day. He was there for me all the time. --Cindy

Jesus, in essence, said to the woman at the well, "Your search is over. Go no further. The relationship you are looking for is with Me." Unfortunately, many single women listen to what the world says and buy Satan's lie that a good relationship with a man will solve all. Some women go from man to man (and even some married women go from husband to husband–their's or someone else's) attempting to get their needs met. God is the only one who knows what our most intimate needs are and He is the only one who is powerful, gentle, and sensitive enough to meet them. The question is, will we wait and have confidence that He will do so?

Jesus told her about herself and her past life. *"Go call your husband and come here." "I have no husband." "You have well said....for you have five husbands, and the one you now have is not your husband...."* (John 4:17,18). Jesus forgives but we still have to face past failures. Wouldn't it be wonderful if we could go into a phone booth like Superman and come out a different person? Ever feel like it would all be okay if you could go back and do it all over again? God made no such provision. He heals, He restores, He has forgiven. But part of our healing oftentimes requires going back and facing the horror of the past.

Author Dorie Van Stone determined to go back to the orphanage where she suffered terrible perverted sexual treatment. As the tour guide showed her one particular room, Dorie recalled the events that took place there.

> This is the room where sexual abuse took place.... The part-time matron responsible for the abuses used to take me into this room and force me to participate in sexual activities with her. She was tough, overweight, and spoke in a harsh voice. She would grab me by the neck and slam my head against the wall. When she twisted my arms and legs and threatened cruel punishment, I had no option but to do as she ordered. No one had to tell me that such unnatural sexual experiences were wrong. Thankfully, that matron was eventually dismissed from her responsibilities and institutionalized. But memories of those horrible experiences dogged me for years. [1]

The woman giving the tour commented that Dorie did not show any signs of bitterness on her face or hate in her voice. This was Dorie's reply: "No, ma'am. You see, downstairs in the parlor, years ago, I met a Man named Jesus, and over a period of time He took away the bitterness and the hate. And now I am whole."

After Dorie completed the tour, and the woman had left with the others to go down to the lobby, Dorie took hold of the knob of that door where the abuse took place and prayed.

> Tears flowed down my face as I spoke to my heavenly father, my Friend who had saved me in that very building so many years ago. "Lord, thank You for letting me take this one last look at my past. Thank You for letting me know that all this is behind me. Thank You that I know that You have touched me and made me whole." That day as the woman closed the door to that last room, she didn't realize how firmly she was closing the door to an ugly chapter of my life. It was as if the past were forever put behind me and I could say 'It's all right.' And it enabled me to allow God to use me to help others close the same door. [2]

God is not trying to torture us by making us face our past. But He knows if we don't open some doors and reexamine the events, this time with His help and His perspective—we will never be able to move beyond certain points in our lives and effectively live for Him.

Jesus clears up misconceptions.
The woman said,.... "I perceive you are a prophet. Our fathers worshiped in this mountain, and you people say that in Jerusalem is the place where men ought to worship." Jesus said.... "Woman believe me, an hour is coming when neither in this mountain nor in Jerusalem shall you worship the Father. You

worship that which you do not know; we worship that which we know for salvation is from the Jews. But an hour is coming and now is, when the true worshipers shall worship the Father in spirit and truth; for such people the Father seeks to be His worshipers. God is spirit, and those who worship Him must worship in spirit and truth" (John 4:19-24).

The woman at the well had to come to know Jesus for who He really was, not by what she had heard about Him. Part of the healing process is to experience Jesus for who He really is not our preconceived notions of Him. "The boogie man is going to get you" is one phrase I heard most of my growing up years. I thought he lived in dark closets and I was always hesitant about opening closets in a dark room. It took several years of opening closets before I finally convinced myself that there is no boogie man in there and he is never coming out to do anything harmful to me.

In the same way, several things have been said about God that are misconceptions or outright untrue: "God will never forgive you for that." "God is not pleased with you." "If you keep doing that, God will leave you." No doubt this woman at the well thought less of herself because she imagined God thought less of her also. She was a Samaritan, a people that the Jews looked down upon and ostracized. Jesus let her know that God is no respecter of persons. At the cross, we are all "low down sinners" and all have the same problem. His love and forgiveness are the same for all.

The Word of God clears up the misconceptions we may have about who Jesus is and our relationship to Him. But you need to study it for yourself. When I study, I find that many things people have said, even preached about who God is, are just not true. But the Word of God has very reliable information and the straight facts. When you study it, ask Him to personally show you the truth of His Word. *"You shall know the truth and the truth will set you free"* (John 8:32)!

Jesus Set Her Free

The woman said to him, "I know that Messiah is coming.... When that one comes, he will declare all things to us." Jesus said,... "I who speak to you am He.".... The woman left her waterpot, and went into the city and said to the men, "Come see a man who told me all the things that I have done; this is not the Christ, is it" (John 4:25-29)?

When we get to this part of the story, we often forget that this is the same woman who was drawing her water at midday because she was ashamed to be seen. Now she ran into the city to tell the people, "Come see a man." After we encounter Jesus, the past is left behind and we are able to run and move forward. The chains have been broken and the heavy load removed from our shoulders.

In this particular case, the woman had one conversation and was set free. But that does not always happen. Sometimes, depending on a woman's individual experiences and how far she has strayed from God's principles, it may take time to peel off some of the layers before she truly realizes that God has truly set her free of her past. Such freedom, however, is possible and God wants you to have it.

Jesus could have walked up to this woman and simply said, "You are healed, emotionally and spiritually." But that is not His way. She needed to walk with Him through the entire process. Why? Why doesn't God just touch us and it is all done and cleared away? Because as God walks us through the process, with each step we become closer and closer to Him. As He peels off each layer we become more and more in love with the Person setting us free. That's exactly what happened to the Samaritan woman. He is waiting for hurting women today.

Many single women have met Jesus as the woman at the well did, and experienced the freedom and joy of being forgiven and given a fresh start. But I've often wondered how the Samaritan woman fared after that day. Did she go and pack her things and become one of the women who followed Jesus? Or when she got home, was the man she lived with there to meet her at the door, questioning her about where she had been? I wonder if he started touching her and tempting her to continue her life with him and Satan? Did she stand strong? Or did she give in? The next chapter includes practical steps a single woman can take to experience consistency in her Christian life and be that chosen vessel for God's use.

NOTES

1. Dorie VanStone and Erwin Lutzer, *No Place to Cry*, (Chicago: Moody Press, 1990), 37.

2. Ibid., 38-39.

Chapter 20

Countering Satan's Attack on Singles

One Sunday night at evening service I stayed and talked to one of the church counselors about some of my struggles and temptations. She went over several scriptures with me and we prayed together. I felt so renewed and ready to start over again. But as soon as I got to my apartment Satan started to rake up some of the same old thoughts. As long as I'm single, will it always be like this?–Alice

It doesn't matter if you are just leaving your teens and entering young single adulthood, if you have been single for a while, or if you suddenly find yourself single again. God is aware of the challenges you face. And as we have seen in the last two chapters, His loving arms and tender care are available to the single woman. But I do not want to leave it at that. In this chapter my goal is to arm the single woman with as much ammunition as I can to help her counter Satan's attack in the sexual areas.

GET A FRESH PERSPECTIVE
See your singleness in a new light. Ask God to help you see your time of being single, no mater how long or short, as a special gift from God. The first thing you should do when someone gives you a gift, even if it is something you don't want, is to thank that person for it. Maybe you need to get down on your knees right now and offer to God a prayer of thanksgiving for allowing you to have this time as a single woman.

I remember opening a gift from a friend once, and after I thanked her for it I had to ask, "Now what is it, and what am I suppose to do with it?" One of God's favorite things to do is give us information. Jeremiah 33:3 says, [*God speaking*] "Call to Me and I will show you great and mighty things that you do not know." God wants the single woman to come to Him and ask what He wants her to do with this time of singleness and how it can effectively be used. He will not leave us alone to figure it out.

One might automatically think God is going to tell singles to read the Bible half of their free time and to exclusively do church activities or Christian work with all the rest. This is not necessarily true. There are many things God may direct the single woman to do with this time God gives her. Even the single parent may be able to incorporate her children into a new adventure God shows her. God may encourage her to develop her career skills or change careers, to go back to school or get training in a new field, to take a temporary or permanent position in another country. This may be a time to develop a dream she has always tossed around–to start a business or offer a service. This may be a time to get some intense counseling for a personal problem she has yet to overcome. Finances may need some attention, and this may be the time to get a second job or learn how to invest. God may even want you, the single woman to work on your physical appearance, lose weight, learn what colors are best for you, and enhance your hair and make-up skills. It may be a time to organize your home or apartment–perhaps take a few classes in home improvement or interior decorating.

> A few years before I met George, I was paging through a technical school catalogue asking the Lord if I should take a few courses in something. For some reason I kept going back to the auto mechanic section and reading it over. Now mind you, I have never had an interest in cars and have always paid someone to have mine serviced. But for some reason, I decided to take this basic course in auto repair–thinking God wanted me to save money on car repair bills, or He could see that I might get stuck somewhere as a single woman and needed to know what to do. Anyway, the teacher made the class so interesting that after I took the basic course I ended up taking two more. By the end of the third class I could tear down a car engine if I had to and rebuild it, and I started working on my own car.
>
> A couple of years later I met George, who happened to own an auto repair shop. After we married I became his office administrator and I fit right in because of the courses I had taken a couple of years before. –Joyce

What Satan wants you to do is spend all your time moping, grumbling or complaining about lacking a man. Or he wants you to spend your single years doing all the wrong things, like working a job just for the money; with no personal growth or advancement opportunities and little or no personal satisfaction. He wants you to feel hopeless and stuck in your situation. But with God, nothing is impossible. If there is something God wants you to do, it can be accomplished in His timing and will.

The point is not to spend your time focusing on the fact that you are not married. More accurately, don't spend all your time focusing on the fact that you are not in a sexual relationship. Be honest with yourself. Ask yourself how much of your motivation to be married is based on sex itself. If it is the only motivation or most of it, then there is spiritual work yet for God to do in bringing balance to your life. Simply put, make sure you have given all your tendencies toward mere lust to God, allowing Him to replace them with a desire to give and receive genuine Christ-like love.

If we give the need for sex such a high calling in our thoughts we are not taking on God's perspective. We are no different than the rest of the world which deifies sex by plastering notions of it on the walls of buildings and billboards, flashing it constantly on the television screen, and singing about it, all too carelessly in the words of songs. So challenge yourself to get busy, first seeking God's view, and doing the things God puts in your mind to do. Pray about what things to do. They just may be in preparation of being the wife you so long to be. Remember the industrious woman in Proverbs 31 that we all admire so much? She is married, but she did not suddenly become a woman of virtue at the moment she said "I do." She prepared. Your first role is to be a vessel for Christ and His work. Prepare for and live it daily. Your sexuality, even as a single woman, is entwined with your role as God's vessel.

See your virginity or time of abstaining as a gift. Along with seeing your singleness as a gift, so should you value your virginity or celibacy. We have already extensively dealt with the definition and the biblical concept of virginity. But for the single woman who is past her teen years, has been sexually active for a long period of time, or is suddenly single again, it is necessary to rethink this area and make a new commitment to abstain. Just as you re-examined the whole idea of your singleness, begin to see your new virginity as a gift from God and give it back to Him. He wants to use your testimony as an example of His power and what He is able to do in a person's life.

As a symbol of your commitment, buy yourself something expensive, fragile, and beautiful. Set it so that you can see it daily to remind yourself that it represents your virginity, something special and expensive that needs to be handled with the utmost care. Imagine yourself giving this outward symbol to your husband on your wedding night if you marry or remarry. Remind yourself of how much this gift costs when you are tempted or impatient about giving it away.

Society has made virginity a shameful word and the idea of abstaining from sex before marriage a joke. As believers we, however, need to view it differently. Ask God to help birth in you a new appreciation for seeing and doing things God's way and not simply following the trends of the world. Ask Him to give you a sense of self-worth, not shame, about your commitment to abstain. When your friends who are sexually active tease you about what you are missing, ask God for the boldness and courage to hold your head high and confidently know within yourself that you have made the right decision.

Sex is God's gift to a married couple to accomplish unity in their relationship. Now Satan will attempt to add to God's original purpose, claiming it as a valid form of recreation for unmarried people, a way to experience true intimacy, a way to get over a broken heart or the death of a spouse, or a way to get and keep a man. But these are all **LIES FROM THE PIT**. When you listen to and follow Satan's lies instead of God's truth, you are now serving Satan as your 'god.' As a result, you will be more depressed and broken hearted than you thought you were before. You have actually given place to Satan in your life.

> At the age of eight, I was sexually abused by the senior pastor of my church and by my mother's boyfriend. As a result, during my teen years, I rebelled against church and any morals.

> In my early twenties, I came back to the Lord after two Christian men witnessed to me. I had been dating a man, I'll call him Bo, for five years. He was a 33rd degree mason who was heavily involved in the occult. I remember watching Bo masturbate at times and his face would take on forms that were not human. He would look like a monster. In fact, he told me that a lot of his sexual activity was done to gain more demonic power.

> I broke up with Bo after becoming a Christian: however, he did not want to let me go. He would harass me constantly. He was very possessive. He would come to my house morning, noon, and evening to see if I was there. He would stand outside my window and beg me to take him back. He promised me anything I wanted. He offered me expensive gifts. Sometimes he would even bring expensive products with him to show me from the window. He had been taking care of me before we broke up. He used to pay all of my bills. It was hard for me to resist his offers especially when my bills were due, because I did not have a job. But I did not let him back into my life.

In the first months of my Christian life I experienced a lot of strange things, for example, my Bible falling off my shelf, shadowy figures in the room, and pricking sensations in my toes. Sometimes Bo would call me and I would experience excruciating headaches just like someone sticking a pin in my head. I would call on the name of Jesus and the pain would stop immediately. Bo would just laugh.

One day, an overwhelming, unnatural lustful feeling came over me. I felt like if I did not do something to release it, I would burst. I really did not want to have anything to do with Bo but I couldn't help myself. I felt like I was out of control, something was driving me. I called him at work and asked him to come over. Of course, he was happy to accommodate me and was at my door within five minutes.

During intercourse, it felt like something entered me. I felt so dirty afterwards. He got up and just laughed uncontrollably. He gave me money for my bills and left. Not long after that, I felt I had to get away from him so I moved. I knew he wouldn't leave me alone, especially since I had invited him back and had sex with him that time. Since he came to check on me before going to work, at noon and in the evening, I had arranged for nothing to appear abnormal in the morning and to be gone by the time he came back at noon. It worked and I did not see him for six months.

In the meantime, I had gone to a church service that emphasized deliverance. I had no intentions of going up to the altar for prayer. I was very skeptical of all that was going on in the service. But something drew me to the altar and knocked me on my knees. They prayed for me and I felt a definite release of a bondage. I knew something had left me.

Not too long after that, Bo ran into me at a gas station and followed me to my new apartment. I had not told him what happened at the church service, but it was evident from one of the first comments he made that he knew about the deliverance experience. To this day, I believe he had knowingly transferred a demonic spirit into me during that last time we had sex. He knew the demonic influence he had over me had been broken.

I maintained celibacy for another six months. This was a very long time for me. Then I met another guy, nicknamed Satan. The first time I kissed him, I saw yellow slanted eyes. I was hooked again. This time, I conceived my son.

I wanted to stay with the baby's father and still be a Christian, but he did not want anything to do with Christianity. I was backslidden and wasn't going to church. Then one day, my cousin, a Christian, told me he had a message from God. The message was, "Daughter, I am calling you."

That made an impact on me and I started going to church. One day the preacher spoke some verses from the Word that I knew were especially for me. He said, "Repent or I'll remove my candlestick." It was like the Word went all through me. The Lord helped me get back on track by taking my son's father away from me. I did not see him for seventeen months. My experience of seeing the demonic aspects of sex and hearing God's clear voice to me has kept me celibate for over twelve years. His grace has been sufficient. He has not even let me get into a situation where I've been tempted. The enemy has sent his tools but God has been faithful to make me aware of them. --Sherise

This is why it is important for those who are not married to stay sexually pure. It is possible that demons can be transmitted through sexual encounters. One of the ways God intended for couples to become one flesh in marriage was through their sexual relationship. When people have sex outside of marriage (including lustful petting and touching) they open themselves up to unclean spirits. The unclean spirits may have access to their bodies, minds and emotions or their circumstances.

For on account of a harlot one is reduced to a loaf of bread, and an adulteress hunts for the precious life.... The one who commits adultery with a woman [man] is lacking sense; He who would destroy himself [*herself*] does it, [i.e. destroys his own soul] (Proverbs 6:26; 32).

Corinthians also emphasizes that when one is joined with a harlot, *"the two become one flesh"* (1 Corinthians 6:16-18).[1]

View your sexual urges positively. It would have been ideal if God had designed us with a turn-on turn-off switch for our sexual urges. But He did not. These feelings are a part of His special design and they need to be appreciated, not hated. They keep us from being hard-hearted and they prevent us from taking emotional stances reflected in such statements as, "I'll never get into another relationship with a man." They help us to be warm and tender toward the opposite sex, and to constantly desire to develop friendships and relationships with men.

Rick Stedman, the author of *"Pure Joy"*, offers these suggestions for dealing with sexual urges:

Use the attraction as a reminder that God has created you to be a relational person, and make it just one more opportunity to commit yourself to developing personal wholeness and whole relationships. When this happens to me, rather than staring at the woman (or billboard, or TV commercial, or whatever), I glance up to the heavens and offer up a prayer like this:

I thank you, God, for this reminder that you created me to be a relational person. I re-commit myself here and now to developing whole, godly relationships that reflect Your image.... I will not engage my mind with this picture. Instead, dear Lord, I pray for those other, quality relationships that I am now working on. First I pray for my friendship with _____. [2.]

The author explains that he is not trying to give a simplistic answer to temptations and sexual urges. He is not saying to just pray about it and, like magic formula your urges will go away. But he is saying that we need to include God in every detail of our lives. This is a positive way to put God's light on something that could turn into something very dark, like lust, sexual fantasies, or even the outright immoral sexual act. This kind of praying also keeps sexual urges in the positive position that they should be.

Be sure not to feed your sexual urges with things that are not pleasing to the Lord. Keep your eyes from things that make tempting situations easier to give in to. Movies and television programs, soaps operas with sexually explicit scenes, pornography, and sensual novels should always be evaluated with this thought in mind. Keep men out of the bedroom of your mind and it will be easier to keep them out of the bedroom of your house. The hymn "Yield Not to Temptation" has a line in it that says, "Each victory will help you, some other to win." Each time you do not allow yourself to give into prolonged sexual thoughts and sexual behaviors, it gives you more positive self-worth in the form of more confidence that you can win other difficult battles.

Some women address their sexual urges by masturbation. We have already discussed the biblical aspects and disadvantages of this behavior in Chapter 10. However, some single women have practiced this activity and by now it has become a habit.

In order to break free from this habit Berry St. Clair and Bill Jones in *Sex: Desiring God's Best* offer these suggestions:

(1) Be honest with God (1 John 1:9); (2) make up your mind that this is gratifying the flesh (Galatians 5:16) and that you will no longer engage in such activity; (3) realize you need the power of Jesus Christ to help you (Ephesians 3:16); (4) renew your mind (Romans 12:1-2); spend time with God in His Word daily; (5) stay away from lustful books, magazines,

programs, movies or whatever may cause you to have lustful thoughts (Matthew 6:22-23); (6) discipline your body (1 Corinthians 9:27); (7) talk to someone about the problem (Ecclesiastes 4:9-10); (8) press on despite failure (Matthew 18:22); and (10) be confident that you can be free (Romans 6:11-14).[3]

When you feel prone to engage in lustful thinking or masturbation, invite God into those times of struggle through prayer. He's already there watching you, so realize He is available to you. Thank Him for His presence, ask for His strength, and confess the battle waging inside. This is a time when meditation on victorious scripture verses is helpful. Practically, get busy with some physical exercise, keep busy, and nurture healthy relationships with other people.

AVOIDING SATAN'S "HE" TRAPS
All of us, married or single, want to be liked, appreciated, and given attention. As we have just seen, our sexual urges and attractions are built into God's design. But when a man comes into our lives and a relationship ("relationship" means any contact you have with a person that goes beyond passing on the street–from talking socially every now and then to exclusive dating) starts to develop, Satan can weasel his way in and turn it into a situation that is not pleasing to us or God. Below are some guidelines and suggestions to help us keep Christ in the center of all of our relationships.

Before you get into a relationship with a man. As I mentioned in the section called "Seeing singleness in a new light," get busy cultivating new interests and activities. Learn to love yourself and to appreciate YOU outside of a relationship with a man. This is especially important for a person who is recently widowed or divorced. You need to define who you are apart from a man. God has given you special worth of your own.

Learn to cultivate female friendships. I've heard so many women say that they do not have any friends. This is sad. One of the ways in which God wants to fill our relationship needs is through female friendships. Married women who have a good friendship relationship with their husbands can tell you that they also appreciate their female friends. There are certain needs that only woman-to-woman relationships can meet. It also keeps you from just overwhelming a man with all your problems, concerns, personal struggles, and life history.

Develop other ways to channel your physical energies. Our bodies are not just for sitting and eating. Many of us have physical ailments because we don't do any physical exercise. Grab a friend and commit to walking in the mall early in the morning. Join a health club. Purchase an exercise machine and make a date with it every night during the ten o'clock news.

You will feel much better mentally and physically. I am told that when we exercise, we release certain chemicals in our bodies which help ward off mental illness, depression, and stress.

Find a prayer partner to pray with you regularly and specifically about your relationships with men and your sexual temptations. She should be someone you can call on anytime for support and encouragement to do the right things. Be honest with her about your struggles. Give that person permission to do whatever is necessary to help you through a difficult time. Talk to God about who to choose. If necessary, have your confidante talk to the person who may be pressuring you to act contrary to what you know is right.

Have your prayer partner pray with you, particularly at certain times during your menstrual cycle. Beginning a certain number of days after a woman's menstrual period hormonal changes in her body cause her to desire sex more than at other times. Study your body to determine when those times are. Be aware of your urges during this time, and make sure these particular days are covered with prayer and that you keep out of compromising situations.

As soon as you see a man and you say to yourself, "M-M-M, I wonder who that is!", your next line should be a prayer to the Father, "Lord, take control of my thoughts and actions from here on out. If this is a person you want me to get to know, please work it out in Your own time and Your own way." Sometimes we pray this prayer after the relationship gets rolling. By that time, our thoughts may be out of control. In our minds we may have already taken him to the marriage altar, had the honeymoon, and raised two kids. Invite God in as soon as you can for His help and control of our thoughts.

Think through personal guidelines for your relationships. You may think this is only for parents to do with teens who are starting to date, but having these guidelines filed away in your mind just might keep you out of a compromising situation as well. Here are a few to get you started.

- Only date Christians. Be aware of your own needs for attention and affection. You may meet someone who does not share your spiritual commitment. He may begin to meet some of your companionship needs, but you know this relationship is not God's will or God's best for you. Take a tip from Solomon; his wives led him away from his relationship with God. You need a Christian who is headed in the same direction you are.

- Beware of close associations with men who are baby Christians. When a new man joins the church, sometimes the single women pounce on him like white on rice. The man needs time to grow. The men in the church should disciple him, not an available single woman. You may find that this man is saved from the waist up but that he has not yet sanctified himself from the waist down.

• Do not touch or allow yourself to be touched in ways that go beyond normal affection for a friend or a brother in Christ. In 1 Timothy 5:2 Christian men are instructed to treat young woman as sisters, "in all purity." This is the way you should insist on being treated.

Once the relationship gets going. Learn to develop friendships with men, without any expectations, without deep emotional attachments, and without pressure. Men will really appreciate it.

I just wanted to have a few female friends, someone to attend activities with, and to talk to from time to time. But as soon as I attempt to do this with a few ladies, especially in the church, I find myself being given all kinds of firm ultimatums, sensual signals, and even marriage proposals.
–Henry

If you are in a friendship with a man and have been for quite a while, beware of the grey areas in the relationship. "Hazy relationships are attractive but never wise." speaks to that time between friendships and that solid commitment to get married. Spend some time alone with the Lord and let Him help you get your thoughts straightened out. Don Merideth, in his book, *Who Says Get Married,* clearly helps singles understand how to deal with grey areas in relationships.

This time may seem grey to you but there are never any grey areas with God. God's purposes in a relationship are always specific concrete and absolute. We should never fool ourselves into believing God's will is hazy. God will always say no to a relationship until he says it is time to say yes. We all want to do what we want to do. There is something in all of us that hates absolutes. And we hate the absolute no's in dating for two reasons. They keep us from dabbling in sexual areas and they keep the wrong relationships from developing into marriage. Especially when we are desperate, simply to get married.

The following guideline is a accurate way to evaluate this troubled state. We need to be asking, where is this relationship going? Am I in God's will? I encourage singles to continue in the friendship relationship as long as the following statements are true:

- Neither person's life goal, such as job, friends church goals, recreational artistic pursuits are being negatively affected by the relationship.

- Neither person's spiritual life is negatively affected by the relationship.

- Neither party begins to participate in or depends on activities that God intends for marriage. For example, sexual involvement, inordinate emotional dependence, too much time together, all of which upset the balance of other commitments. [5]

If you believe God is moving you into a serious, more committed relationship, let the man take the initiative. Women should not try to manipulate the relationship and push the man into a corner. Allow the Lord to deal with your heart and feelings toward this person. You just continue to build the friendship.

Beware of playful or serious teasing, and be aware of double messages and game playing. Ask God to examine your ways and conversation. Are you verbally saying no to sexual involvement in the relationship but dressing sexy or making seductive innuendoes? Are you saying you are going to allow the Lord to lead in the relationship, but then accept expensive gifts which make you feel obligated to spend more time with the person than you ought? Be careful to be honest with God, yourself, and each other. If you are a new Christian and have been sexually active up to this point, you might consider having a mature Christian woman give you some pointers on dress, make-up, and an overall appearance that does not attract ungodly attention from men.

> When I became a Christian, I had no idea how I was to conduct myself as a godly woman. At first the women in my church just talked about the way I looked and acted. That really hurt because I really didn't know what I was doing wrong. Finally an older woman took me under her wing and began to disciple me. She gently helped me to understand the sensuous way in which I carried myself and she gave many helpful suggestions. Thank God for older godly women. –Sue

AVOID SATAN'S REMARRIAGE TRAPS
One way Satan will take advantage of a woman considering marriage the second time around is through confidence. "I'm older now; I know what I want. I've been this route before." Satan can use that self-assured attitude to deceive you into marrying the wrong man.

Do not marry an unbeliever. The Bible says, *"Do not be bound together with unbelievers..."* (2 Corinthians 6:14). Scripture teaches very clearly that a Christian woman is not to marry a non-Christian man. If you have any doubts about why this is not God's best provision for you, talk with an honest Christian woman who has been married to a non-Christian man for years. Such a discussion may help you make the right decision. If he is the one for you, God can save and grow him up in the Lord before you get married.

Marrying a prince who turns out to be a toad. One author, Zig Ziglar, in *Courtship After Marriage* suggests a two-year courtship in order to really get to know a person. On the other hand, those who warn against sexual temptation recommend a short courtship. They encourage the couple to take the plunge, the rationale being that you don't really know a person until you are married to him anyway. I will not debate this issue here. But I will echo the words of Mrs. Ruth Stanford Peale: [6]

> Study your man. Study him as if he were some rare, strange, and fascinating animal. Study him constantly because he will be constantly changing. Study his likes and dislikes, his strengths and weaknesses, his moods and mannerisms. Just loving a man is fine, but it's not enough. To live with someone successfully you have to know him. And to know him, you have to study him.

> **Observe in various settings the man you are about to marry.**
> If you want to get to know someone, you don't do it by spending long days and late nights together.... Life is not made up of moonlit walks. Spend time in groups–different kinds of groups, young kids, old kids, friends, families, co-workers, Christians non-Christians. Do things together that allow you to see him shine like a star, as well as fail miserably. Reality is day-to-day life, not intimate conversations hour after hour. [7]

Don't make sexual pressure the sole criteria for marriage. Do not base your decision to marry on sexual needs. Satan can use this to keep a single person from being in God's will. Satan will constantly badger your flesh and even encourage you to make a hasty decision to marry. Remember, he does not want you to make an objective, well-thought out, prayed-over, Spirit-led decision. .

Be sure that the marriage is the right thing for your children. If you have children, consider them in your decision. This is not just a new husband for you, but also a new father for them. They should be included in some aspect of the premarital counseling process. They may have attitudes of bitterness, resentment, and hostility that need to be worked out.

A CHALLENGE TO YOU AND THE CHURCH

Being a single adult woman may not include the same kinds of pressures that can beset a teenage girl, but it still has its satanic traps. Because adult singles are just that–adults–the world can look upon a woman's decision not to follow God's ways regarding singleness as just a matter of personal choice. As sad as it is, too many times even our churches share this same view. The pastor, the leaders, and the congregation all look away when women and men allow their chronological maturity and experience to dictate their lifestyles before God. As Christians, however, our choices are always to include God and His will even if no one else, including the church, seems committed to His ways.

I challenge YOU, however, to see your singleness and your commitment to live a life of sexual purity as more than just a benefit to your spirituality and relationship with God. See it as a testimony to all young women in your home, your neighborhood, and especially your church. Living the life that God prescribes is possible indeed, even as we move through the various stages of adulthood. Your example of a godly mature single adult may be just the incentive a young woman needs to continue living her life for Christ.

> In my twenties, I attended a large church that taught the young people to abstain from sex before marriage. In fact, that was a message that was often preached. What confused me, though, was that there were single women my age, some with positions in the church, who had pretty blatant relationships with men that included sex. In a couple of cases, the young women became pregnant, one of them twice. I have to admit that at the time, I was not living the way God wanted, either. But seeing these women kind of gave me an excuse to continue doing what I was doing. After all, if the pastor didn't say anything and the church didn't seem to notice, I thought maybe no one took God's commandment about sex seriously.

> I am now in my forties, still single, but now living the way God wants. It is always encouraging to me to learn of other women my age who are living the celibate life, or to hear of churches who even teach it as a modern-day principle. When I ask my friends about what their churches have to say about sex before marriage among adults, I am still amazed at the number who say their churches don't even talk about it and they ignore what they see. If that is all the encouragement we get from our leaders, it comes as no surprise that more single adults are not living by the Word.
> –Beth

In a loving way, which God can reveal to you, challenge your church to take a stand against sexual sin among adults. First start by being an example, by clearing up your own sins, if you have some in this area. Ask God to help you let go of any relationship where the person insists that you have sex with him. In fact, pray that God will begin to lovingly convict him of his own sinful behavior.

Talk to your church leaders about your concerns for the young people. Ask for permission to begin programs or activities to encourage young and older unmarried women to remain sexually pure. Perhaps part of the plan could be a mentor program, a Bible study on sexual purity, or even a prayer gathering on just this one subject.

Find other women who are committed to God's way. If there are none in your church, ask God to turn some other women's hearts around to doing things His way. Finally, pray for your pastor that he may see the spiritual appropriateness of taking a courageous stand against sexual sin in the congregation. Pray that God will prepare you, and the entire congregation, to receive and be obedient to God's mandates of sexual purity. The prayers prayed and the examples set by this generation can have a profound impact on how much or how little Satan sexually attacks our future women and girls.

As we conclude this section on the single woman, I hope you come away with a renewed sense of God's presence and care, and more excited about how God wants to mold and re-shape His unmarried vessel to bring Him greater glory during this time in your life.

NOTES

1. Dottie Hewitt and Donna Morse, *Deliverance Training*, (Water Park Florida: House of Beth-el Ministries, 1989), 10.
2. Rick Stedman, *Pure Joy*, (Chicago: Moody Press, 1993), 109-112.
3. St. Clair and Jones, *Sex: Desiring God's Best*, 101-114.
4. Mary Yerex, *I'd Rather be Single for the Rest of My Life Than be Married to the Wrong Guy* (San Bernardino: Integrated Resources, Division of Campus Crusade for Christ) audio tape.
5. Ibid.,
6. Zig Ziglar, *Courtship After Marriage*, (Nashville: Thomas Nelson Inc., 1990), 26.
7. Yerex.

EXERCISES

1. Look up scriptures which address or minister to particular needs you have as a single woman. For example look up the words <u>widow,</u> <u>divorce,</u> <u>virgin,</u> or <u>not married</u> and see what God has to say about these concepts. Ask yourself these simple questions: What is God saying? What does He mean? (You may need to use a dictionary, a study Bible, or a commentary to answer this one.) What does He want me to do? Do I change my thinking? Do I change my way of living?

2. Think of ways you are pleasing God now in your single state.

3. Write down the benefits of waiting on God, especially in the sexual areas of singleness.

4. Use these guidelines to help you develop a list of activities that should be avoided to not feed temptations. Think of things to replace these. Write down the victories and immediately confess the failures.

5. Pray for a female friend or friends who may also be struggling with their singleness. Ask God to help them give their single state to Him to be used and completed according to His will. Pray that all the single women in your church will stand firm on God's commandments regarding sexual activity. Before you begin any of these prayers, pray for yourself. Ask Him to help you gain victory in your own struggles with singleness.

6. List the times God saved you from bad relationships or sinful activity. Thank Him for each one.

7. Keep a prayer journal and keep track of what God is teaching you about singleness from His perspective. Every day thank God for at least one reason for being single that applies to that day.

8. Ask God if there is an activity that He specially wants you to do to help single women in their efforts to remain sexually pure.

Section Four

Satan's Sexual Attack on The Married and Older Woman

SEASONED AFFECTION

Chapter 21

Intimacy in Marriage

When I was a little girl, I remember finding some long lacy curtains in my grandmother's basement. I remember holding the panels on the top of my head and pretending that I was a bride. Most little girls do this kind of thing. We all think about our wedding day, our Prince Charming, and living happily ever after.

The sad reality is that more than one out of two marriages in the United States ends in divorce. Of the couples who stay married, many are unhappy. In new marriages, the sexual intimacy that the world promotes as the ultimate experience is often disappointing. When expectations do not match the experience, a couple must be careful not to allow the chief enemy of marriage and the family to bring in feelings of insecurity and distrust. Left unattended, these thoughts and anxieties can grow and undermine the very foundation of the marriage.

While writng this book, it was interesting to note that, when I mentioned the subject matter to married women, several of them did not see a need to read it. Their response was, "Oh, I've got a teenage daughter and I'm sure this will be helpful to her," or "I've got a single friend who has been sexually abused and she needs this book." Somehow Satan has convinced the married woman that he no longer attempts to destroy her by sexual means since she is now married. This is one of Satan's biggest deceptions.

After all, God ordained the institution of marriage and gave sex to married couples as a very special gift. Sex was meant to be an act of not only physical but spiritual bonding. Sex in marriage unites two people with Him, intertwining them, giving the world a picture of God's love and oneness with mankind. Satan would be overjoyed if he could cause married people never to experience sexual satisfaction and oneness. If he succeeds, the couple will not be as effective in living out God's purposes and plans.

Without a doubt, Satan is on his job. Women sometimes cheat on their spouses the same as men. Often Satan entices women when marital and sexual bliss are not present as expected. The disappointed wife looks elsewhere for romance or more sensitivity to her emotional needs.

Some women, on the other hand, stay with their husbands, but resign themselves to marital disharmony, depression, or bitterness. Some turn their attention away from their mate and smother their children with too much attention or spend all their time developing a career. Satan loves this kind of dysfunction in families. It not only upsets families but the women's relationship with God is usually casual and distant as well. The woman may blame God for letting her marry this man. She may even think that God tricked her into believing marriage would be wonderful when, for her, it is the worst time of her life.

> No one in my family ever got a divorce. I'm not going to be the first one. But I'll let you in on a little secret. I hate my husband. Everyday I wish he would die. Getting married was the worst mistake I ever made. –Laura

Before we look at the specific ways Satan causes havoc with the sexual intimacy of married couples and related emotional problems, let's look at what God wanted from this relationship. If we don't know what God intended originally in this area, it is a lot easier for Satan to play on our ignorance and sow his lies.

GOD'S SEXUAL INTIMACY INSTRUCTION BOOKLET

To understand what God had in mind when He ordained marriage, especially in the intimate areas–the Song of Solomon is an ideal place to go. Here God lays out His ideal couple for those who are planning to marry and for those already married. As we look at this model, we can see how Satan has eaten away at what God wants, injecting misery and thwarting emotional and spiritual growth. Many of the following concepts are based on information from *A Song for Lovers,* a commentary by S. Craig Glickman.

The book. I realize in the Christian community that there is an ongoing debate as to whether the Song of Solomon speaks of the relationship between Israel and God, Christ the groom and the church His bride, a Christian individual and Christ, or a husband and wife. I believe there is much we can learn in this book about all of these relationships. I would love to take the time to parallel them and present a picture of how much God loves us and how much we can love Him in return.

I also believe God wanted to paint a picture of courtship and marriage in the Song of Solomon, to give us specific guidelines on these important matters. Other passages in the Bible deal with marriage, but this is the only place that addresses in so much detail courtship, marriage, and intimacy within marriage.

The Song of Solomon is not a book that can simply be picked up, read, and understood like some other books in the Bible. This one takes a little time to study through and understand the imagery and symbolism. I encourage every engaged couple and every married couple to take the time to do so. There are books that can help you interpret the message. It is well worth the time and effort to see and understand God's original design for courtship, marriage, and intimacy. Then we can clearly see the areas in which Satan has attacked this beautiful union which was created to glorify and exemplify Jesus Christ's unity and relationship with us, His children.

Let me say here at the beginning, that one of the conclusions a married woman might come to once she looks at the love Solomon receives from the Shulamite woman is, "This is impossible! I could never love my husband this way," you say. You think this especially considering all of the misunderstandings, hurts, and wounds that have been inflicted during the marriage and before. Remember, the Bible is a book of high principles and standards most of which are unattainable if we try to reach them through our own ability and power. When we say, "I can't," God says, "I'm glad you realize that, so you are going to have to rely totally on Me, and I CAN." God wants women to trust Him daily to make the necessary changes in their lives.

I would love to outline the Song of Solomon word for word but that would be another book all by itself. I will just highlight certain parts pertaining to our subject. Basically there are two people here who are developing a relationship which ends up in marriage. In the historical account Solomon is the male person and the author of the book. The Shulamite woman is the woman he falls in love with and marries.

GOD'S EXPECTATIONS IN THE COURTSHIP RELATIONSHIP

What happens before a couple marries will determine quite a bit of what happens within the marriage. In the friendship and courtship interactions, good or bad habits are being developed which may be sustained in the marriage. This is a time when the couple either can make some wise decisions which will strengthen their relationship or plant some destructive seeds that will spring up to do major damage to the relationship after the marriage takes place.

The male should be the aggressive one in the relationship. "May he kiss me with the kisses of his mouth" (Song of Solomon 1:2). The Shulamite starts out longing and waiting for Solomon to be the initiator in the relationship. In the next two verses, she continues to desire and encourage him to make the first move. [1]

It is popular and acceptable in our times for a woman to see a man she likes, call him up, ask him out, and even take the initiative in seducing him. Many times the woman will do all the work in keeping a courtship going. Guess who will probably do all the work in keeping the marriage together? God told the *man* to leave mother and father and cleave to his wife (Genesis 2:24), placing the responsibility for the marriage staying together on the husband.

Understand clearly that a single female in a relationship should still be making her own decisions about the direction of her life. Husband headship and wifely submission belong in marriage only, not in courtship. However, she should allow him to be the initiator in the relationship. He should ask her to marry him, not the other way around.

The person you are to marry should have good character. Not only did the Shulamite love Solomon and think highly of his character, but those around her thought highly of him, too. "Your name is like purified oil, therefore the maidens love you" (1:3). Many times young women are so enthralled with their young prince that they cannot see that he is really a frog. That's why premarital counseling is a must–to give both persons a more realistic look at the other, at strengths and weaknesses which could cause conflict in the marriage.

The Shulamite also called Solomon a shepherd. It may not necessarily mean that he was one professionally, but she may have been reflecting on his shepherd-like character. Shepherds are gentle, kind, and caring, but also strong and courageous.

The person we are about to marry should not be someone we are ashamed of, or someone we feel is ashamed of us. *"He has brought me to his banquet hall" and "his banner over me is love"* (2:4). Solomon took her out and showed her off. He wanted everyone to know this was the lady he was to marry. And she felt the same way. [2]

> Everyone thought I shouldn't marry the person I married, my parents, my brother, my pastor, and all my friends. I was so in love I didn't care what anyone had to say. We ran off and eloped. Now that we are married I wish I had listened to what every one was saying. The old saying is true, "Love is blind, but marriage is an eye opener." – Maggie

The marriage bed should be undefiled. In the seventh verse of chapter 1, we see the Shulamite concerned about where and when she meets with Solomon. "Tell me, O you whom my soul loves, where do you pasture your flock, where do you make it lie down at noon? For why should I be like one who veils herself beside the flocks of your companions?" In that culture, a veiled woman was a woman of questionable morals or even a prostitute. She did not want to give the impression that she was like this kind of woman. Up to the time of marriage she carried herself with decency and respect.[3]

God also realizes once a man and woman commit themselves to be married, they desire to express their love physically. The Shulamite says, *"I am lovesick"* (2:5). God knows all about the human fleshly war that will rage within our members. Satan will take advantage of this vulnerable time and attempt to give couples every excuse in the book not to wait. God, however, says wait.

God wants couples to wait until marriage because, first of all, courtship is not marriage, and sex is to bring unity and warmth to the marriage relationship. To open God's gift before it is time is like taking a cake out of the oven when it's only half done. Oh sure, it will taste okay, but it will be flat and doughy and will not bring the satisfaction that it would have had it been allowed to cook fully. Sex before marriage spoils the fullness of pleasure God intends.

> It was hard, but my boyfriend and I made a commitment to not have sex before our wedding. Instead of sitting around our apartments trying to keep our hands off each other, we volunteered to help the youth minister in our church. After that, we rarely had any time to be alone. If we were not going somewhere with the youth, we were counseling one or two of them, or having them for dinner or a sleep-over. I really got a chance to see what my future husband might be like as a father. It made me appreciate him more. I'm glad we decided to give that time to the Lord. I know it has made a difference in our marriage. And that honeymoon night–it was great! –Amy

The relationship should mutually build up one another. The Shulamite often compared herself with other women and felt insecure, but Solomon built her up and helped to strengthen her self-perception. *"If you yourself do not know, [you are] most beautiful among women...."* (1:8). A woman who engages in sex before marriage usually looks down on herself for giving in. The prospective spouse who keeps pressuring her to sin in this area is obviously trying to get his own "needs" met, without concern for how this activity might be affecting her spiritually and emotionally (and none of this is to say that he should not be concerned about his own sin).

The man about to marry should be helping his future bride to grow, develop, and mature spiritually and emotionally. He should never cause her to be brought down. A man who cannot accept a woman's godly convictions cannot have her best interest at heart.

The relationship should include God. It appears that one of Solomon's and the Shulamite's favorite things to do was to take long walks together, talking and enjoying the beauty of God's creation (1:17). It's unfortunate when two people are so engrossed with each other that they forget about God and His desire to be recognized in their relationship. If prayer, Bible study, Christian activities, and ministry are not a part of your courtship, they probably will not be a part of your marriage.

Both parties should be single-minded about the other. *[You are] like a lily among thorns" (2:2). "Beloved is mine and I am his"* (2:15). In other words, "I only have eyes for you." Beware of a man who is engaged to you, but his eye is still roving.

> I knew my boyfriend had a problem with other women, but I thought once we got married, I would have him and he would be totally mine. Well, marriage made no difference to him. I married him but a lot of other women still were getting a piece of him. –Wilma

Love needs time to develop and it can't be forced. *"...That you will not arouse or wake my love until she pleases"* (2:7). Solomon says this several times throughout the book. He is exhibiting patience toward his future bride. They first develop a friendship, followed by courtship and then marriage. The first two stages enhance the sex in marriage. Sex is meant to bring a deeper bonding and commitment, and takes the relationship beyond the commitment levels present in friendship and courtship. When this special tool to boost the relationship along is used before marriage, its full impact and force are diminished, and the marriage can stagnate or actually sink.

Both parties should be protective about anything that harms the relationship. Sex before marriage is harmful to the relationship but so are pride, selfishness, and unforgiveness. *"Catch the little foxes for us..."* (2:15). Both Solomon and his loved one are trying to keep harmful things out of the relationship. Both the man and the woman need to understand potential problems from God's perspective so they both can work hard at operating on a level that is pleasing to the Lord. Without a mutual godly perspective, the little foxes may be next to impossible to put away. Left unbridled, they can surely damage the sexual relationship.

> My husband struggled with homosexuality years before he met me. When we were engaged to be married, he confessed this to me. I insisted that he

go through counseling and committed myself to go through it with him. We went into this marriage with our eyes wide open, knowing the possible problems. Now that we are married, we still go periodically to talk with our counselor about trouble spots in our relationship. I think the key is that we are both committed to working on this thing together.—Doris

I was dating Gil, who said he had a relationship with the Lord. But when I would tell him that I needed to pray about something, he would ask, "Why do you need to pray about it?"—especially when it seemed to him that the answer I was seeking was pretty clear. There were several other things that I felt uncomfortable about with him, too. But that one attitude and those comments really made me leery of how he would approach problems if we were married.—Tia

THE WEDDING NIGHT AND THE MARRIAGE
The wedding night together should be special. Solomon is not sleeping off a hangover on his wedding night as too often is the case today. Instead, he is able to talk with his bride. He realizes this is a special night for her but that it also might be frightening. He appears patient and is ready to slowly guide her through this time.

First of all, he expresses his adoration verbally. He is not just interested in one part of her, but he starts at the top of her head and he works his way down, talking with her, complimenting her, making her feel special (4:1-7). *"How beautiful you are, my darling, How beautiful you are!"* (4:1).

He realizes that she is a virgin and that she might be apprehensive. He describes her fears and reservations as dangerous places, *"the den of lions and the mountain of leopards,"* and he encourages her to come away from those places with him. He is affectionate and tender (4:8-11).[4]

Solomon does not poke fun at the fact that she is a virgin. Instead he praises her locked garden (4:12), which symbolizes her virginity. Finally she responds to all his soft words and invites him into her garden. It is not forced or surrounded by shame or doubt; she is assured of his love and commitment to her and to their marriage (4:16). This is a sacred, precious moment between a husband and wife, one Satan attempts to ensure will never come to be. Notice, too, how secretly and beautifully the Word of God describes this moment. It is so tastefully done. Satan has brought sex out into the open and made it crude and animalistic.

The ups and downs of marriage are not denied. It would have been fine for the Song of Solomon to end on the honeymoon. They could have faded out with the two in each other's arms. But God gives us a glimpse into Solomon and the Shulamite woman's marriage in chapter 5.

Solomon describes a time when the Shulamite was already in bed when Solomon came. She doesn't open the door for him—maybe she's tired, angry at him, pregnant, or has a headache. He goes away and later she feels badly about what she had done and goes to look for him. She finds him and instead of being angry with her and holding a grudge, he's glad to see her and they make up quickly.

The sexual intimacy in marriage should grow and develop. God gives us one more intimate sexual scene between this couple. The next time Solomon and the Shulamite are intimate together, it is different than the first. It is obvious their relationship has matured in this area. He is more confident. He knows her body. He compliments her more and not less (7:1-9). He is still talking, touching, and keying into her feelings. Now she feels freer to be more forward and aggressive in their relationship. She suggest things for him to do and she tell him what pleases her (7:10- 8:10).[5]

> I have a friend who taught me a valuable lesson, and he's not even a Christian. He's really intrigued by attractive, but somewhat conservative women. He says they present a challenge to him and that they are often full of surprises; of course, he means when it come to sex. So he likes to try and find out what they're like when no one is around. My friend's comments say to me that the women who intrigue him are probably symbolic—in some ways, at least—of the way God wants us to be until we are married. I believe God does want single women to keep men guessing about the most intimate things, so that when they do get married, the husband will know a side of them that no one else knows. —Ollie

There should be no regrets about the marriage. The Shulamite woman thinks back over their meeting and courtship without regret. She and her husband want their commitment to each other to grow and last forever (8:14). Unfortunately, many married couples look back and wish they had done things differently in their past before they got married, things that now contribute to problems in the marriage. But a woman who finds herself in a marriage that is less than sexually satisfying does not have to give up and resolve herself to misery and bitterness the rest of her days. God is able to help her restore His original plans in her marriage. He can counter the lies and damage Satan has done. She and her marriage can be whole again.

NOTES

1. S. Craig Glickman, *A Song for Lovers,* (Downers Grove, Illinois: Inter-Varsity Press, 1976), 29.
2. Ibid., 30.
3. Ibid., 32.
4. Ibid., 19.
5. Ibid., 71-73.

DON'T IGNORE THE PROBLEM

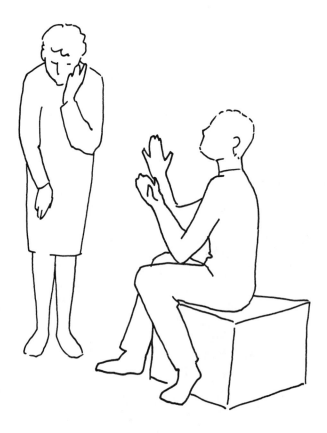

Chapter 22

Lies Satan Tells the Married Woman

It was strange. I never imagined our first major fight as newlyweds would be like this one. We had just finished making love. Usually my husband would hold me for a long time afterwards, but this time he hopped right up into the shower.

He dressed quickly but he wasn't late for work, he hadn't previously mentioned anything or other place he had to go that morning. I began to wonder if I had done something wrong while we were in bed together. Finally, as he sat on the bed to put on his socks and shoes, I asked him about his hasty exit from the bed and his quiet demeanor.

"Just got a lot on my mind," he said. "It has nothing to do with you. Everything was great as usual." With that he gave me a quick kiss on the lips and talked about going to the auto supply store before going to work. Then he was gone.

The argument did not begin until after my husband was gone. "So you're bored and unhappy already," I started to argue with my husband in my mind. "We haven't even been married a month and our sex life is unsatisfactory already. Do I need to lose weight? Wear sexier night gowns? Be more aggressive?" It was as if someone were filling in my husband's lines and keeping the argument going.

After a while I thought, "This is ridiculous. I'm having a full blown argument with my husband and he is not even here."

Unfortunately, the busyness of my day did not dispel the flow of negative thoughts against my husband or about myself. I finally realized that this was not an argument with my absent husband but a battle with the enemy himself. I had allowed Satan to infiltrate my mind that morning with lies

that fed thoughts of doubt and insecurity about our sexual relationship.
–Georginna

One of the biggest problems we as married women face in marriage is that we miss the truth God speaks and often embrace Satan's lies. It is my pleasure to expose some of these lies that he whispers in a married woman's ear so that the next time she hears these lines she will know the source behind them and will be able to counter them with truth. Believe it our not, these lies are some of the major causes of strife related to sex in marriages.

Lie: Sex is for the pleasure of men. Woman just have to endure it.

Truth: As has been said throughout this book, the sexual relationship was given to a married *couple* not just one individual in the marriage. God physically equipped both the male and female to enjoy sex within marriage.

The husband may seem to be enjoying sexual intercourse more than a woman because a woman may initially experience some early discomforts during sex. If a woman is a virgin, the stretching and the eventual breaking of the hymen can be a painful experience. It may also take time for a woman to learn how to relax her muscles to receive her husband in this private place. It should be a learning experience for both, which is the reason that lovemaking is to take place only inside a committed marital relationship. It may take months, weeks, or even years for sex to become mutually satisfying for both.

Unfortunately, most of us are not married to a Solomon who knows how to converse sensually and, along with it, has all the right moves. In our society males often grow up describing their experiences with females in terms of a baseball game. In locker rooms men talk about "making it to first base" (meaning they were able to kiss her). Second base means they got a little further, and a home run is going all the way. Many men go into marriage with this kind of sport mentality–kiss, pet, fondle, and insert. This is not an easy pattern to break. Change in this type of pattern is not usually seen until the wife feels secure and free enough in the relationship to discuss her sexual needs and responses with her husband. When she becomes more comfortable and appreciative to God for her own and her husband's body, she is able to include God in her marital sexual relationship.[1]

"Sexual expression that is rooted and grounded in love is fulfilling, even when lovemaking is awkward, humorous, or initially embarrassing. Each encounter can be a new revelation rather than an end in itself, a fresh look into the husband with whom you have made a covenant to share life's journey."[2]

Lie: Sex is nasty.

Truth: Women have held on to this lie much more than men. Usually such attitudes are developed in childhood. A child who has experienced shame and guilt for normal genital exploration may feel that touching genital organs is nasty and should not be done, even as part of a godly sexual relationship. One needs to change her perception of the body and sex, based on the Word of God. God created sex and everything God created is good. Everywhere in Scripture where the body is addressed, read it and write down what it says. Ask God to help you to see yourself as being specially made by Him (Genesis 2:18).

Re-study the Song of Solomon using one of the guides suggested in the list of resources at the end of the book. Ask God to help you appreciate his gift of sex in marriage. If possible, go through this study with your husband or with a mature Christian woman.

Lies: All men "mess around" or cheat on their wives. It is just one of those things you'll have to accept about your husband. If your husband has an extramarital affair, it is all your fault.

Truth: The Bible states, "*Let each man have his own wife and let each woman have her own husband*" (1 Corinthians 7:2). Since we know that God only ordains sex in marriage, women on the side must go. Not all men sleep around and you don't have to accept it. There are ways in which you can sometimes detect a husband who is being unfaithful: a wandering eye, long lunches, a new friend about whom he gets angry when you inquire, or secrets among his co-workers or friends. If you suspect your husband is being unfaithful, ask God to make it clear to you what is going on and what you specifically need to do. If possible both of you should get some marriage counseling immediately.
***
I had only been married six months before I realized my husband had not let one of his old girlfriends go. My initial thought was to kill him, then resurrect him, then divorce him. But then I started thinking rationally. I decided I would pray for him for a whole month. I didn't mention anything about what I had found out, I just prayed. I asked two girlfriends to pray with me on the three-way line each time he left the house possibly to see the other woman. We would pray for him, the woman, and for me. One of my prayer partners gave me a copy of James Dobson's book, *Love Must Be Tough,* which talked about confronting your mate.

After the month was over I talked to him and told him what I knew. He confessed and said he didn't want to separate. I told him he had to get counseling and he did. Things have not been without problems, but I'm confident that we would not even be together right now if it hadn't been for that month of prayer. –Peggy

Some wives blame themselves for the extramarital affair. However, some men have a problem with lust, and an unbiblical mindset about faithfulness in marriage. Some may be immature and not ready to get married and be committed to one woman. For some men it would not have mattered if the wife had sex with him around the clock, lived in seductive night gowns, and performed belly dances around the bedroom, he still would have ended up in someone else's bedroom. I once heard a man joke that all the men in his family had an extra woman on the side. These men do not understand marriage from God's perspective and are clearly not following biblical principles.

Usually adultery occurs in marriages that are already experiencing problems. The husband may be trying to fill a need for something that he feels is missing in the marriage by finding an intimate relationship with someone else.

Kay Marshall Strom, author of *Helping Women in Crisis* offers some helpful suggestions for a woman whose husband has been unfaithful or whom she suspects is involved in an extramarital affair.

1. **Speak with your husband about your concerns.** This can be a starting point for a discussion of what actually happened, what it means, and what can be done to prevent it from happening again. If her suspicions are wrong, it can lead to discussion of other problems in the marriage.

2. **Consult a qualified Christian marriage counselor.**

3. **Act immediately.** The sooner the problem is faced, the greater the chance of saving the marriage.

4. **Understand your inner conflicts.** Come to terms with the hurt and anger you may be feeling. This needs to be done so that you can make clear, rational decisions.

5. **Be hopeful.** Do not scoff at your husband when he says he loves you. It may be true. The marriage is not necessarily over. Healing can take place.

6. **Do not blame yourself.**

7. **It is necessary to hold your husband accountable.** Don't allow an unfaithful partner rights as husband and father while he is still engaged in an adulterous affair. By his actions, he has given up those rights as head of your home.

8. **Don't think divorce is your only answer.** Scripture allows freedom to divorce because of adultery, but it will not necessarily be a solution to the problem. Divorce can sometimes spawn a whole new set of problems even more difficult to solve.

9. **Consider the alternative of forgiveness.** While it is true infidelity hits hard in marriages, it does not have to be the death of that marriage. Rebuilding trust in a marriage is very hard, but it can be done. While forgiveness is not easy, it is God's way for us. It is also the best way for us to deal with destructive emotions we feel towards others. God wants us to see that His way of handling pain, bitterness, anger, hatred, is to learn to forgive. This keeps us from experiencing the physical backlash of these destructive emotions.Many marriages can be healed by God's power. Couples who have successfully worked out their marriage difficulties (even infidelity) report that the rewards made the effort worthwhile.

10. **Be loving and forgiving after reconciliation has taken place.** The past is not so easily erased. The wound will heal; however, the scar will remain. Although the memory is not erased, the hatred, malice, and anger can be.[3]

Lie: If you are angry with your husband you have a right to withhold sex from him.

Truth: A woman needs to understand that a man's sexual needs are different from her own. It is unwise for a woman to deprive a man sexually for long periods of time. In fact, the Bible warns both spouses about this practice. It directs both parties not to deprive each other so they will not be tempted, for lack of self-control to fulfill their needs elsewhere (1 Corinthians 7:5). A woman is playing with fire and right into Satan's hand when she uses sex as a manipulative tool.

Lie: Your husband will never meet your sexual needs.

Truth: "Nothing is impossible with God" (Genesis 19:26). All through the Bible God performs the humanly impossible. He can certainly handle problems we have in these areas.

There may be a number of reasons that a man is not meeting his wife's physical needs. There might be a physical reason. Both the husband and wife should get a good physical exam. He may have a problem with premature ejaculation (inability to control one's orgasm long enough to complete intercourse and satisfy the woman). This quick release pattern may have developed from the use of pornography and masturbation. Masturbation is quick and powerful; thus a man trains himself to quickly reach orgasm after arousal.

Emotional problems or personality conflicts may be the culprit. Some men have fears about their performance and are afraid of disappointing the wife. Some wives have hang-ups about sex and want it over quickly, so the man learns to reach orgasm quickly and prematurely.

Whatever the problem, the first thing to do is seek the Lord concerning it and ask Him what direction you should go. Each marital situation is different and there is no one universal answer that is going to solve every couple's problem in this area. If possible, talk to your husband about how each of you can help to achieve sexual satisfaction in your relationship. There are many books, tape series, and seminars available to help married couples strengthen their marriage and which specifically address sexual intimacy. Help is available.

Lie: You will never satisfy your husband's sexual appetite.

Truth: Women do need to understand that a man's sexual needs are different from their own. A healthy man is usually physically ready for sex every forty-eight hours. [4]

One woman commented to me that during the times when her husband's relationship with God is not strong, his desire for sex seems to be insatiable. Instead of obtaining feelings of comfort, encouragement, self-esteem, and intimacy from his Heavenly Father, some men use sex to try to meet these needs. There is nothing wrong with a couple engaging in sex to comfort one another through difficult times. However, there is no substitute for one's personal relationship with God. A wife should pray about her husband's relationship with the Lord and, if she can, talk to him about her observations.

Some men (and women) do have sexual addictions, the same as people have alcoholic or drug addictions. And they will need similar help (good information on the subject, determination to stop the addictive habit, counseling and/or a support group) in order to break the addiction.

Both the woman who had no sex before marriage and the one who had an immoral sex life can have a satisfying sexual relationship in marriage. Satan will try and use both situations to make you feel that you can't. For the one who is a virgin, look to the Holy Spirit to be your guide. It has been proven that women who marry as virgins have a more satisfying sexual experience in marriage.[5]

The woman who was sexually active before marriage should look to the blood of Jesus Christ that was shed on Calvary. In Christ you are a new creature; the old things are passed away and Jesus makes ALL things new! (2 Corinthians 5:17). Each day you may need to establish who you are in Christ and what is available to you in Him. Use Ephesians 1 as a guide.

Lie: You are to submit to whatever your husband asks.

Truth: Scripture provides guidelines regarding a couple's sexual behavior which is pleasing to the Lord. Debra Evans in her book, *The Mystery of Womanhood*, gives some excellent suggestions using Galatians 5 as a guideline to better understand whether a couple's sexual behavior is pleasing to the Lord:

- Is it <u>loving</u>?

- Is <u>joy</u> expressed in our attitude toward each other? (<u>Strong's Concordance</u> defines joy as "calm delight.")

- Do we feel the <u>peace</u> of God after we have finished?

- Are we demonstrating <u>patience</u> with one another?

- Do we see God's <u>goodness</u> manifested in the physical love we share with one another?

- Are we <u>faithful</u> to each other?

- Are we being <u>gentle</u> with each other?

- Are we able to <u>control</u> our thoughts and action when we are apart? To the extent that we are able to serve one another's needs when we are making love? [6]

If you can answer yes to each of these questions, you know that your sexual behavior is pleasing to the Lord.

Sex should include only what makes both people comfortable. Some requests are distorted by pictures, articles or movies that emphasize sex in unusual ways. A marriage is not a master-slave relationship. We are to submit to one another in the fear of Christ (Ephesians 5:21).

It is a big deal if your husband asks you to engage in distorted sexual behavior that does not seem normal or right to you. Talk to him about his past. There could be some disorientation in your husband's childhood, adolescence, or even earlier adulthood. Again, these expectations could have come from pornographic material. He may need help. If he refuses, you can get help for yourself. You may start to understand more about how to deal with his problem. Satisfying his request will not help. And even if his behavior is not really bizarre but you just do not feel comfortable with his unusual request, talk to him about your own feelings and refuse to do it.

> You are not in any way obligated to act out sexual situations with your husband that are derived from a fantasy life fed by pornography. By just saying no, you can enable your husband to grow closer to the Lord as you pray for healing in this area of his life. You are not merely a body for your husband to have sex with in whatever way he pleases. Your husband is called by God to love your body as he loves his own. When your husband forcefully dominates you during intercourse without considering how it is affecting you, he is not loving you according to God's plan for your marriage. [7]

Pray about any problems and ask God to let the two of you come to a common understanding and point of acceptable agreement.

Lie: All men masturbate, indulge in pornography, and are lustful. It's a "man thing," normal and harmless.

> Truth: It may be common, meaning most men have at one time engaged in these activities, but it's effects are not harmless. The practices of masturbation and pornography can lead to impotence, premature ejaculation, and sexual addiction. Most men start this practice early and by the time they get married can have a hard time satisfying their wives sexually.

If your husband is looking at erotic or pornographic magazines his view of female sexuality is probably not biblical. Many of these materials depict women as sex objects, in violent sex scenes, or acting in perverted ways.

"Let the marriage be held in honor among all, and let the marriage bed be undefiled; for fornicators and adultery God will judge" (Hebrews 13:4). Sexually explicit materials cause men and woman to see sex in a way God never intended.

Jesus emphasized the fact that adultery does not just mean a physical extramarital affair. *"You have heard it said, 'Do not commit adultery.' But I tell you that anyone who looks at a woman lustfully has already committed adultery with her in his heart"* (Matthew 5:28). When your husband invites another woman into your bedroom, even if it is only in his mind, this is adultery and it hurts a marriage. Many times the husband will deny that what he is doing is sinful and the wife may know something is wrong in the marriage but not know what it is. These are ways Satan can come in and cause severe damage to the relationship.

Find out as much as you can about this subject and encourage your husband to do the same. Several Christian men have begun to publicly talk about their struggles in these areas. They are getting help for themselves and are attempting to help others.

One pastor's wife wrote an article about her experience after her husband confessed his sexual addiction and deep involvement with pornography, adult book stores, and message parlors (which eventually lead to adultery).[8] After his confession, she made a commitment to help him work through his problems. Even though biblically she could have left him, she stayed because she saw a genuine commitment on his part to change. She clung to God's Word for her own healing and restoration. She trusted God with her fears (of getting AIDS, for example). She was eventually able to forgive her husband and walk in love (1 Peter 4:8). She was able to see what happened as a trap Satan set for them. She praises God for re-establishing their marriage.

Lie: Pain is a part of the sexual experience.

Truth: No it is not. Get a complete gynecological exam. Try to explain to the doctor exactly where and how having sex hurts. Vaginal warts, hormone deficiency, or any number of causes could be responsible.The problem could be vaginismus (when the muscles in the vagina involuntarily have spasms during intercourse, making it impossible for the penis to enter or causing pain and discomfort).

Look at past sexual activities. If a woman has been sexually active before marriage, vaginismus could result. If she petted heavily but did not go all the way, her body may have learned to shut down at a certain point.[9]

When physical causes are ruled out, emotional issues should be examined. Perhaps problems related to past sexual abuse are beginning to surface in physical ways. Talk to your husband if you do have such a past. Then pray for the stability in your marriage during this difficult time and seek God for the best means of correcting the problem.

Lie: There is something wrong with you because you don't have orgasms.

Truth: There are a variety of reasons women do not have orgasms: early childhood experiences, improper foreplay, prior abuse, fatigue, depression, or distractions to name a few. A woman's sexual response is usually developed over time. Once again, start with a physical exam and rule out any medical causes.

There are things a man can do to help his wife. The solution could be as simple as more understanding, more foreplay, more attention, and more patience on his part. There are many sources that offer advice and practical help with improving sexual orgasmic response. While you and your husband work toward improving your orgasmic response, learn to appreciate one another in other sexual ways. There is a lot to be said for physical bonding without the presence of an orgasm. We have just reviewed a beautiful example from the Song of Solomon in the Bible.

Today, too many have made sex a god and bow at the alter of orgasms. The goal of the sex act should be much more than that. The couple in Song of Solomon expressed their feelings; they touched each other, and enjoyed bodily closeness and movements. Sex is supposed to bring two committed individuals intimately closer.

I recall one young wife sharing with me, "My husband gives me a body rub before we have sex. For me, that's the best part." Most people, if they heard the wife's comments, would say that her husband needs to take some love-making lessons and learn how to sexually please his wife. But who are we to stand in judgment over what goes on in someone else's bedroom and what they mutually enjoy? If a body rub is what the wife enjoys, and it does not pose a problem for the couple, that is good sex. Maybe he gives a better body rub than he performs sexually! The question is: are they both happy with whatever they are doing?

Lie: If you lack sexual desire, there is nothing seriously wrong with you.

Truth: In a normal marriage, God does intend for the couple to use sex for procreation and pleasure. If one or both persons in a marriage have no desire for sexual contact, there could be a problem. This may be an indication, barring physical reasons, that there are some serious relational problems in the marriage.

Sometimes sheer busyness is the culprit stealing a woman's sexual desire. It is one way Satan keeps a married couple from having a fulfilling sexual life and enjoying the bonding that is so healthy to the relationship. Living life in the fast lane usually leads to stress. The Lord made our bodies with the need for work and rest. Stress can affect a woman's sexual responsiveness. If you are extremely busy, make it a priority to allow time for you to relax. There are also a host of physical and intellectual activities to pursue. Remember, anything that keeps you away from your husband in bed is a trick of the enemy. [10]

Lie: Your husband's impotence is your fault.

Truth: Impotence occurs when a man has trouble achieving or maintaining an erection. Many men experience episodes of impotence during some period in their lives. Alcohol consumption, job stress, excessive weight, or physical ailments could cause this problem. Some medications and even drug abuse cause instances of impotence.

The cause could also be emotional and may include pressure related to a job or even the approach of mid-life or retirement. The husband may even be dealing with the resentment of his wife pressuring him to perform.

The husband should contact a physician first. Past sexual activities need to be examined. Childhood sexual abuse, molestation, incest, shame in association with normal genital exploration, and masturbation, are all possible reasons for impotence. At any rate, the problem likely has nothing to do with you. (Chapter 24 will offer more solution as to how a wife can handle with this problem.)

Lie: You are not a whole woman because you are unable to have a child.

Truth: Once a woman fulfills her life long dream of having a beautiful wedding and getting married the next item on the agenda is to have a baby. When a woman is unable to become pregnant or maintain a full term pregnancy in order to have a child, Satan can fill her mind with all kinds of lies. "Something is wrong with you." "Your husband will not be pleased with you because you cannot give him a child." "God has overlooked you." A friend of mine who has gone through this experience offers these helpful facts and suggestions.

- **Trust in the fact that you can and will recover.** Not being able to have children is a big disappointment and hurt. Some couples have had several miscarriages and with each one the pain is excruciating. But realize this is a phase in your life that God can heal and you can go on with life without anger and bitterness. As I have passed through this phase I am able to see now why God did not allow us to have children. One reason is the ministry I have to other women who are in the same circumstances. The pain I experienced in my life was great, but the victory He has worked in my life as a result of this experience is even greater.

- Some things will be very hard for you. Baby showers, hearing other mothers talk about their children and holding a newborn are just some of the experiences which will bring a rush of emotion. Each time you have a period (or if your period is late and you think you are pregnant then it comes), these will be very painful times for you.

- **Realize that God is in control.** God will give you what He wants you to have. Maybe there is a reason why God has not given you a child. For example, maybe he wants you to adopt or He has a ministry for you that needs a young couple without a family.

- **Don't be overly concerned with what people have to say.** One of the hardest things to deal with when you are not able to get pregnant is what people have to say. After you have been married for about five years and still do not have any children people can be very insensitive with their comments. "You haven't had a baby yet?" "Don't you want children?"

- **You will probably need support.** Get with other women who have experienced victory in this area. There are several books on the subject. It's a difficult phase of you life and you will probably need support and encouragement to get through it.

***

Many times Satan is able to make his entrance into the sexual relationship in marriage and fill it with lies because this area is not seen and handled from a spiritual perspective.

I'll never forget listening to a seminar speaker challenge the women at a retreat to use sexual intercourse as a time to pray for their unsaved mate. She also jokingly added, "This is a time to really lay hands on him."

My husband was not unsaved but I began to implement this in our sexual relationship. When I had my quiet time in the morning and prayed for my husband I would also include prayer for our intimate relationship. I would ask God to use me to minister to my husband in this way and he to me. If I needed to be the aggressor, or more passive, or just physically affectionate for God to make me aware of what my husband needed that day. Also, when we have sex I use this opportunity to pray not only for our time together but also for God's guidance in our activities and that both of us will be able to minister to the other in a way that is pleasing to God.

I also pray for each part of his body as I touch or feel it. When I touch his head, I pray for his mind and thoughts–that they would be filled with the knowledge of God and His Word. When I rub his back, I pray for him to continue to be strong and in good health, also that he would be bold in his stand for Christ. I even pray for his sex organs, that they too would stay healthy, free from cancer or infections, and that we would be able to enjoy an intimate relationship on into our senior years. I also pray that we would be faithful to each other, and that we would be continually sexually aroused and excited by the sight and touch of each other and not any other person or thing.

This has made a significant difference in the bedroom for me. First of all, I look forward to having sex with my mate and want to do it as often as possible so I can pray for him. I feel like God is included and our intimacy is something that gives God pleasure, like an act of worship. I see what I do with my husband in this area as one of the ways I can minister to his needs. I approach sex less selfishly and surprisingly I seem to experience more satisfaction than when I was concentrating on what he was doing right or wrong. I also have less of a tendency to worry about our marriage and what is going to happen. Each time we have sex I commit the future of our sexual relationship to the Lord. –Annie

NOTES

1 Debra Evans, *The Mystery of Womanhood* (Westchester, Ill.: Crossway Books, 1987), 58.
2. Ibid., 74.
3. Kay Strom, *Helping Women in Crisis*, (Grand Rapids: Zondervan Publishing, 1986), 93-94.
4. Haman Cross, Jr. *The Wild Thing*, (Atlanta:Intercultural Resources), 1992, 4.
5. Debra Evans, *The Mystery of Womanhood* : 74.
6. Ibid., 110.
7. Ibid., 259.
8. Bonnie Fehlauer, *The Other Side of Pain*, Ministries Today, (April-March, 1995): 35,36.
9.   Cross, *The Wild Thing*, 7.
10. Debra Evans, *Mystery of Womanhood*, 116.

Chapter 23

Battling Satan During Mid-life

> When I hit thirty, I was very depressed. A toddler around my ankle, a baby in arms, and I looked and felt terrible inside and out. My husband was busy tackling his career and he was excited about his future. But I couldn't see past the baby bottles and mountains of diapers. I wondered if the stains and smell of baby spit-up would ever come out of my clothes. I thought I'd never make it through those early thirty years. But I did and the years did pass quicker than I thought. By the time I reached forty I was ecstatic. I never knew life could be so good. My kids can walk and I don't have to carry them every place I go. I can talk to them instead of trying to figure out their cries and whines. I'm in the middle of a new career and I think I look the best I ever have. I can't wait to hit fifty. –Mary

Unfortunately, everyone may not be thrilled about hitting their mid-life years. During mid-life (roughly between thirty-five and sixty-five) women go through a physical, emotional, and maybe even a spiritual transition. Changes sometimes catch us unaware and knock us off balance for a while. Satan tries to level any fragile pieces in our lives into an emotional heap, rendering us unusable for our heavenly Father. If we are not careful, wounds at this stage can be firmly engraved in. Even when a couple is twenty, thirty, or forty years into the relationship, Satan can use sexual problems and enticements to cause marriages to disintegrate. It is a good idea to know as much as we can about this stage of our lives so as to counter his attacks.

Naomi, whose life is somewhat chronicled in the book of Ruth, is a biblical example of a woman who had to work through several changes in her life. When the narrative opens in the first chapter, we see a family moving and starting a new life together. I am sure they anticipated a better life than the experience of hardship and famine they had left behind in Judah.

But before the chapter ends, tragedy has taken place and Naomi's response to her circumstances is bitterness.

The passage does not specifically give us the timetable of Naomi's life, but I imagine she might have started this journey in the early years of her life. She was watching her sons grow and mature into men like their father, and she was full of hope for their marriages and her grandchildren. But the unexpected happened. Her husband died, then eventually both sons died. She was left with two childless daughters-in-law. Her changes left her bitter and unhappy with life.

ADJUSTING TO MID-LIFE

So it can be with women today who have to make difficult adjustments in life. Life will always be filled with challenges which can cause us all to think and act below our God-given potential if we are not spiritually secure. As we grow older, Satan's attacks often come in the form of what we call the "mid-life crisis" or adjustments to the aging process.

> I'd watched my friends suffer with the "empty nest syndrome" and I was determined not to go through it. Before my last son became a freshman in high school, I started taking classes part-time and working on a new career. I was excited about the potential and personal challenge of my education and new job. I just knew this would keep me from going through the "blues" I had witnessed with my friends. But when we said our last good-byes to my youngest son who was attending a college just two hours away, I cried all the way home...and all that next week...and stayed teary-eyed whenever I thought about him for months after that. My children did need me, but not like when they were going through school. I felt so silly, but it actually took me a little while to adjust to the fact that all of our children could function on their own. –Sue

Satan attacks the self-perception. One way in which Satan often tries to throw people off course during these adjustment periods is through their own self-perception–either based on our intellectual or our physical capabilities.

When a woman is also a mother, once her children are all grown up and have left home, she often questions her usefulness. This is especially true if during the child-rearing years the mother did not work outside the home. What can she do now? Is there anything she knows besides how to raise children? Is she too old to learn anything new? After all, the children are gone and she no longer gets any strokes for being a wonderful caretaker. Young people are, in fact, perceived as having all the answers.

Contrary to widespread belief there is no generalized intellectual decline with aging. Many women find themselves entering school or the work force for the first time and proving themselves productive and creative.

If Satan cannot get a woman to question her intellectual abilities as middle age begins, he may try to get her to develop a negative physical self-perception. This is especially true of women, since generally women are more noticed for physical detail than are men.

A woman may look at the younger, firmer women and remember the days when her breasts didn't sag, when she didn't have to cover up veins, or smooth out saddle bags, or add pieces to thinning hair. This is all in contrast to how the world views an aging man. When a man gets a little gray around the edges or a few lines in his face, he is considered distinguished and admired. When a women has the same characteristics, she is just considered "getting old."

> One day I noticed my breast in the mirror. They had fallen down about three inches and flattened out considerably. It seemed like it happened overnight. My attitude had been positive until that happened. Then everything in me seemed to want to fight against this aging process. –Justine

MENOPAUSE–IT COULD BE THE BIG ONE

Perhaps you remember a segment from *All in the Family* where menopause was discussed. Archie Bunker told Edith "if her "gri-o-no-co-lo-gist" insisted that she go through it, she could, and he would give her thirty seconds to complete the process.[1] How we wish the process would pass that quickly.

A marker of life. In reality, menopause does last longer than a few seconds but is just "a marker of life–not the end of the line."[2] Too many Americans view menopause as signaling that a woman is now useless. Many problems result from this conclusion that makes middle age a declining time.

Menopause, often called the "change of life," can be the biggest natural physical occurrence in women's lives that Satan may attempt to use to tear at the fibers of self esteem and healthy sexuality. However, with an understanding of the process and the concomitant emotional responses, a woman can fortify herself against embracing negative feeling about herself and her physical changes.

The enemy should not be allowed to use body changes to wreak havoc with us as women. His plentiful lies include things like, "You can't think straight anymore," "You are old, wrinkled, and ugly," "You are no longer sexually desirable," or "Sex is no longer satisfying." All of these changes could be the result of our BODIES changing. In fact, many women have felt that way and have overcome, either with medication or just with time and patience.

What does it mean? The "change of life" is medically called the "climacteric." The word stems from the Greek and means "rung of the ladder." This implies another step of healthy development. Cessation of menses may occur at any time between ages of forty-one and fifty-one. Pre-menopause may last two to six years, generally beginning between ages thirty-eight and forth-two. This is when egg production is diminished and the remaining eggs are more resistant to complete development. The menstrual period may become erratic–light, heavy or even missed entirely. PMS-like symptoms may appear due to estrogen and progesterone deficiencies. [3]

Some women say menopause was the best time of their lives. Others report that portions of it were miserable but brief. Still others desired to rob banks, shoot in-laws, and leave home for Rio.[4] Common symptoms include insomnia, numbness and tingling sensations, fatigue and weakness, irritability, mood swings, personality changes, apprehension, and anxiety. The cardiovascular system is affected and a woman may experience heart-pounding, chest pains, shortness of breath, varicose veins, and swollen ankles.[5]

Estrogen depletion is responsible for a number of menopausal symptoms, including night sweats and hot flashes. A true hot flash is a rather sudden occurrence that involves feelings of warmth from the chest to the head, which may be mild or intense. Some women say it feels like a blowtorch has been burned on their upper body.The feeling may last for just seconds or up to an hour and may be followed by their night equivalent–night sweats. Some women may have three to five of these episodes a day.[6]

During menopause the skin becomes drier and itchy, loses its elasticity and bruises more easily. There may also be an increase in facial hair. The thinning of the tissues of the bladder and urethra cause increased frequency and urgency to urinate. The affected tissue becomes thin, delicate, and dry. Intercourse may cause bleeding and tearing and can be painful. The breasts become smaller and softer, and may sag.

Satan will attempt to use all of these to communicate to the woman moving through mid-life that she is no longer attractive or useful. This is contrary to the biblical account of so many women who were probably in mid-life when they accomplished their greatest feats for God–Miriam, Jochebed, Deborah, Dorcus, Anna–just to name a few.

SATAN ATTACKS THE MARRIAGE

Menopause is a major portion of the mid-life stage for women, but both men and women go through this phase of living. It is like moving from childhood into adulthood when one is an adolescent. What makes mid-life a time of crisis rather than a smooth transition is too many changes all at once.

> It's not terribly difficult for most people to handle one or two stresses in their lives. If you are a healthy person, you should be able to handle the normal stress of the mid-life transition. However, if your children are going through a rough transition from childhood to adolescence or adolescence to young adulthood; if you are having a difficult career adjustment; if your husband is having a horrible mid-life crisis and wants to resign from his job, divorce you, split up the estate, and sail around the world with his secretary; and if your father had just died of a heart attack, you are likely to have a crisis. [7]

MEN AND WOMEN IN MID-LIFE

Both men and women in the mid-years are influenced by changing bodies and a generation on each side of them—adolescents with their youth culture and aging parents. They may not feel needed as much, may have a lower self-image, and may be feeling unfulfilled in marriage. Because a man and a woman may react differently to these feelings, a woman is the wiser if she understands not only her own responses to aging but her husband's as well.

Pace adjustments. At mid-life, a man may begin to question his career, become bored with it, while his wife may be just developing hers. This especially may be the case if the wife delayed her development in order to focus on the children. She may be returning to school, her aspirations are just starting to blossom while her husband's are fizzling out.

The man may want to slow down at mid-life, while the wife may feel that her life has been on hold for years. The man may have spent most of his years on a career and now wants to spend more time with his kids who are grown now and busy with their own lives. The wife, on the other hand, may feel like she has spent most of her life with the kids.

A man's body, his wife, his family, his job—all may be viewed as enemies during mid-life crisis. If only he could get rid of all of these things, he would be happy. He may want to walk away and be free of all responsibilities. He could even become angry with God for the way He made him—his drives, his sexual desires. He may feel that God has left him to work everything out. He is very alone. No one understands what he is going through, and he blames everyone else for his struggles.[8] Anger is another common male response to aging. A man may become angry at everybody and every thing, unable to stand imperfections and distractions of life.

In the bedroom, the man wants more of a girlfriend and a lover, not a mother or a household manager. The wife, on the other hand, may feel too tired to play girlfriend, preoccupied with her outside accomplishments and new ventures. The way some men respond to these feelings is to withdraw. Some men who have had substance abuse problems in the past may resort again to drinking or drugs. They stop by the bar after work or have a couple of beers at home, thinking this will help relieve the stress and pressure that they feel. They may sleep, sit out on the porch all day, or watch endless hours of television.

Some men try to change their image. They may start exercising excessively wanting to become a macho man. Men who always bought conservative family cars now want something classy or sporty. The same goes with clothes. We've all seen the middle-aged men wearing outfits their teenage sons should be wearing–all in the name of trying to stay young and slow that aging clock. When he looks in the mirror, he wants to say, "I may be forty-five but I can run and keep up with any twenty-five-year old."

What does all of this have to do with a woman? How does a husband's mid-life crisis affect a wife? Unfortunately, these changes cause some men to start chasing after younger women. This can be very disturbing for a wife who is also working through several of her own aging issues. In reality, only about 3 percent of men who go this route actually divorce and marry the "other" woman. Yet, these little flings sometimes do irreparable damage to the marriage relationship.[9]

Tied to this general desire to be young again is a man's concern and insecurity about his sexual functioning. Mid-life can be a time when a man seeks out an extramarital affair to assure himself that, sexually, everything still works well.This also may be a time when he gets interested in pornography or some other bizarre sexual behavior.

> Around fifty my husband began to deal with impotency and premature ejaculation. I tried to talk to him about it and encouraged him to seek some medical attention, but he wouldn't listen. Instead he had an affair with a couple of women to see if he was still able to function with someone else. He was not and he came crawling back to me because he knew I'd accept him regardless of his sexual ability. I took him back and he finally went to the doctor. It was just a matter of making a change in a medication he was taking. There is still a part of me that just will not forgive him for his affairs. Every time he touches me, I think of him touching those other woman. Only God can help me get past this one. –Amy

With the threat of AIDS and other serious diseases, and the risk of severe damage to the marriage, it is not so easy to say, "Oh, let him sow his wild oats and he'll be back when he's had enough." If it seems that your mate is headed in this direction, seek counsel for both of you.

The Christian community seems to be getting more sensitive and aware of this process of growing older and is beginning to provide more seminars, books, and magazines on the subject. Get as much information as you can to keep your marriage strong. Satan can and has used all of these changes to put a wedge between husband and wife.

Surviving the crisis. How can a woman help her husband through mid-life? First, understand the stage. Listen to him. Give him time to sort out his values. LISTEN and don't set out to set him straight. Be available. Don't hover, but when he wants to go out or spend time with you, be available. Make your life flexible enough to deal with his. Re-evaluate your priorities to accommodate your husband's needs for understanding and support.

Wait until he asks "What do you think?" before you jump right in there with solutions. Be gentle. Ask questions rather than explode. Help him get his thoughts and feeling out, rather than hitting him over the head with biting, accusing words. Be patient; this process could last several years.

Think back to when you and your husband were courting. What attracted you then? What kept the relationship interesting? Rekindle those interests and build a new exciting relationship around them. Commit to an unconditional relationship. Tell him, "I love you no matter what. I'm your friend no matter what."

And remember that God can always provide answers for your husband when it appears that neither you nor anyone else can.

At first when my husband retired it drove me nuts. He was depressed all the time and anything I suggested he didn't want to do. Finally, I prayed about it and left it in the hands of God. Not too long after that he was appointed to head the building committee for our new church. This seemed to give him a renewed sense of purpose and the depression lifted.
–Anne

Sex at mid-life. Mid-life is a significant time of transition in the sexual lives of both men and women, just as it is in other areas of life. The actual adjustments are usually less traumatic than our society suggests they will be. Couples respond to the aging process in their own unique way. Depending on how they respond to aging, their sex life can be better than in their youth. [10]

At mid-life, the couple is not trying to figure out what to do. There are fewer distractions like little children and careers. Men may be more mature, have less sexual urge, and are usually more sensitive. Love-making can become more artful and varied when the couple feels secure and the wife is more involved. The focus shifts from performance to pleasure.

If boredom has set into your middle-age sex life, be open to new ideas, places, and times for sex. It is more important than ever to recognize it as a priority. Be rested and make appropriate time available for it. It would be easy to start to use excuses like, "We're too old for all of this." "I don't feel good and I need my rest", or "I just don't want to be bothered." Don't fall into this trap. At mid-life, God still uses intimacy in marriage as a means of bonding couples together.

Do not be discouraged if your bodies have changed and one or both of you may now need aids for the sexual act. For example, a woman who has gone through menopause may need to use estrogen cream because the vagina has become dry and sensitive to friction. Since natural vaginal lubrication is reduced and slower, there are many helpful aids on the market for both men and women.

On the other hand, some men may need more physical and visual stimulation in order to have an erection. The wife may need to wear more alluring clothing (or no clothing at all) to bed, or give him a sexy back rub. This can become a fun and stimulating activity for the couple. The emphasis is on pleasure rather than performance.[11]

At mid-life and through retirement there may be more pressure on the wife to help her husband. She may resent having to physically and emotionally stimulate him more than before. She can withhold the direct stimulation which her husband may now need to function. Or she can cease to look attractive, overeat, gain weight, ignore him, and focus only on her own activities. These are ways Satan uses the wife to cause problems in the marriage. She must be careful to avoid these traps.

I encourage married couples to persist in maintaining a regular and frequent sex life. In fact, infrequency actually contributes to vaginal dryness and decreases the size of the vagina. Some couples, too embarrassed to try lubrication or seek medical advice, just cease their activities. They could have had many more years of pleasure.

All married couples, young and old need to see sex as more than intercourse and an orgasm. Intercourse sometimes takes more psychic and physical energy than a person can muster, but he or she may, nonetheless, long for sexual intimacy. The sexual appetite can be satisfied in a variety of ways. Each couple must learn to know themselves and work together for the solutions. If problems in the marriage existed before mid-life, they will loom larger during this stage. Couples who have been supportive of each other and have a healthy marriage have minimal sexual adjustments as they age.[12]

STAY ALIVE

If you are a woman approaching or presently experiencing the autumn and winter years, don't let Satan rob you by filling your mind with negative thoughts of yourself, aging, or your sexuality. Bring into this time of life a beauty and wisdom appropriate and fitting for your years.

Continue to give yourself permission to be sexual, taking advantage of the variety, and the many niceties in the marketplace that help us to feel sensual and attractive. If you are without a partner, allow for touching by maintaining a social life that includes good friends. Become a hugger. These things will radiate your good feelings about yourself and your sexuality. You are still special to God and others.

Keep up your appearance. Make regular hair appointments, treat yourself to a manicure, and maybe even a pedicure or a facial. Join the local health club and enjoy the sauna and jacuzzi. Work at keeping yourself active and vital. Exercise and stay in shape.

Don't be afraid to seek advise and talk openly with others who have or are also passing through this stage of life. Take a class, go to a seminar, purchase some of the publications on aging. Determine that these years will be the best you have ever experienced, despite many adjustments. The virtuous woman in Proverbs 31 smiled at her future (Proverbs 31:25).

Most important of all, this is a time of continuing spiritual growth and personal development. Remember, the mature woman is called to pass on her wisdom and the benefit of her experience to the next generation of women (Titus 2:3-5). Find comfort in ordering your life in God, forgiving yourself for all past mistakes and shortcomings. Ask God how He would have you use all your experience, including your failures to help others. Then get busy doing it. It is your calling as a chosen vessel of God.

> My daughters are in their springtime, my wife is in the middle of summer, and my mother is walking through autumn to step into winter. Together they form a chord of womanhood–three different notes creating a harmonious blend. [13]

At the beginning of the book of Ruth, Naomi called herself Mara, which means bitterness. Yet by the end of these four short chapters, God moved quickly through her dedicated daughter-in-law and godly new son-in-law. She was now filled with joy. A new grandson sat on her lap and those around her sang her praises. Little did she realize when she turned her face toward Judah, her home town and the place of God's blessing, what God had in store for her during the silver years of her life. Satan had her convinced that everything was gone, that her changes in life where too much to bear. But God still had plans for Naomi in spite of her self-perception and weak faith. He used her as a link in the chain to bring forth one of the greatest kings in Israel.

May the Lord fill us with anticipation as we encounter various changes in our lives—anticipation of what He can do in the midst of mid-life and in the years that follow.

NOTES

1. Mary Ann and Joseph Mayo, *The Sexual Woman*, (Eugene, Oregon: Harvest House, 1987), 88.
2. Ibid., 88-89.
3. Ibid., 90.
4. Ibid., 91.
5. Tim and Beverly LaHaye, *The Act of Marriage*, (Grand Rapids: Zondervan Publishing House, 1976), 272-273.
6. Ibid., 272, 273.
7. Ibid., 125-127.
8. Ibid., 126.
9. Ibid., 127.
10.Ed and Gaye Wheat, *Intended for Pleasure*, (Old Tappan N.J.: Fleming H. Revell Co.,1977), 203.
11. Ibid., 205.
12. Ibid., 205-206.
13. T. D. Jakes, *Woman Thou Are Loosed!* (Shippensburg, Penn.:Treasure House, 1994), 165.

Chapter 24

Over 65 and Sexually Alive

"Life truly begins when the dog dies and the children leave home."[1]

The sex lives of teens, young adults and even middle-aged adults make front-page news. Everywhere we turn, we read the statistics about the sexual attitudes and activities of these age groups. On the other hand the sexual activities of the over sixty-five seem to be of little interest to the world. On television, we see this group selling denture cream and other products associated with aging. Rarely are older couples depicted touching, holding, or communicating sexually. Some people believe sex, sensual urges, and even interest in sex stops at a certain age, but my friends in the winter years might respond, "If only they knew."

Because of the lack of information about the winter years, Satan can have a field day with myths and false perceptions. He attacks this time of life and attempts to render the person a useless bag of bones, ready for the graveyard when, in fact, most people have almost a third of their lives left. God has not finished polishing this vessel and displaying the older woman as one of His finest accomplishments. The Bible says, *"Wisdom is with aged men* [women]*, with long life is understanding"* (Job 12:12). This is where we should turn to find golden nuggets of God's wisdom that have matured with time and experience.

As a woman ages, the quality of her life, including her sex life, depends on her walk with God, her attitude, her general health, and the overall satisfaction she feels with the way she has lived her life. If she has always had a close relationship with the Lord and admits that she has made mistakes, but overall she feels the Lord is pleased with decisions she has made concerning marriage, parenting or a career, she will probably approach and move through this stage of her life with satisfaction and peace. However, not all women are positively dealing with their final stages in life.

God knew that women at this point in life would be grappling with questions that only He and His Word can answer. If we look closely enough, we can see that the Bible sheds some light on the role of women's sexuality, even in their older years.

OLDER WOMEN IN THE SCRIPTURES

Sarai is one biblical character we can watch move from one stage in her life to another. We are introduced to her in Genesis 11:30. She was the wife of the famous patriarch, Abraham.

Sarai suffered several losses. In this same passage, we find that Sarai had a problem. She was barren, meaning that she and those around her had concluded that she would not bear children (Genesis 11:30). In those days, a woman who was unable to have a baby was open to scorn and ridicule, and suffered a lot of shame. Often the husband would take another wife because children in that society meant everything–wealth, the future of the family, and someone to take care of the parents when they became older. Although Sarai might have had a status in her life as Abraham's wife, she could not have received all due respect because of her barren state.

Sarai was also called to be with a man who was following God. This required her to give up her home, relatives and friends. By any standards, this constituted great loss. I have met very few women who did not feel some negative effects as a result of moving. Packing and starting all over is a major challenge for a woman, even if she is excited about a new place.

Abraham and his family were on their way, following God's call. Something happened that, I believe, affected the entire caravan. Terah died. He was Abraham's father. Little attention is paid to the verse in Genesis 12:32, which reports this tragic event. Sarai was already dealing with being barren. She was moving to a place she had never seen, following a God who had, at this point, only spoken to Abraham. Then she lost her father-in-law.

When you lose something precious at a young age, there is always the hope of getting another. But if something is lost when we are older, we grieve more because it is very unlikely that it will ever be replaced. Money, jobs, physical health, and even family and friends are things we take for granted in those early years of life.

At that time in Sarai's life, she probably valued things and people dearly. One does not usually appreciate what one has until it is lost.

Sarai's loss reminds us of not only the agony of bereavement, but also of our security, our lifestyle, our own ways of doing things. For example, one thing we very seldom think about is the loss of our privacy. In some health institutions, husbands and wives are physically segregated, prohibited from staying in the same room together, not to mention sharing the same bed. How hard it must be when a woman has to cope with living in the midst of others when she has been so accustomed to privacy. How lonely she must feel when she can no longer enjoy physical bonding with her mate.

The loss of sexual intimacy can also occur when disease or illness strikes. However, a person still has a need for closeness, touching, and sensuality. Infants who are cuddled, held, and loved are more likely to gain weight, thrive, and develop normally. The rest of us are simply happier when we are touched. Unfortunately, older couples sometimes forget that fact and rarely touch at all.

Loss can be gain. Madeleine L'Engle has written a moving book that looked back on forty years with her husband. On the pages of this book, she takes us through the illness which led to his death. She writes:

> I go to my lonely bed, thinking of Hugh alone in his hospital room, grateful for the nurses who are so good to him. During the night I reach out with my foot through force of habit to touch his sleeping body. And he is not there. Nevertheless, we have been making love during this time in a profound way. He is making love with me in the pressure of his fingers. I am making love when I do simple little bodily services for him. How many times he has taken care of me! And that is intercourse as much as the more usual ways of expressing our sexuality.[2]

Just as Madeleine L'Engle found out, true intimacy transcends sexual intercourse. The passage of time may mean making adjustments in the way we express our intimacy. However, grounded in deep and loving relationship, new, sometimes even non-physical ways of expressing intimacy can be just as meaningful in keeping a strong relationship together and even taking it to deeper levels of commitment. God does not take away good things without replacing them with better ones.

As a woman attains these golden years, it becomes even more important to remember that her sexuality is much broader than those things related to it: sexual arousal, orgasms, or the sex act. It is what distinguishes a woman from a man. Since all women are different, our sexuality is a very personal and individualized thing.

By now you should know what attributes God has given you as a woman and what your special gifts are. Perhaps, you have taken all these qualities for granted and might need to refresh your memory by writing them down. In fact listing your special talents and abilities on paper is a great exercise, to boost your self-esteem.

Think about your role as sister, aunt, or mother. Are you a great nurturer and encourager? Even though you may not have little children, you can use these wonderful qualities positively with your adult children, nieces and nephews? Or if you already use these talents with your family, what about taking on the responsibility of encouraging a young woman, or even a middle-aged woman, who may not have a family of her own? There are some things that only a woman can do with her feminine touch and ways. God may have your generation in its golden years to begin teaching all the women following you the true meaning of sexuality.

If you have not already done so, ask God to prepare you at this stage of your life to take your adjusted role as a woman and a sexual being. Then ask Him to show you how yo prepare others whom you now have an opportunity to influence. You can talk to your granddaughters about the pitfalls Satan may have prepared for them as they grow into each phase of womanhood. Be an example of a godly woman. These are suggestions, but God has your individual list designed for you, if you will only ask. Perhaps you have wanted time to be more involved in the nurturing of others. Maybe this is the time that God has set aside for you to do just that.

In your role as a wife, are there things you can say or do to your husband that no one else can? Perhaps there is a special place that he loves to go alone with you. Will he allow you to give him a massage? Or maybe regular strolls down memory lane through the pages of old photo albums and scrap books will bring warm thoughts of especially happy times. Most of these things you can do even if your spouse cannot perform as he once did sexually. They are appropriate and loving things to do within your role as his wife, and they will continue to bring intimacy to your relationship.

Alone. Loneliness is a very real struggle when a woman has lost her husband by the time she reaches her golden years. It is especially important for such women to pray for God's wisdom about how He would now use them as vessels for his work. However, a woman at this stage can be lonely for other reasons. Perhaps she has never been married and still longs for the kind of companionship God says we can only experience when we are married. Likewise, a woman can feel alone even when she is married. Perhaps her husband has turned away because he is facing his own physical or emotional anxieties.

I believe there are times in our lives when no person will be able to understand or to dispel our emotional confusion. If you already have a relationship with the Lord, it is at those times that you know you can turn to Him for comfort, encouragement, and answers for your complexities. If you do not already know Him, it is not too late to begin turning to Him now. If you do not know how to begin, don't hesitate to ask around about a reputable, Bible-teaching church in your area that will help you get to know Jesus Christ and grow in your relationship with Him.

In a woman's winter years, bitterness can rear its ugly head. It may be prompted by frustration with an inattentive spouse. You think your communication with your spouse should be better at this point. Or perhaps you and your husband never achieved the status in life you wanted. Perhaps, as Naomi, you are bitter because your husband or maybe even other loved ones have died. It could be that you never married and so desperately wanted to. Resentment can take on many forms.

> Once the kids all moved and we were finally financially stable I thought life was going to be different. Finally the house was quiet and we could play the music we wanted and even walk around the house naked if we choose to do so. We finally had the money to take those sensuous hide away weekends and not have to rush back for the kids. But with this stage also came my husband's impotence. Instead of joy at this stage of our lives this area is very unfulfilling for me and full of confusion and tension.
> −Amy

Remember that Satan causes bitterness. He would love to have one more stab at trying to make you unhappy. As always in our lives, even in the midst of trials, this should be a time of joy and thanksgiving. Repent by asking God to help you agree with Him about the value of your life, and spend the rest of it doing as He directs. Give no place to the devil.

Believing God for the impossible. Even if your marriage seems irretrievably broken, or your sex life has gone away, or you feel terribly lonely, always know that God is full of miracles. When God told Sarai that she would bear a child, she laughed. To her it was a joke. As she looked at her barren body already past menopause and then, at Abraham who was also very old, she could not fathom God doing something extraordinary. In fact, she and Abraham both tried to help God out by allowing Hagar to have a child for them. But this was not God's plan. The seed was to come from the bodies of Abraham and Sarai. When the angel of the Lord reported this fact to them He added, *"Is anything too difficult for the Lord?"* (Genesis 18:14)

When you look at your less than ideal marriage even now, can you believe God for the impossible? When your simple suggestions to get a check-up and discuss problems in the bedroom are met with a great deal of stubbornness and anger from your husband, can you believe God for the impossible? Maybe your physical health has affected your desire to have sex. Can you believe that your desire can return? Can you believe that God can do the impossible? Or will you laugh like Sarai and ask, *"After I have become old, shall I have pleasure, my lord being old also?"* (Genesis 18:12)

God did pull off a miracle for Abraham and Sarai. He resurrected their sexually dead bodies, restored them to normal, and a child was conceived. He did not supply all of the details of this story just to fill up the pages of Scripture. He could have put Abraham and Sarai's historical account into two sentences: *Abraham followed God's call and went to Canaan. Eventually Abraham and Sarai had a son who was to continue the promise to Abraham about becoming a great nation.* That could have been it. Instead, God shows us the trials this couple suffered and their happy ending. Why is it here? Among other reasons, to give us hope in our silver years. God is the same today and He is still able to do miracles. The following is a true account of a woman in whom God has done exactly that.

ONE WOMAN'S STORY

I was raised in a Christian home and accepted Christ at four years old. My family read the Bible every day and I picked up the habit early in life.

In high school, my eyes locked with one of my classmates. I had never really paid him much attention before, but for some reason that day, I knew in my heart that he was the one that I wanted. Sure enough, not long after that we were married. Like most married couples, the early part of our lives was filled with having children, my husband changing jobs, moving, and adjusting to new places and things.

We both were virgins when we married and in a word I would describe our early sex life as "awkward". He was quick and simple; I was slow and complicated. The turnabout in this area did not occur in the bedroom, but in God working in both of our hearts. About the same time, the Lord revealed to both of us our self-centeredness. Without saying anything to the other until much later about what God had said, we each decided to place the other person's needs ahead of our own.

Allen, my husband, and I had always attempted to have devotions together. Like our early sex life, I would also describe that time as awkward. But once we discovered our selfishness and made a commitment to change, our devotional life also changed. We each began to ask the other about just one thing that we could pray for on the others' behalf, and each morning we would pray out loud for whatever that was. Then at the end of the day, we usually asked each other what happened that day with the prayer request. This opened up a whole new area of intimacy that took place outside the bedroom, but the commitment to unselfishness, and the new spiritual intimacy led to a great improvement in our sex lives as well.

During mid-life, I had a hysterectomy. I had no idea how this would affect me or our sexual relationship. By this time, though, I had matured spiritually and finally understood what it meant to live the Spirit-filled life. Each day I yielded myself and my family to the Lord. I began to understand that nothing that I had belonged to me, but that it all belonged to God. Daily I would pray, "Lord, take my hands, my heart, my home, my husband, and my children. They are yours. Take and use them according to Your will." By the time I had the surgery, I had already learned to place the outcome in His hands. I knew there would be adjustments, but I didn't know what to expect.

As it turned out there was no change in our sexual relationship at all. I know it sounds unbelievable, but I can only give credit to my heavenly Father. My husband and I continued to have a growing loving relationship in this area.

When Allen retired, we asked the Lord what He would have us do. We ended up working for several years on the mission field. This was great for our sex life. As many times we were given a room with two twin beds and a dresser in the middle, we had to be creative. This creativity kept things interesting.

After leaving the mission field, Allen and I settled down with a ministry in our church. In our late sixties, we found out Allen had prostate cancer. Now, up to this point Allen and I continued to have a growing, fulfilling, and wonderful sex life. Because of the cancer treatment, he lost 85 percent of his sex drive. His sexual appetite went down, but mine didn't. I had to decide what I was going to do.

I did not want to change our beautiful sexual relationship. But I wasn't sure how to proceed. Should I just ignore it and say this is it, and try my best to push aside my sexual desires? Should I masturbate and take care of my needs that way? This was definitely a time of transition. I didn't know if I should push my husband in this area or to hold back. I knew that whatever I said during this time was very crucial. I had to be very delicate. This was one of the most difficult and private things I had ever gone through. I knew this was a time to be very quiet before the Lord. I take no credit for what eventually took place. It was all God's doing. Gradually the most beautiful sex life between my husband and me returned.

One of the first things I determined was not to masturbate because this didn't include Allen. I didn't want to exclude my husband; I loved him so much. I was so afraid of bringing pleasure to myself and shutting him out. We had always shared and been so involved in each other's life I did not want to exclude him then. I cannot say what is right or wrong for others, but I believe this decision is one of the reasons God restored our sexual relationship. I was determined not to be self-centered.

Another thing I determined is that I would not complain. God had given Allen and me over fifty years of marriage, with a beautiful sexual relationship. I decided that if He chose to take it away, I would be grateful for what He had already given us. I see His restoration in this area as a very special gift.

After the cancer, I later noticed that because sex had not been as frequent, my husband and I were not touching as much as we did before. Again, I can't take credit for this idea that I got because I believe God gave it to me. After we had breakfast, we would spend a considerable amount of time in devotions and intercessions for several people, then go back to bed. One day I suggested to Allen that when we returned to bed, we should take off our clothes and just lie there next to each other. That has done wonders for his arousal. And we've had the best sexual intimacy during this time. This is a gift. It really is a miracle.

When we came up against this sexual barrier in our marriage, we took our time. We let God work it all out. I chose not to get selfish and just take my needs into consideration. All these things, I believe, have contributed to our being able to continue to relate sexually, but most of all, I think it's our relationship with the Lord. We both individually have sought the Lord for answers and have been obedient to His guidance in our lives. We always tried to work things out in our marriage. We've made our share of mistakes, with each other and our children. Both of us are willing to admit that. But in the midst of everything, we have been able to see the hand of God throughout our lives and even now as we approach the uncertain years ahead. Unless the Lord takes us both at the same time, one of us is going to have to face life alone.

One thing God has taught me with every challenge He has placed before us: it is God's business. God can work anything out any way He chooses. I feel really grateful that God has chosen to bless us in this way.

I also realize not all women have been as fortunate as I have. I have counseled several women who were abused as children, did not come up in a Christian home, and have had very upsetting circumstances in their marriages. Many envy what Allen and I have. I say to them that God is able, that there are no limits to the constant rebirth and the rebuilding available in God. He can restore that which Satan has sought to destroy. My counsel to those women is that they find a path of honor, one with respect for themselves and their husbands. They need to be honest with themselves about their needs. But most of all, they need to cultivate their relationship with the Lord so they will know what to do in each situation and change that occurs in their lives.

NOTES

1. Mary Ann and Joseph Mayo, *The Sexual Woman*, (Eugene Oregon: Harvest House, 1987), 86.
2. Madeline L'Engle, *Two-Part Intervention*, (New York: Farrar, Strauss and Ciroux, 1988), 184.

EXERCISES

1. How is the intimacy in your marriage? Write a brief statement concerning the following in your marriage relationship:

- Communication
- Sex
- Ability to work together
- Enjoyment of each other's company
- Ability to weather a storm together

2. Now list what you believe God wants from your marriage relationship. (Review chapter 21 if you need help.) What do you plan to do to improve your part of it?

3. Are you growing older gracefully or grouchily? Why? List some things you could do to improve your overall attitude.

4. Write out an honest prayer to God about this stage of your marriage and your personal life. Ask Him to help you know where to begin making changes, especially in the sexual areas. (This is where we sometimes try to leave God out.)

5. As a single or widowed woman in her winter years, think of at least three ways that you have not already put into practice in which God can use you as a single vessel

6. If you are struggling as an older single woman in the sexual areas of you life or in engaging in practices that you know are not pleasing to the Lord (living with someone who is not your husband, reading romance novels or watching movies, soap opera and any other thing that causes sexual arousal and lust), confess your ungodly behavior, find and meditate on Scripture passages pertaining to these behaviors, and ask God to do a work in your heart. Make a list right now of things that may be coming to mind that you need to change.

Chapter 25

Conclusion

He restoreth my soul for <u>His</u> name sake.... (Psalm 23:3, KJV, emphasis mine)

I was born into a family with several problems. My father left my mother when my brother and I were small children. From that point on, I lived in a house where I witnessed several men coming in and out of our home, and doing all kinds of sexually perverted things with my mother. She spent her evenings in night clubs and bars, taking my brother and I along. For some reason whenever she got drunk, which was often, it always caused her to do some kind of sexually grotesque thing like stripping. Inevitably, the police would be called and she would be taken to jail. Therefore, my brother and I spent quite a bit of our time alone and on the streets.

In our desperation for love and affection—which was definitely not coming from our mother—we clung to each other. But we had no idea how to love each other. All we had witnessed was the sexual distortions of our mother and her relationships. Therefore we engaged in all kinds of sexual abnormalities with each other.

Finally, after years of this kind of living, which also included severe verbal, emotional and sexual abuse from my mother and sometimes her live-in boyfriends, I was moved to my father's home. He had married again. Even though he and my stepmother offered a home environment better than the one I came out of, they were not able to give me the love and affection I craved.

My father was not a Christian and did not attend church. But somehow in my teen years I ended up at a Christian camp one summer. I heard the gospel. I embraced the love of Jesus with a whole heart and I know that is when He came to live inside me.

Yet I was still so mixed up and confused about relationships with men, love, and sex. I ended up marrying very young. The marriage was abusive and stormy. Eventually my husband abandoned me and my little girl. During the marriage and after, I repeated the lifestyle I had learned from my mother (short of the stripping in public places).

Even though my lifestyle through the week was a sexual mess, I went to church on Sundays. I went to a Christian conference. It was there that a couple shared with me the hope of getting free from the garbage of my past and that Jesus could help me live a whole life. I really embraced this truth and from that point on I began to allow Christ to do what was necessary to heal me.

At that time I had made this commitment, I was carrying a child and not married. After much prayer and agony I gave my baby up for adoption. Somewhere in this world, I have a child that I have not seen since day of her birth. I think about her often. I would love to meet her, tell her that I'm sorry and that I love her. I pray for that opportunity but at this point the Lord has not allowed that to happen. –Jessica

After Jessica told me her story, I stared at her in amazement. One might imagine that someone with this kind of past would have all kinds of personal hang ups, would be spiritually crippled, or even have no thought of serving God. It would be understandable, though unfortunate, if she chose to live her life licking her wounds and using her past as an excuse for negative thoughts and behaviors. But Jessica's hang-ups have been hung up on the cross of Jesus Christ. She has given herself back to the Potter, every single piece, and has asked Him to remake her all over, a new vessel again. *"But the vessel that he was making of clay was spoiled in the hand of the potter; so he remade it into another vessel, as it pleased the potter to make" (Jeremiah 18:4)*. I have to admire His restoration work.

I know Jessica personally and I know of her ministry. She is a warm, loving, giving, and caring person. She has the ability to minister to professional women, those who are down and out, and everyone else in between. She counsels and speaks to women with spiritual wisdom, insight, and depth. Her ministry has even reached outside this country. She has gone to dangerous places abroad and felt it her spiritual duty to touch, hug, and love people that others would not go near for fear of catching a deadly disease. She has continually opened her home to those who are homeless, in need of foster care, and pregnant women with no place to go. Her husband and children would praise her as one of the best wives and mothers around. Her tender, maternal spirit has even reached my children on occasion and they have been impressed by her unselfish love.

This is an example of a woman in whom God has made up for the years the locust has eaten (Joel 2:25). Yes, Satan had a plan from the day of her birth to destroy her and he still tries. But, praise God, Jesus came to earth and died on Calvary to destroy the works and plans of the devil (1 John 3:8).

"...[Jesus came to give] a garland instead of ashes, The oil of gladness instead of mourning, the mantle of praise instead of a spirit of fainting. So they [women] will be called oaks of righteousness, the planting of the Lord, that He may be glorified" (Isaiah 61:3).

God also had a plan to use Jessica to touch the lives of many people with His love. As a friend of mine says, "God was the first into recycling. He can take the junk allowed in our lives and recycle it for His glory."

Wherever you are, whatever you have done, or whatever has been done to you **is fixable**. The wounds in Jesus' hands after He was resurrected gave witness to the fact that Satan does strike and seek to destroy people. But God's power is greater. "...*Greater is He* [Jesus] *who is in you than he* [Satan] *who is in the world*" (1 John 4:4) . Do you want to be a whole woman? The power is available in Christ. The knowledge, guidance, and practical ideas are in the Word of God. The Holy Spirit stands ready to lead you every step of the way.

Every Christian is told to serve God with a whole heart. But before we can do that, many of us need to take every single piece of our broken vessel, no matter how big or small, back to the Potter, the God who originally made us. The Potter works at His wheel. If the vessel that He made does not turn out as He wished, this is no problem for Him. God has the power, wisdom, and ability to re-knead it into a lump and start all over again (Isaiah 64:8; Jeremiah 18:3-4).

God is more than willing to take on the job and stay at the task of restoring you, no matter how long it takes, no matter how messed up you think you are. Do you want to be healed? Will you commit to Him the original work of His hands? He can give you a new beginning. You can be His whole vessel again.

I Can Begin Again
(words and music by : David Clark and Larnelle Harris)
Used by permsission

ALONE AGAIN, IN A CROWDED ROOM
CORNERED BY THE QUESTIONS IN MY MIND
IT'S SO HARD TO UNDERSTAND
HOW THE LIFE THAT I HAD PLANNED
STOLE MY JOY AND LEFT ME FAR BEHIND.

THOUGH ALL I HAVE, IS LOST IT SEEMS
IN THE SHADOW OF A DREAM THAT USED TO BE
I CAN LOOK BEYOND THE SKIES
DEEP INTO THE FATHER'S EYES
AND SEE THAT THERE IS HOPE FOR ONE LIKE ME

I CAN BEGIN AGAIN
WITH THE PASSION OF A CHILD
MY HEART HAS CAUGHT THE VISION
OF A LIFE THAT'S STILL WORTHWHILE
I CAN REACH OUT AGAIN
FAR BEYOND WHAT I HAVE DONE
LIKE A DREAMER WHOSE AWAKENED
FOR NEW BEGINNINGS ARE NOT JUST FOR THE YOUNG

I FACE THE DAWN OF EACH BRAND NEW DAY
FREE FROM ALL THE DOUBT THAT GRIPPED MY PAST
FOR IV'E FOUND IN TRUSTING HIM
THAT EVERYDAY STARTS AGAIN
AS I LOOK TOWARD THE THINGS OF LIFE THAT LAST.

One Last Testimony...

In the first chapter, we told you Tammy's story. To show that God truly does bring us full circle and restores, here is an update on Tammy's life in her own words.

I have accepted Christ and am finally turning my life over to the Lord in a real way. I am so glad! I am so excited. I am so relieved! It has been a long and rough journey. I'm sure the journey I have ahead will be longer and harder still. But I am confident in Christ that it will be both rewarding and fulfilling. I am so excited and eager about the adventures that lie ahead. I didn't write what I wrote earlier as a plea for sympathy or pity or even prayer. And now I write this as a testimony to the sheer power, mercy, goodness, and infinite love of our Lord Jesus Christ.

God is delivering me and all that I am from myself. And making me see the magnitude of all that I am and all that I have done. How much more a sinner can a person be? Yet, God is changing me. It is truly remarkable. In spite of everything, I can look forward to a life of awesome testimony for the Lord. That is why I am so excited. I can empathize with the abused child, the sexually promiscuous woman, the child aborter, the drug addict, the liar, the deceiver, and a host of others who are lost to Christ in the same manner that I was.

Even with all that I've done, God has gifted me with remarkable abilities. I am articulate. I am intelligent. I am personable. I am creative. I am so many other positive things. And now, through Christ, I am learning to adorn the armor of Christ. I am learning about how to use the spiritual tools He has placed before me. I am so excited to think of all I can do!

God can turn *your* life around.God wants you to seriously consider letting Him have the job of managing your life. He is truly capable of restoring your broken vessel. And if you need a reference, I give Him an excellent recommendation. He is worthy to be praised!

Resources

SATAN'S SEXUAL ATTACK ON LITTLE GIRLS
Sexual Abuse

Beauty for Ashes, Joyce Meyer. Tulsa: Harrison House, 1994.

The Wounded Heart. Dan Allender. Colorado Springs: NavPress, 1990.

When Child Abuse Comes To Church. Bill Anderson. Minneapolis: Bethany House Publishers, 1992.

Released to Love. Alfred Ellis. Nashville: Thomas Nelson, Inc., 1990.

In the Voice of a Child. Judy Emerson. Nashville: Thomas Nelson Inc., 1994.

Helping Victims of Sexual Abuse, Lynn Heiritter, and Jeanette Vought. Minneapolis: Bethany House Publishers, 1989.

Family Secrets. Michael and Julie Mask, Jeanne Hensley, and Steven Craig. Nashville: Thomas Nelson, Inc., 1994.

How Our Family Coped With Incest. Jessica Martin, Paula Stanford, and S. Daniels. Avon-By-The-Sea, N. J.: Magnificent Press, 1989.

Stages. D. McKenzie. Indianapolis: Price Write Publishing Services, 1994.

Beauty for Ashes. Joyce Meyer. Tulsa: Harrison House, 1994.

Glenda's Story. Glenda Revell. Lincoln: Gateway to Joy, 1994.

"Abstinence: The Radical Alternative to Sex Education." Andres Tapia. *Christianity Today*, 37, no. 2, (February 8, 1993) 24-29.

No Place To Cry. Doris VanStone and Erwin Lutzer. Chicago: Moody Press, 1990.

Sex Education

How to teach you Child About Sex Abuse, Grace Ketterman, Old Tappan, N.J. : Flemming H. Revell, 1981.

The Wild Thing, Haman Cross, Jr. Atlanta: Intercultural Resources, 1992.

How and When to Tell Your Kids About Sex. Stanton and Brenna Jones. Colorado Springs: NavPress, 1993.

The Story of Me. Stanton and Brenna Jones. Colorado Springs: NavPress, 1995.

What's the Big Deal? Stanton and Brenna Jones. Colorado Springs: NavPress, 1995.

Facing the Facts. Stanton and Brenna Jones. Colorado Springs: NavPress, 1995.

How to Teach Your Child About Sex. Grace Ketterman. Old Tappan, N.J.: Fleming H. Revell, 1981.

Decent Exposure. Connie Marsher. Nashville: Wolgemuth and Hyatt, Publishers, Inc., 1988.

The Myth Of Sex Education. Josh McDowell. Nashville: Thomas Nelson, Inc., 1991.

What You Need to Tell Your Child About Sex. John Nieder. Nashville: Thomas Nelson, Inc., 1988.

Before I Was Born. Carolyn Nystrom. Colorado Springs: NavPress, 1995.

A Betrayal Of Innocence. David Peters. Waco, Tx: Word, Inc., 1986.

Dating: Going Out in Style. Barry St. Clair, and Bill Jones. Wheaton, Ill.: Victor Books, 1993.

Sex: Desiring God's Best. Barry St. Clair, and Bill Jones. Wheaton, Ill.: Victor Books, 1993.

Talking With Your Kids About Love, Sex, and Dating. Barry and Carol St. Clair. Wheaton, Ill.: Victor Books, 1993.

"Sex Education: Failing to Make The Grade." Marian Wallace. <u>Family Voice</u>, 15, no. 9, (September 1993): 4-10.

SATAN'S SEXUAL ATTACK ON TEEN AGE GIRLS

Bondage Breaker. Neil Anderson. Eugene, Ore.: Harvest House Publishers, 1990.

The Way Of Escape. Neil Anderson. Eugene. Ore.: Harvest House Publishers, 1994.

The Messies Manual. Sandra Felton. Old Tappan, N.J.: Fleming Revell Inc., 1986.

"Prom Night Sex: Just Say No." Frison, Aretha. The D-Town Collaboration of Advanced Studies Journalism. 1995, 1.

Where Does A Mother Go to Resign? Barbara Johnson. Minneapolis: Bethany House Publishers, 1994.

Parenting Streetwise Kids. Victoria L. Johnson, and Mike Murphy. Elgin, Ill.: David C. Cook Publishing, 1995.

How to Help Your Child Say "No." Josh McDowell. Waco, Tex.: Word Publishers, 1987.

Raising Kid in a Violent Society. Mike Murphy, and Victoria L. Johnson. Elgin, Ill.: David C. Cook Publishers, 1995.

SATAN'S SEXUAL ATTACK ON THE SINGLE WOMAN

Addicted To Love. Stephen Arterburn. Ann Arbor, Mich.: Servant Publications, 1991.

Helping Women Recover From Abortion. Nancy Michels. Minneapolis: Bethany House, 1988.

Free To Love Again. Dick Purnell. Nashville: Thomas Nelson, Inc., 1989.

Pure Joy. Rick Stedman. Chicago: Moody Press, 1993.

Yerex, Mary. *"I'd Rather Be Single For The Rest Of My Life Than Be Married To The Wrong Guy."* San Bernadino, Calf.: Integrated Resources (Division of Campus Crusade for Christ).

SATAN'S SEXUAL ATTACK ON MARRIED AND OLDER WOMAN

Battered Into Submission. James and Phyliss Alsdurf. Downers Grove, Ill.: InterVarsity Press, 1989.

Torn Asunder: Recovering from Extramarital Affairs. David Carder with Duncan Jaenicke. Chicago, Ill: Moody Press, 1992.

Women In Mid-Life Crisis. Jim and Sally Conway. Wheaton, Ill.: Tyndale House, 1978.

The Mystery of Womanhood. Debra Evans. Westchester, Ill.: Crossway Books, 1987.

A Song For Lovers. Craig S. Glickman. Downers Grove, Ill.: InterVarsity Press, 1976.

"The Other Side of Pain." Bonnie Fehlauer. Ministries Today, (March April, 1995): 35.

The Act of Marriage. Tim and Beverly LaHaye. Grand Rapids: Zondervan Publishing House, 1976.

The Haunted Marriage: Overcoming the Ghost of Your Spouses' Sexual Abuse, Andres Tapia and Clark Bashiner, Downers Grove: InnerVarsity Press, 1995.

Two-Part Intervention. Madeleine L'Engle. New York: Farrar, Strauss and Ciroux, 1988.

The Sexual Woman. Mary Ann and Joseph Mayo. Eugene, Ore.: Harvest House, 1987.

Intended for Pleasure. Ed and Gaye Wheat. Old Tappan, N. J.: Fleming H. Revell, 1977.

Liberated Through Submission. B. P. Wilson. Eugene, Ore.: Harvest House, 1990.

Courtship After Marriage. Zig Ziglar. New York: Ballantine Books, 1990.

ADDITIONAL RESOURCES

Lord, Heal My Hurts. Kay Arthur. Portland, Ore.: Multnomah Books, 1989.

Woman to Woman: Perspective From 14 African-American Christian Women. Novella Carter, (ed.). Grand Rapids: Zondervan Publishing House, 1996.

Restoring the Wounded Woman. Melinda Fish. Grand Rapids: Chosen Books, 1993.

Why Do I Feel Like Hiding? Daniel Green and Mel Lawrenz. Grand Rapids: Baker Book House, 1994.

Inner Healing for Broken Vessels. Linda Hollies. Joliet, Ill.: Woman to Woman Ministries Inc., Publications, 1991.

Woman Thou Art Loosed! T. D. Jakes. Shippensburg, Penn.: Treasure House, 1994.

The Parent Warrior. Karen Linamen. Wheaton, Ill.: Victor Books, 1993.

Ordering Your Private World. Gordan MacDonald. Nashville: Thomas Nelson, 1985.

Chosen Vessels: Rebecca Osaigbovo. Detroit: Dabar Publishing Company, 1992.

Keys to Change: *A Guide to Spiritual Growth*. Rebecca Osaigbovo. Detroit: Dabar Publishing Company, 1996.

Breaking Bondage. Ruthanne Garlock and Sherron Quinn. Ann Arbor, Mich.: Servants Publications, 1994.

Biblical Counseling With African-Americans. Clarence Walker. Grand Rapids: Zondervan, 1992.

Breaking Strongholds in the African-American Family. Clarence Walker. Grand Rapids: Zondervan, 1996.

Eros Defiled. John White. Downers Grove, Ill.: Intervarsity Press, 1977.

.Faith Training. Joe White. Colorado Springs: Focus on the Family, 1994.

ORDER BLANK

QUAN	ITEM	COST	YOUR COST
	Restoring Broken Vessels: Countering the attack on Female Sexuality by Victoria Johnson	$12.95	
	Parenting Streetwise Kids (A Leader's Guide) by Victoria Johnson and Mike Murphy	$19.95	
	Raising Kids in a Violent Society (A Leader's Guide) by Mike Murphy and Victoria L. Johnson	$19.95	
	Woman to Woman: Perspectives of 14 African-American Christian Women (Available January 1996)	$12.99	
	The 7 P's (An Easy Guide for Personal Bible Study) by Victoria L. Johnson Pack of 25 (Available January 1996)	$2.00	
	Postage and Handling For the first item Each additional item.	$3.00 $1.75	
	Amount enclosed		

(Make checks payable to: CWER (Christian Women's Educational Resources)

Name_____

Address_____

Zip_____Phone_____

Send order blank with payment enclosed to:

Victoria L. Johnson
P.O. Box 10105
Milwaukee, Wisconsin 53210